Perfect

The Inside Story of

Baseball's Seventeen Perfect Games

JAMES BUCKLEY JR.

TRIUMPH
B O O K S

CHICAGO

This book is for Patty, who, after all, is also.

Library of Congress Cataloging-in-Publication Data for first edition

Buckley, James Jr., 1963–
    Perfect : the inside story of baseball's sixteen perfect games / James Buckley Jr.
      p. cm.
    Includes bibliographical references (p.) and index.
    ISBN 1-57243-454-6 (hardcover)
     1. Pitchers (Baseball)—United States—Biography. 2. Pitchers (Baseball)—Rating of—United States. 3. Baseball—Records—United States. I. Title: Inside story of baseball's sixteen perfect games. II. Title.

GV865.A1 B85 2002
796.357'092'2—dc21
[B]

2001055549

This book is available in quantity at special discounts for your group or organization. For further information, contact:

Triumph Books
601 South LaSalle Street
Suite 500
Chicago, Illinois 60605
(312) 939-3330
Fax (312) 663-3557

Printed in Canada
ISBN 1-57243-716-2
Interior design by Eileen Wagner Design

Contents

Foreword

No one ever expects to pitch a perfect game. It's an extreme rarity that every pitcher dreams about, but it has only happened 17 times in the entire history of major league baseball. For me, it was the highlight of my professional career.

My perfect game was a total surprise to me, but I can still remember it like it was yesterday. It was Father's Day 1964, and we were playing the Mets at Shea Stadium in the first game of a doubleheader. The weather was sunny, hot, and humid—just the kind I liked. My wife, Mary, and our daughter, Barbara, had driven to New York for the game and were in the stands watching.

During warm-ups I didn't feel particularly sharp, but in the first inning I got away with a few bad pitches and I felt like the good Lord might be smiling on me that day. I had complete command of my fastball and slider, and after the fifth inning I developed a really good curve that I could throw for a strike at any time.

As the game went on, being perfect became a mission. I was letting all my teammates know about it and trying to loosen them up on the bench. Baseball superstition demands that players in the dugout not talk about a no-hitter or a perfect game so that they don't jinx the pitcher. But I had never believed in superstitions. I kicked the foul line and broke all of the little "rules" that many players swear by. Plus, just three weeks earlier, I had taken a no-hitter into the eighth inning in a game against the Houston Colt 45's, but our team became so uptight about the no-hitter then that it ended up costing us the game.

I wasn't going to let that happen again. So after every inning I kept talking to my teammates in the dugout to relieve the pressure, urging them to buckle down and to stay sharp. And they did. In the fifth inning my second baseman, Tony Taylor, made an unbelievable diving stop on a hard ground ball hit to his left and from his knees threw out Jesse Gonder by a step. Dick Allen also made a sparkling play on a smash into the hole at third base to rob a sure hit.

After the game was over and the initial thrill had worn off a bit, I realized that the best part about a perfect game is that your teammates are perfect with you. In my professional career I have never felt anything else quite like it, except maybe the elation that came when I won a seat in the U.S. Senate in 1998. But that victory took the work of so many more people—volunteers, supporters, and staff—while on the diamond, there were just nine of us. That made it a little more special because on that one summer day in 1964, our team was flawless—in pitching, fielding, and communicating on the field—and the thrill that comes with working so closely, so perfectly, with your teammates is beyond words for me. Baseball might be a series of one-on-one match-ups between the pitcher and the hitters, but on that day we won—and were perfect—as a team.

Only a handful of pitchers have thrown perfect games, and I'm very proud to be part of that group and part of this book. Sometimes a perfect game is the only great game of a pitcher's career; sometimes it's just another milestone in a Hall of Famer's career. But that doesn't really matter. Because the thrill and emotion from a perfect game last a lifetime.

— SENATOR JIM BUNNING
JANUARY 2002

Preface to the 2005 Edition

Two and a half years early, Randy Johnson came through. In the first edition of this book, we wrote that perfect games occur, on average, every 7.3 years. On May 18, 2004, Randy Johnson beat the odds—in more ways than one, as you'll read in a new chapter on his game—when he followed the perfecto crafted by David Cone in 1999 by just under five years.

One of the many delightful things about perfect games is that you just never know . . . another one might be thrown tonight—or not. Every game opens up two new possibilities for perfection. We all watched Ichiro Suzuki attack the single-season record for hits, day after day, at-bat after at-bat, the inevitable conclusion a fixed signpost on the road ahead. But a perfect game has no road map; it shows up in a pitcher's path like a deer standing in a road on a dark night, accelerating your heartbeat before it zings to safety. Did you really see that, you think, as your heart slows down?

After writing this book, I now watch games with a new and particular passion, my interest level waning slightly as soon as each team gets a base runner. The games start out with an empty scorecard, awaiting zeroes. As each pitcher fails, perfection—as hard to catch as a hummingbird—disappears until next time. That's a hard judgment, of course: to be branded a failure simply for giving up a hit or a walk, or after seeing your teammate commit an error. But in the context of perfect games, there are no second chances—until your next turn through the rotation.

This edition is our second turn through the order of perfect games. While discussing the first edition with readers and commentators, I was struck by the fact that people focused as much on those who did not quite make it as on those who did. As much as I enjoyed celebrating the worthy achievements of the 16 (now 17!) perfect-game pitchers, I was also humbled at the care that readers showed for those who, while outstanding, were not perfect (see the Appendix). And because, frankly, all of us are just that (outstanding, but not perfect) to varying degrees, the sentiment gives me some hope for the world yet.

Thanks to Randy Johnson for spurring us to revisit perfection, near-perfection, and baseball history. See you in another 7.5 years (or less!).

Acknowledgments

Thanks first of all to the 17 pitchers who fashioned these perfect games along with the help of their teammates. Obviously, without their talents and accomplishments, I'd have nothing to write about.

Thanks also to the intrepid Bob Woods, who braved the Yankees clubhouse to gather a number of perfect-game stories from a variety of players and coaches.

During research for the book, dozens of people inside and outside baseball generously gave their time to reminisce about these 17 perfect days in the sun. I thank all the players, coaches, broadcasters, writers, and others quoted directly in this book, who spoke to a guy who was a stranger to nearly all of them. Some of them were players reliving their greatest moments; others were players looking back on days they didn't much enjoy remembering. For the most part, all of them were thoughtful and interested and helpful.

Thanks to David Fischer, who provided tons of diligent research, wrote a great Appendix, and acted as a sounding board for stories along the way.

In addition, some special thanks to people who are not quoted directly within but who provided help, support, or encouragement: Jon Scher, *ESPN Magazine;* Tim Mead, Anaheim Angels; John Blake and Amy Gunter, Texas Rangers; Wes Seeley, *Total Sports;* Cara Tayback and Stu Weiner, MSG Networks; Mike Renard, Senator Jim Bunning's office; Bill Francis and Bill Burdick, Baseball Hall of Fame; Jason Zillo, New York Yankees; P. J. Loyello, Montreal Expos; Brent Shyer and Dave Tuttle, Los Angeles Dodgers; Mike Swanson, Arizona Diamondbacks; and Keri Naeger, MLB Players' Alumni Association. Thanks also to alert reader Jeff Sharp for a helpful stat that found its way into Chapter 17.

The fine reporting of many, many writers and reporters over the years contributed to the stories in this book. Among the many periodicals consulted for their record of days gone by: the Associated Press; *Baseball Digest; The Baseball Research Journal; The Baseball Timeline;* the *Boston Globe;* the *Cleveland Plain Dealer;* the *Los Angeles Times;* the *Los Angeles Herald-Examiner; The National Pastime;* the *New York Daily News;* the *New York Post; The New York Times; The Sporting News;* the *Toronto Globe and Mail; Sports Illustrated; USA Today; USA Today Baseball Weekly;* and the *Washington Post.*

A special thanks to a secret sports treasure trove: the Amateur Athletic Foundation Sports Library in Los Angeles.

The staff there was consistently helpful, enthusiastic, and resourceful. I recommend their services to all sports historians.

Thanks to my family—Patty, Conor, and Katie—for keeping the noise to a dull roar as I typed for days at a time. Thanks to the Wheezers for helping me always remember why I love this game in the first place.

Thanks to Mitch Rogatz, Tom Bast, Linc Wonham, and Blythe Hurley at Triumph for believing in me and this project from the very beginning, and for their patience as they waited, toes tapping, for my final chapters.

Finally, thanks to you for reading. I hope you will enjoy it.

The zeroes on the scoreboard and the joy on David Cone's face both tell the story: he has just thrown the 16th perfect game in baseball history, joining the game's most exclusive pitching fraternity. *Photo courtesy of AP/World Wide Photos.*

Introduction

Imagine . . .

Imagine the most perfect day you could ever have.

Maybe it's your wedding day . . . beautiful weather, you look great, your soon-to-be spouse looks better. No one trips coming down the aisle; the caterer is on time and on budget. The band plays every tune perfectly. You don't get lost on the way to the honeymoon hotel, and, well, everything else is just perfect, wink, wink.

Oh, but wait, Aunt Mildred wears the same dress as Aunt Sophie. And boom, just like that, your perfect day isn't perfect after all. It's close but, sorry pal, 'tweren't perfect. And worst of all, it wasn't even your fault.

Or perhaps it is the day your child is born. You make it to the hospital in time, the doctors all smile, the insurance paperwork is a breeze. Labor comes and goes like a Nolan Ryan fastball, and bingo, a child is born. A perfect, healthy, happy, smiling child.

But oops, you forget the batteries for the flash, so you can't capture the one-moment-old photo.

Bang. Insert *almost* before perfect.

Something that small—a blip on the radar screen, a hiccup in the proceedings, a minuscule scratch on the CD—that's all it takes for the day to go from perfect to nearly perfect.

And so it is in baseball. A perfect game is almost unimaginably hard to attain. Each game presents hundreds of ways that perfection can slip away. A pitcher can mow down batter after batter, hitting his spots with laserlike precision; his fielders can make play after play, from routine grounders to *SportsCenter* "Web Gems." Yet if just one of those batters manages to squib out a hit, or, in the immortal words of Crash Davis, to come up with "a bloop, a bleeder, a Texas leaguer, a ground ball with eyes," the perfect game disappears like cigar smoke in the Wrigley Field bleachers.

And that's just the opposing batters crossing out a chance at "perfect."

If the pitcher himself misses the plate by a fraction of an inch on a ball three, it's good-bye, perfect game (just ask Milt Pappas, who did just that in 1972). Or a pitcher can plunk a batter, as poor old Hooks Wiltse did to the final batter in his near-perfect game in 1908 (and to make matters worse, it was the opposing pitcher!). Bill Singer and Dick Bosman each committed the intensely ironic errors that kept their no-hitters from being perfect. Brian Holman was one of several pitchers to give up a hit to the 27th batter in a game, after having erased the previous 26 in a row; Holman's perfection breaker, in 1990, was a home run, for emphasis. (You can read more about these "almosts" in our Appendix on page 272.)

Each pitch, each ball put in play, each new batter is a chance for perfection to vanish. But each completed set of 27 outs, combined with a win by a team, earns a permanent place in baseball history.

The concept has even entered popular culture. One of the many hilarious ESPN *SportsCenter* ads had host Dan Patrick flubbing a word late in a broadcast, thus ruining his attempt at a "perfect show."

This book, whether perfect itself or not, will examine each of the 17 official perfect games pitched in the major leagues since 1876. But first, an overview of just what perfect games are . . . and are not.

Perfect Games Are Rare

Since 1876, when the National League was founded and the "major leagues" semiofficially were born, there have been more than 173,000 games played. In each one of those, two starting pitchers took to the mound, so, in fact, you can double that number to find out just how many chances there have been for a perfect game to occur. In perhaps the single-most telling stat to show just how difficult it is to catch lightning in a bottle and throw a perfect game, only 17 have ever been thrown. That's one every 20,350 games, a nearly invisible .00004 percent. The chance that you'll see one next time you go to the park is actually smaller than the chance that you'll be hit by lightning while walking to the stadium from your car. In 2000, for instance, more than 350 people were hit by lightning. Zero people saw a perfect game in the major leagues . . . because there wasn't one.

Compare the occurrence of a perfect game to that of baseball's other rarest feats: hitting four home runs in a game and making an unassisted triple play. Both have happened about a dozen times, fewer even than perfect games. But the former, while stunning, is doing the best thing possible four times; a pitcher does it 27 times. And, though not yet achieved, there remains something better, something "more perfect"—five home runs in a game. As for the triple play, that's very much an incidence of sheer luck rather than any particular skill or practice.

In a 1995 article in SABR's *Baseball Research Journal*, writer Charles Blohaus actually figured out the mathematical chances of pitchers throwing perfect games in their careers. Using a formula so complicated I won't bother to explain it, Blohaus determined that Sandy Koufax had a 0.337 percent chance of throwing a perfect game. And, in fact, Koufax's long odds came in with his 1965 perfecto, as did number four all time on Blohaus's list, Catfish Hunter. But Bob Gibson's 0.254 percent chance didn't pay off, nor did Whitey Ford's even-longer-shot 0.170 percent.

And just how often do perfect games occur? On average, about once every 7.3 years.

The point of all these numbers is just to get a little mathematical perspective on the fact that perfect games don't happen very often. But don't let your guard down . . . the next one might happen during the next game you see.

Perfect Games Are Fickle

As is often noted, the list of pitchers who have not thrown a perfect game is as stunning as the very fact that even 17 pitchers managed the feat. Among the Hall of Famers who, à la Red Buttons, "never got a dinner," are Christy Mathewson, Bob Feller, Grover Cleveland Alexander, Whitey Ford, Bob Gibson, Tom Seaver, and Warren Spahn.

Nolan Ryan threw an unthinkable seven no-hitters . . . and exactly zero perfect games. His wildness cost him in each case, as walks proved his undoing in each of the seven games. Roger Clemens has six Cy Young Awards but is still waiting at this writing for his first perfect game . . . heck, even for his first no-hitter.

The difference between pitching a perfect game—and earning your own chapter in this book, which, we hope, is far down the list of awards that these pitchers received for their feat—and pitching a no-hitter is razor-thin.

Is it fair? No, of course not. There's no crying in baseball; who says there should be fairness? The lattice of coincidence (thank you, *Repo Man*) that assembles to create a perfect game can snap at any one of a dozen points. Literally hundreds of things must go just right for a perfect game to happen. Over the course of a season or a career, all those things go right many, many times. It's putting them all together in one game that is the tricky part.

Perfect Games Are Baseball's Own

Baseball rewards imperfection more than any other sport. Imagine a football kicker making only 3 of every 10 field-goal attempts—a .300 average that would make a batter an All-Star—and then watch that kicker start looking for a job. Yet a pitcher can regularly have a .500 record and year after year keep getting a paycheck (especially if he's left-handed). A team that wins only 60 percent of its games usually gets to play in late October. Perhaps because of that inherent imperfection, baseball also is the only sport that so specifically celebrates perfection, especially as defined by the perfect game. There may indeed be no crying in baseball, but there likewise can be no "perfect" game in football, basketball, golf, etc.

The NFL has the "passer rating" system that grades quarterbacks using a formula so complicated that I'm getting a headache just thinking about trying to define it for you. Suffice to say that there is a maximum grade of 158.3 (please don't ask why). Yet even a quarterback who reaches that number in a game can lose, and, oddly, can have statistics that aren't as good as another quarterback who reaches the same grade. Do they call that a "perfect" game? No.

Similarly in basketball, a player might make all of his shots from the field and the foul line, but there is no way to grade perfection in other areas, such as assists and rebounds. So, no special epithet is given this 100 percent shooting performance. In fact, it will rate nothing but a footnote in the evening highlights.

OK, yes, you can bowl a perfect game, 12 consecutive strikes for a score of 300. Guess what? Thousands of people have accomplished that feat, so, while it certainly is hard to do, it's also not so unique as to boggle the mind. Someone also mentioned that we should compare our perfect games to a perfect 10 in gymnastics, but I advised him to come in out of the sun.

Baseball rewards imperfection and at the same time exalts above other performances the game's single version of perfection. But why?

You might put it down to the almost freakish nature of the feat. It just comes along so rarely that when it happens, everyone stops to notice. It's just another victory, in most cases, just another game in a long slog of a season. A pitcher doesn't get extra credit for the event, though some have enjoyed instant bonuses from friendly owners, as well as a lifetime of card shows and memorabilia autographing. It might be the last truly great game a pitcher throws, like (possibly) David Cone; or win number 380 in a 511-victory career, like Cy Young; or the only time that a pitcher stepped into the spotlight, as in the case of journeyman lightning-catcher Charley Robertson in 1922.

If you think of a baseball season as being a long book in a series of long books that make up baseball history, a perfect game is like an old bookmark left between two pages that pops up unexpectedly. But that bookmark isn't just a scrap of paper . . . it's a thousand-dollar bill. So that's the excitement, the thrill, the out-of-nowhereness that is celebrated as much as the physical acts of pitching and fielding. Yes, a perfect game is a great feat, but it's an unlikely one, a rare one, and that's why we talk about them. Most of the pitchers I spoke to said they had had better stuff in other games; certainly fielders have made many more spectacular plays than have been made in perfectos; and many pitchers have gone longer than nine innings without issuing a walk. Yet it is in that tidy little one-shot bundle of zeros that perfection is achieved.

Unlike a no-hitter, for example, another one of baseball's highest, though far less rare feats of achievement, a perfect game is the total of many parts. In a no-hitter, a pitcher can walk the lineup (the record is nine, most recently by A. J. Burnett of Florida in 2001) and still celebrate a no-no. In a no-hitter, a pitcher's teammates can flub their way through nine innings, committing error after error, and still the pitcher gets a place in the record book (assuming he goes nine innings and wins, that is).

But in a perfect game, perfection is demanded of all nine players on the field. As John Thorn and John Holway point out in their 1988 book, *The Pitcher*, it's hardly fair that a pitcher can get the job done—induce a candy-hop grounder, for instance—and then fail to reach perfection when his second baseman throws it to Keith Olbermann's mother (not that Chuck Knoblauch ever cost a pitcher a perfecto, just the opposite on two occasions, in fact . . . I just like that image).

"It just does not seem fair that, when a shortstop makes a sensational play to rob a batter of a sure hit, the pitcher is given a perfect game, but if another shortstop boots an easy grounder, the pitcher is penalized," they write.

"A perfect game is a team accomplishment," Thorn said. "A no-hitter is a pitcher's accomplishment."

"It's a total team effort," says Jim Bunning, who should know, because he pitched a perfect game in 1964 with Philadelphia.

But who gets credit? The team? Nope. It's the pitcher, that's who. All the members of his team must be perfect in the field, and the team must score at least one run, by hook or by crook. Yet perfect games are not recorded by teams but by pitchers. Again, is that fair? No, that's baseball.

Perfection can be denied by something completely out of the pitcher's control. That's not fair, really. But them's the rules, Katie, and that's how they score the game.

Perfect Games Are Narrowly Defined

Baseball officially defines a perfect game as one in which the pitcher allows no base runners in at least nine innings of a complete-game victory. Shoot down 27 out of 27, as Pedro Martinez did for Montreal in 1995, and then give up a hit to number 28 . . . sorry, Pedro, no es el perfecto (or should we say, in deference to L'Expos: "non est parfait"). Or, even worse, as in the famous case of Harvey Haddix, you can nail down 36 consecutive batters, then watch perfection, and even victory, get flushed away in the thirteenth inning with an error, a walk, and a dinger (OK, officially a double, but Joe Adcock did hit the ball out of the yard). Many observers have called Haddix's the greatest game ever pitched. The man retired 36, count 'em, 36 hitters in a row, a feat since topped by others (although each of them over several or many games), yet he is more famous not for that level of achievement but for the ignominious way that he and the Pirates lost the game. It is his imperfection that is famous, his and the Pirates' inability to achieve perfection that is noted. Again, in the context of an inherently imperfect sport, the rare is the thing that gets the ink.

Thorn and Holway point out that Waite Hoyt, then with the Red Sox, once pitched 11⅓ perfect innings during a 13-inning game against the Yankees (he gave up hits in the first and thirteenth innings of an eventual 2–1 loss to the Yankees). Yet you almost never hear about Hoyt's feat when it comes to talking about perfection. He pitched a four-hitter that day and wound up losing in thirteen on a sac fly. His achievement, while impressive, not only was not a winner, it was also overshadowed by teammate Babe Ruth's 28th dinger of the year, setting a new single-season record.

But were those pitchers perfect? No, not officially, as of 1991, when a special Major League Baseball commission rewrote the rules, "kicked out" several no-hitters from the official list, and erased Haddix and Ernie Shore from the perfect-game list. (Shore, of course, famously relieved Babe Ruth in a 1917 game after Ruth had walked the opening batter and then punched the ump. Shore got the next 26 men in a row. His feat for years was included on the perfect-game list, but not anymore.)

Thanks to that ruling, and now with the assembled weight of history behind it, ya gotta get the W, and we don't mean W. Bush, to make the short list of perfect-game pitchers.

Perfect Games Are Devoutly Desired

It's really stunning, when you stop to think about it. As I did research on this book, I watched every game with the hope that it would turn into a perfecto. That's not normally how you should watch a game, of course, and of course, I was disappointed time and time again. Each time, as the first batter reached base for each team, hope vanished. A walk, a hit, an error, even a hit batsman, and, poof. It was like the game was over; the result really didn't matter, only that perfection remained once more elusive.

On May 26, 2001, Curt Schilling of the Arizona Diamondbacks got my hopes up. The former Phillies' fireballer was going through Padres like a church with an angry congregation; he was perfect for 22 batters. I was watching *Baseball Tonight* on ESPN, and they kept teasing viewers with progress reports of Schilling's impending gem. I tried to get the game live on Internet radio through mlb.com, but some program bug made that impossible. So I was bouncing back and forth from my TV in one room to the computer in the other, watching *Baseball Tonight* on one and the pitch-by-pitch "GameCast" on espn.com on the other.

In the sixth, down went another set of Padres.

This is it, I thought, another chapter for the book. Big sales in Arizona!

In the seventh, Schilling put up notch number 22, retiring Phil Nevin.

Then up stepped Ben Davis.

The GameCast screen reset with the words, "Davis infield hit." And like a PC monitor going dark, poof, Schilling's bid for history was over. Of course, that unadorned line of type in the little computer box didn't show the details of Davis' hit, a bunt single against an infield at normal depth. Diamondbacks manager Bob Brenly excoriated Davis, who, only slightly cha-grined, pointed out that his hit had brought the tying run to the plate in a 2–0 game.

(Not long before we wrapped up this book, the Yankees' Mike Mussina came as close as anyone has ever come to a perfect game without achieving it, giving up a clean, non-bunt single with two outs in the ninth and two strikes on Boston's Carl Everett. Mussina's near-perfect game is relived in the Appendix.)

The controversy over Davis' hit merely called attention to the stunning rarity of and baseball-wide amazement at the very idea of a perfect game. The reaction of fans and players was to the fact that Davis could so brazenly—or wisely, depending on your point of view—flout the baseball gods by ending the bid with a less-than-manly move. It was as if the perfect game was a special, sacrosanct thing, to be created in purity and not sullied with chicanery. In his 2001 book about David Cone, *A Pitcher's Story*, Roger Angell called a perfect game "Puritan." The baseball world so hungers for this display of pitching perfection that it rises up in anger when that chance is snatched away from it in a way it felt was less than, well, "right," whatever that means in this case.

Yet even the appearance of a chance of another one makes the baseball world rush to their computers and TVs and radios in hopes of being part of the miracle. (The fact that millions can now share in what was once able to be shared by only thousands is a theme I'll cover briefly in the chapters on Wells and Cone. Whereas you could probably find 200,000 people who say they were in Yankee Stadium to see Larsen's game—there were actually only 64,519—today, millions can say they saw Cone's—or at least a part of it—and they won't be lying.)

Perfect Games Are These

There were two in 1880. Two bolts of lightning struck just five days apart. J. Lee Richmond pitched the first one for the old Worcester club of the National League. John Montgomery Ward fired the other for Providence against Buffalo. Ward later became a fine-hitting shortstop, a lawyer, and the founder of the short-lived Players' League.

The first perfect game of the 20th century was thrown by the man who came to define pitching greatness with the award named for him. Cy Young cleaned out the Athletics in a game he called his biggest thrill in baseball.

Four years later, Addie Joss threw what was perhaps the most clutch perfect game or no-hitter in baseball history, with the possible exception of Don Larsen's in 1956. With his Cleveland team battling for a pennant they would eventually lose, Joss threw a perfect game against Ed Walsh, who himself set a league record with 15 strikeouts while allowing only three hits.

My vote for most obscure player to pitch a perfect game is Charley Robertson, whose 1922 perfecto was the only way that baseball would have remembered him today, because the rest of his career was subpedestrian in every way.

Thirty-four years would pass before the next perfect game, and this would be the most famous one of all time: Don Larsen's 2–0 victory over Brooklyn in Game 5 of the 1956 World Series. It was the only postseason no-hitter ever, to say nothing of a playoff or Series perfect game. Larsen's game put the perfect game permanently on the baseball map, firmly fixing it atop the roster of pitching accomplishments in a way that it had not been prior to that day.

There were three more in the 1960s, by a trio of Hall of Fame pitchers: Jim Bunning in 1964, Sandy Koufax in 1965, and Catfish Hunter in 1968.

The 1970s were not only a quite imperfect decade, but those years also passed without a perfect game.

The 1980s saw three more, but this time around a trio who would each eventually visit Cooperstown only with a ticket, not a plaque: Len Barker in 1981, Mike Witt in 1984, and Tom Browning in 1988.

Dennis Martinez became the first Latin pitcher with a perfect game in 1991, while making the Dodgers the first team to have a pair of perfect games thrown at them (Browning tossed the first one). Kenny Rogers found lightning in his arm on a hot Texas evening in 1994.

And in 1998 and 1999, perfection came again to Yankee Stadium when first David Wells and then David Cone eliminated 27 batters in a row in the House That Ruth Built.

Cone's was perhaps the more remarkable of the pair and gives the list of perfect games (so far!) a fitting coda, coming as it did with Don Larsen present in the park, having thrown out the first pitch on "Yogi Berra Day."

And that's it, in a few paragraphs: the entire roster of those pitchers who, for whatever reason, harnessed all that they had to discover perfection.

Most recently, in 2004, Randy Johnson became the oldest member of the "perfect club," shutting down the playoff-bound Atlanta Braves and putting a fitting cap on his certain Hall of Fame career.

––––––––––

To re-create these magic moments of baseball, I spoke to many of the perfect pitchers still alive, to opponents, team-mates, broadcasters, writers, fans, and others. I hope that the stories of these games are told in such a way that you can say you feel like you were there. And if you were there in the first place . . . to discover that you can go there again.

As you read through the accounts of these amazing days, these, in every case, once-in-a-pitcher's-lifetime performances, remember their rarity again and again. The seasons go on, one after another. The games pile up, 162 a year for each team these days, some 4,860 possibilities each season in the majors. Over and over, the pitchers go to the hill, and over and over, they fail to achieve perfection. They win, sure, they even allow no hits sometimes. But that ethereal state of perfection eludes them all . . . save for a chosen few.

Perfect games appear out of nowhere, a mystical combination of nasty stuff, stunning luck, and a blessing from the baseball gods.

If you're a pitcher, here's hoping you're blessed someday with a sip of that heady cocktail. If you're just a fan, here's hoping we can be there when it happens.

The perfect game was born when Providence rookie left-hander J. Lee Richmond, a future doctor, teacher, and high school dean, shut down the Cleveland Forest Citys. *Photo courtesy of John R. Husman.*

CHAPTER 1
J. Lee Richmond
June 12, 1880

The game of baseball doesn't have a birthday. Instead of popping into the world fully formed, it was built over time, like the pyramids except with much less slave labor (though players from the days before the end of the reserve clause might disagree). The traditional histories date the first organized "base ball" game to 1845, played in the now-legendary (and so aptly named) Elysian Fields in Hoboken, New Jersey, under the rules of the Knickerbocker Base Ball Club. References to "base ball" in New York in 1823 and Massachusetts in 1791 have also been unearthed. And there are references in British writings to similar games even earlier. The point is that unlike basketball, for instance, which one man invented in one day, baseball was not born so much as it evolved.

Baseball's perfect game, however, does have a birthday. There had to be a first instance of this rare event (a first instance in the "major leagues," that is), though like a child whose parents can't decide on a name, it wasn't called "perfect" until it was 42 years old. (Imagine calling your dad's brother "Uncle Baby Boy" until he was 42.) And there was indeed just such a birthday: June 12, 1880, in the town of Worcester, Massachusetts, home to a first-year National League team that was so green that it didn't even have a nickname. (Paul Dickson, in his *Baseball Dictionary* definition of the term "perfect game," calls Worcester the Brown Stockings, but *Total Baseball* does not give credit for that nickname, nor does any contemporary account of the game. You make the call.)

The "creator of the perfect game," a sobriquet he earns by doing it first, was a slender left-hander just recently arrived (in more ways than one, as we'll see) from Brown University. After almost no sleep, without a meal in about 12 hours, and pitching his second game of the day (really!), J. Lee Richmond became the first pro pitcher ever to set down all 27 men he faced in one game, defeating the Cleveland Forest Citys 1–0.

The perfect game was born.

But before we head back to 1880 to blow out the candles on the first perfecto, let's make a stop in Toledo, Ohio.

It's a sunny June day in 2000, the 120th anniversary of the first perfect game (OK, it was June 10, two days early, but they weren't perfect, Richmond was). A group of more than 50 of Richmond's descendants gathers in Forest Cemetery, atop Richmond's grave site, to erect a monument to their ancestor in honor of his greatest pitching feat.

Richmond's great-grandson John Richmond Husman had gotten the idea to honor his great-granddaddy when he saw similar monuments to Civil War heroes and other local legends. Husman is a baseball historian by avocation, a member of the Society for American Baseball Research (SABR), and author of several articles on Richmond's life and career. He had contacted all his relatives, and they had enthusiastically ponied up to buy the large stone tablet, and then many arrived to watch its dedication.

At that ceremony, in front of the crowd of relatives, friends, baseball fans, and local media, two little girls step forward. Amid the ghosts of the past, Richmond's great-great-great-granddaughters sweetly sing an anthem to a game loved past, present, and future. A few fans flap back and forth as the words sung by Sophia Forbes Marciniak and Isabelle Richmond Marciniak waft out over the crowd, and a few people join in.

"Take me out to the ballgame, take me out with the crowd . . ."

OK, we can take a hint. Off we go to the ballpark, the West Side Fairgrounds in Worcester, Massachusetts. Set the Way-Back Machine for June 12, 1880, Mr. Peabody.

While we're zooming through space in a very non-Einsteinian way, let's examine baseball as it was played in Richmond's day. While in no way belittling Richmond's accomplishment, it's important to understand just how different the rules of the game, the style of play, the equipment, and the league structures were in 1880.

First of all, the rules. Three outs were still a half-inning, and there were nine innings a game, but by 1880, the number of balls necessary for a walk was only down to eight. It wouldn't drop, gradually, to four until 1889. Three strikes was an out, but foul balls of any sort were not counted as a strike. In the years following, fouls would first be strikes when bunted, then strikes at all times. However, a defensive player in 1880 could catch a foul ball on one bounce and record an out; this was called the foul bound. (Fielders' ability to get to these foul bounds on one hop would prove crucial to Richmond's perfect-game win, as will become apparent when you read about the single weirdest defensive play in any perfect game.)

In addition, pitchers like Richmond could not just rear back and toss the ball wherever they thought it would do the most good (from their point of view, that is). Batters could request a high ball (above the waist) or a low ball. Pitches missing that zone, even though the ball might be right down Broadway, were called balls (maybe that's one reason they got so many).

And just because Randy Johnson has dominated the majors for the past decade as a lefty with a Richmond-like aura of success, don't think the Big Unit would have even made the J.V. in 1880. To start with, his pitching arm couldn't go above his shoulder while pitching the ball. Richmond, like most other pitchers, pretty much threw underhand, much like today's fast-pitch softball players. Johnson might still have a nasty sidearm curve, but that overhand fastball would be illegal. Of course, he'd be throwing it from 45 feet away, so maybe he would be a star in 1880 after all.

The pitchers of 1880 threw from flat ground, not from a mound, inside a four-by-six-foot box, the front edge of which was 45 feet from home plate (which often was a square, not the pentagon familiar today). Estimates of their velocity range from the mid-60s to the low 80s—not exactly radar-gun-busting, but thrown from much closer and with all sorts of nasty spin.

Should this in some way denigrate Richmond's accomplishment? The question of the relativity of statistics continually pops up when comparing players, teams, and eras. Many "records" are actually only records since 1901, when the American League joined the existing N.L. to form the "major leagues." For instance, think Nolan Ryan's 383 strikeouts in 1973 is the all-time best? Wrong. Matt Kilroy whiffed 513 batters in 1886. Rickey Henderson's 130 stolen bases in one season are the most ever, right? Nope. Hugh Nicol swiped 138 in 1887.

Richmond deserves to be first on the list of perfect games because he fulfilled the rules of the game as he knew them: under the rules of play, erase 27 men in a row without one safely reaching first base. He did that. Perfect game.

Let the arguments fly, but the bottom line is this: those records were set, like Richmond's perfect game (and J. M. Ward's perfecto five days later, as we'll see in the next chapter) in the National League, which has played without interruption since 1876. There is an unbroken line between Richmond and the perfect games thrown by Jim Bunning, Sandy Koufax, Tom Browning, Dennis Martinez, and Randy Johnson. A similar line connects Cy Young to Don Larsen and David Cone. And a thick black marker of a line connects all these players together.

The players of the late 1800s, under the rules of play they were given, accomplished amazing things. The beauty of baseball is that we could argue all night about this, and neither side would be completely convinced of victory in the argument. Yes, the game was in many ways dramatically different. But should we punish old-time players because the game had yet to evolve? While they did enjoy rules like more balls for a walk or "called" pitches, they didn't benefit from modern training, equipment, travel, and so on.

Understanding the context of the feats, in my opinion, just adds that much more color and flavor to the story, rather than detracts from the players' successes.

Another thing that was different was that pitchers also threw pretty much every game. Part of the reason was that the underarm style was much less rough on the arm and shoulder. But still . . . Richmond told of one streak where he pitched 13 games in 13 days. The "change pitcher," another fielder, was instructed "not to come in unless I had sun-stroke," Richmond said. And he never did.

Perhaps the most amazing thing about Richmond's perfect game (and there are other amazing things to come, trust me) is that there were no errors. Of course, that's what helped make it perfect, but as historian John Thorn notes, "The fields were rutted and poor, and all the fielders were essentially barehanded. To have a perfectly clean game played behind you was almost as rare as a perfect game."

In fact, only weeks earlier, Providence, another team in the National League, had managed to squeeze 11 errors into a nine-inning game. Thorn notes that his studies for *Total Baseball*, of which he is one of the authors and editors, found that the percentage of unearned runs was about 1 in 3 in those days; to compare, today it's about 1 in 20.

Richmond recognized this unusual feat and made sure to mention it eloquently in future interviews. "I couldn't have pitched it if the fielders had not been so expert in handling the ball. No pitcher can pitch a perfect game if he does not have perfect cooperation."

Finally, pro baseball was just about a decade old in 1880, and the National League was in only its fifth season. For none of the players was this a year-round job, and it was still considered a less-than-fashionable occupation for a gentleman, so most of the players weren't considered gentlemen.

One of those who was considered such was Richmond.

After growing up in Toledo, he went to Brown University in Providence, Rhode Island, where he soon became the top pitcher on the school team. He was so good, in fact, that he defeated professional teams in exhibitions in 1879, including Cap Anson's Chicago White Stockings.

"He was considered the best pitcher in baseball even before he joined the Worcester team," Thorn notes. In fact, for his first full season, 1880, Richmond signed for a record $2,400 salary.

Before turning pro, however, Richmond led his Brown team to the 1879 national baseball title, defeating Yale 3–2 when he struck out the final batter after going to a count of 8–2 (the number of balls needed for a walk would drop to 8 the next year). But his talents were so obvious to the fledgling pro teams that he was repeatedly wooed to play for them. He finally signed with Worcester while still a collegian.

Richmond's new life as a professional led to a major brouhaha about his collegiate/amateur vs. pro status. Richmond, in fact, can quite literally be called the first college athlete to leave school early to go pro. He gave up his final year of eligibility to join Worcester in 1879, and later his example was one used to pass rules banning pro athletes from competing at the college level. (Worcester then officially joined the N.L. for the 1880 season).

In his first start with Worcester (then a part of a minor league), on June 2, 1879, he no-hit the White Stockings in a seven-inning exhibition game. "The game only went on seven innings because the Chicagos had to catch a train," Richmond remembered years later. "Just 21 of the old White Stockings came to bat."

Turning pro looked like the right idea.

Of course, he did go on to graduate, doing so in fact four days after his perfect game, and later got a doctorate in medicine from Columbia. So he didn't exactly toss away his education to play ball. And in fact, he remained one of Brown's most celebrated athletes, with numerous articles honoring him appearing in alumni publications and memoirs popping up on anniversaries of his feats.

Richmond went by the name Lee and had apparently, according to Husman, simply added the J. at some point for style. "It's like Harry S Truman, but with a period," Husman adds with a laugh. "He had a brother J. Otis. I found a baptism record when he was 13 and it says J. Lee and his signature was always J. Lee." Many record books still call him John, but you can now win bar bets by proving that that wasn't his name.

While Lee's was the first perfect game, he did go through some labor pains to deliver this baby, or at least to get to the park on time to deliver it. Mid-June was pretty much cruising time for the young gentlemen scholars of Brown University. Classes were over, exams were in the books, and commencement ceremonies were several days away. Then, as now, this was nothing more than an excuse to party.

On June 11, Class Day was held at Brown, a daylong—and eventually nightlong—series of parties and dinners that young Richmond took part in to the fullest, apparently. A letter written later by a friend describes the future doctor marching to the College Hill baseball field early on the morning of June 12 with an empty champagne bottle cradled lovingly in his arms.

It was 5:00 A.M. on Saturday morning, June 12, when Richmond finally took his place in the pitching square. But he wasn't facing the Cleveland Forest Citys, and he wasn't pitching for Worcester. He was pitching in what was apparently a Class Day tradition; instead of enjoying some of the hair of the dog, the students took up the hide of the horse and played dawn patrol baseball.

"I doubted the time, too," says John Husman. "But I actually went back to Providence and found the site where we think the games were played. And I went out there early in the morning and there was indeed enough light to play."

Though the lack of light may not have been the only reason the players had trouble seeing, Richmond and his fellows wrapped up the game at about 6:30 and headed for bed. And just like Don Larsen would allegedly do 68 years later, the soon-to-be-perfect pitcher burned the midnight oil and then some. Of course, Larsen hadn't spent part of his supposed curfew-breaking activities firing heaters past heated classmates.

"Richmond's got to be the only perfect-game pitcher who threw two games in one day," laughs Husman.

Did we mention that not only did he get to bed at 6:30, but he had to get up to catch an 11:30 train from Providence to Worcester to pitch in the game for which he was being paid? The train was then delayed, and he had to hustle straight to the park from the station "without his dinner [i.e., lunch]," according to the *Worcester Gazette.* So Richmond was fortified with only whatever was left from the previous night's bacchanal as he finally threw the first pitch of the game that would make him famous.

Richmond, 5'10" and 142 pounds at the time, was facing a Forest Citys lineup that was not exactly Murderer's Row; only three of the nine starters entered the game with averages above .250. However, this was very much in line with the standards of the time; the league average was but .245, and only a handful of players batted over .300.

To face these hitters, Richmond used a surprisingly varied list of pitches, including what was perhaps the first curveball put to consistently good use in the big leagues. The curve had been "invented" by Candy Cummings several years earlier, and most pitchers had something like it in their arsenal. Richmond seems to have perfected it. In fact, he once escorted disbelieving Brown professors to the diamond to successfully demonstrate that, as he once said, "a pitched sphere might indeed change its horizontal course during a pitch and that the 'curve' was not mere optical illusion." That Richmond threw this unusual pitch from the left side (he was one of only two southpaws pitching regularly at the time) made it all that much more difficult to hit.

"I also had a fast jump ball that was hard to hit when it was working right, and it must have been working right on that hot afternoon," Richmond told a newspaper interviewer in 1910. "My half-stride ball was also working splendidly."

Um, jump balls are in basketball, right? And a "half-stride" ball? Explanation, please.

Richmond threw basically a rising fastball that seemed to rise even more than would be possible thanks to the upward sweeping motion of his delivery. This "jump ball" appeared to pop up as it approached the hitter.

Here's Richmond on the half-stride ball, which was basically his change-up: "I would only stride half the distance [as I pitched]. The abrupt halt as the ball left my hand caused the ball to do some of the most remarkable things in the way of ducking, diving, and bobbing up again I have ever seen."

Add to this array of pitches a delivery that was uniquely described by a writer in the *Providence Journal:* "Richmond is simply agonizing. Before delivery he works his feet like a chicken getting ready for a dirt-bath. He turns his right side to the batter, looks around at his fielders, then up at the heavens, then commences a painful working of the shoulders, as though something were biting him between the shoulders."

Sounds remarkably like Fernando Valenzuela, doesn't it?

Husman kindly provided me with a copy of the original scorecard of the game, and the wonder of those little marks still shines through. Using only numbers, a few code words, and some lines, the entire game comes to life in front of your eyes. Any father who doesn't teach his kids to score a game should be made to face Randy Johnson armed only with a ruler.

Though not recorded on the scoresheet, it's interesting to note that Cleveland manager (and pitcher) Jim McCormick tried to neutralize Richmond's "portside deliveries." He fielded an all-right-handed-hitting lineup, perhaps one of the earliest uses of this now-typical "matchup" strategy.

Second baseman Fred Dunlap led off the game for Cleveland by grounding out to second. Third baseman Frank Hankinson did likewise. And catcher Mike Kennedy fouled out to the shortstop.

And so it went for four full innings, both teams notching nary a hit. In that span, Charley Bennett, catching for Richmond and Worcester, recorded three "foul" outs, two of which were of the foul-bound variety. Cleveland hit only two balls out of the infield, a pair of fly balls to Fred Corey in center field.

In the top of the fifth occurred the play that stands alone among all perfect games. In the 120-plus years that followed Richmond's victory, perfect-game performances have been aided by diving catches, by strong throws from the hole, by timely hitting, by long runs after fly balls. But none of them was saved by an almost-unheard-of play that is recorded simply as 9-3.

Leading off the top of the fifth inning, 200-pound, right-handed-hitting first baseman Bill Phillips lined a hard shot to right field. Worcester's Alonzo Knight charged the ball and, without hesitating, fired to first base. Phillips was out by a step, declared umpire "Foghorn" Bradley (note that he was the only umpire on the field that day). An assist at first from right field? C'mon, if you put that in a movie script, they'd laugh you out of the theater. But that's what happened; Knight gunned down a guy at first on what was on any other day a clean single.

Did Knight know it was a no-hitter at the time? Maybe, but it didn't mean a thing back then. He certainly didn't know it was a perfect game; not only had the term not been invented, no one had ever thrown or heard of one. So why did he do it? I personally think it was a combination of the way the ball was hit—sharply by all accounts—the slowness of Phillips (perhaps he slipped; no mention is made of it), and Knight's familiarity with fielding balls on one bounce. Remember the foul bound? Whereas players of today wait for a clean hop, whether first, second, or third bounce, players back then knew to charge and catch by one bounce. Yes, Phillips' hit was fair, but it was the order of the day to attack the ball to get it on one bounce. Whether those were Knight's reasons or whether he was just showing off, the play seemed to energize Richmond, as Husman points out in his article in *Toledo Magazine.*

Richmond notched his first strikeout on the very next hitter, right fielder George Shaffer. He had one strikeout in each of the next four innings. Also, the ball left the infield only once more for Cleveland, a fly to Knight in the ninth.

Worcester went on to scratch out a run against McCormick in the bottom of the fifth. Shortstop Arthur Irwin got the second hit of the game to lead off the inning (Richmond himself, batting second in the lineup, had seen his single erased in the fourth by a 6-4-3 double play). Bennett followed with a walk.

Third baseman Art Whitney then grounded back to McCormick, who grabbed the ball, whirled, and fired to Dunlap, covering second base. But Dunlap dropped the throw. Irwin never stopped running, and as he dashed for home, Dunlap made his second error on the play by firing it over the catcher's head. The score was 1–0 Worcester on an unearned run. (Addie Joss, Sandy Koufax, and Mike Witt would all later win their perfect games 1–0 on unearned runs.)

And then Richmond methodically moved along through the lineup: two grounders and a K in the sixth; a strikeout and two flys in the seventh; a strikeout, a ground-out, and a fly-out in the eighth.

After Corey struck out for Worcester to lead off the bottom of the eighth, a storm shower hit the ballpark and play was suspended. The *Worcester Gazette* put the delay at seven minutes, but it didn't seem to affect Richmond a bit. (More perfect parallels: misty conditions affected play during Len Barker's perfect game, rain delayed the start of Tom Browning's perfect game by more than two hours, and David Cone waited out a 33-minute rain delay in his perfecto.)

Sawdust was piled behind the pitcher's square, and Richmond "did some pretty lively work" with it, according to the *Worcester Daily.* To allow a pitcher with Richmond's array of pitches to doctor up further an already wet and soft ball hardly seems fair.

The ninth inning: a fly ball, a strikeout, and an unremarkable ground-out, short to first, completed the first-ever perfect game—27 up, 27 down. It was, said the *Chicago Tribune,* "The most wonderful game on record." The short item didn't mention who pitched it, however.

Though Worcester had managed three hits, they had more importantly committed no errors, a feat that was more remarkable to observers of the time than Richmond's similarly faultless performance. The *Worcester Gazette's* reporter puts Richmond's five strikeouts merely in the middle of a list of how the outs recorded in the game, giving them, and by extension him, equal weight with the fielders. Which, in many respects, is as it should be, but it is far from the exalted position that perfect-game pitchers have come to enjoy.

"Richmond was most effectively supported," the *Gazette* also noted, "every position on the home nine being played to perfection." That last phrase is as close as writers of the time came to coining the term by which we know the accomplishment today.

No mention is made of special postgame celebrations, and reporters didn't exactly crowd the locker room to talk to wet, naked men about what had just happened. That just wasn't done.

"Pitching [such a game] 30 years ago didn't make the same sensation in the base ball world that it does today," Richmond said in a 1910 interview. "I don't recall that any particular fuss was made about it by any newspaper or set of fans when I was fortunate enough to set this record."

Richmond's success didn't carry over very well the next game, either. Facing Cleveland again two days later, he was shelled for 23 hits and Worcester lost 7–1. Easy come, easy go.

In fact, it was only as time went on and when Young and Joss and Robertson added perfect games to the list that Richmond and J. M. Ward, pitcher of the second perfect game just five days later, began to get notice for their feats. Richmond was interviewed by Toledo papers on the 30th anniversary of the game and by a Worcester paper when a local minor leaguer nearly duplicated the feat in 1916. Brown University publications featured him several times, more often for his prowess as a college pitcher, but certainly as an athletically distinguished alumnus.

In all these articles, writers continued to struggle for a definition of the deed. One 1911 article in the *Toledo Blade* includes the tortured phrase: a "no-run game, no-hit game, no-man-reaching-first game." That was also what Richmond called it in a 1916 interview.

The postscript to Richmond's giving birth to the perfect game is the day it finally got a name. In 1922, in response to Charley Robertson's stunning performance against the Tigers (see page 57), a writer named Ernest J. Lanigan finally saved us all from extended use of hyphens by first using the term "perfect game" in his *Baseball Cyclopedia*. (Thanks to Paul Dickson's invaluable *Baseball Dictionary* for this tidbit.)

Richmond finished the 1880 season 32–32 on a team that finished in fourth place—not bad for their first season in the National League. It would, however, be the first of only three Worcester would spend in the bigs. Richmond's career ended for all practical purposes when Worcester disbanded after the 1882 season (he had short stints with Providence in 1883 and Cincinnati in an abbreviated "comeback" in 1886). He had bigger things in mind than pro ball, after all. He went to Columbia and earned a degree in medicine. Returning to Toledo, he became a teacher and principal in area high schools until "retiring" to become a professor and a dean at the University of Toledo.

"I'm just very proud of what my great-grandfather did," Husman says. "Both on the baseball field and throughout his whole life."

Richmond died in 1929. His death was front-page news in Toledo, a city that he had done proud in many ways.

And so, like Richmond did after his long and eventful life, let's go back to that cemetery in Toledo.

After the girls finish singing, Clifford Shields steps up to the microphone. He is dressed in a replica 1880 Mudville baseball uniform, and he intones the most famous baseball poem of all time, "Might Casey and the Mudville Nine." A local baseball club executive offers some words about Richmond and his career. And then three of Richmond's oldest relatives step forward and unveil a 30-inch wide, 42-inch tall granite memorial marker.

A steel diamond is inset in the granite, flanked by the years of Richmond's birth, 1857, and death, 1929. J. Lee Richmond, M.D., it goes on to say, and then details his accomplishments on the field and off.

Husman and the others in the crowd applaud, their clapping echoing the sounds that Richmond enjoyed on so many days in the ballfield.

"He was the first pitcher to ever throw a perfect game," Husman says proudly. "There were some that followed, but there are none like the first."

———————

(Author's note: a special note of thanks to John Richmond Husman for his great assistance in the creation of this chapter. He proudly promulgates the story of his great-grandfather's career, and as a member of SABR, he relies on facts and not legend to tell the tale. Thanks, John.)

John M. Ward's perfect game, hurled just five days after Richmond's, was the first of many successes for one of baseball's most versatile superstars. *Photo courtesy of The National Baseball Hall of Fame and Library, Cooperstown, New York.*

CHAPTER 2

John M. Ward

June 17, 1880

To tell the story of John Montgomery Ward's perfect game, we turn to comparisons that begin five days earlier and last for 85 years (heck, 124 years if you want to be picky).

The first point of comparison is to Lee Richmond. Five days after the former Brown lefty gave birth to (what would one day be called) the perfect game, it happened again when Ward and Providence beat Buffalo 5–0.

That's right—five days!

The next perfect game would not come until nearly 25 years later, while only twice more would perfect games even be thrown in consecutive years (1964–1965 and 1998–1999). It had never happened before, and then it happened twice in less than a week. There's no rational or statistical reason for this; it's just another reason to love baseball.

As for the two creators of those first perfect games, one can't help but lump them together in many ways, beyond simply the fluke of the calendar. Both Ward and Richmond were among the most well-known and successful pitchers in the game at the time, the Randy Johnson and Pedro Martinez of their day (though they played in the same league, of course, there being only the one). Ward and Richmond finished the 1880 season of their double-perfectos ranked second and third in innings pitched, respectively, with startling totals of 595 and 590⅔ IP. Ward had 39 wins on the season, Richmond 32. Ward led the league with eight shutouts; Richmond, remarkably, paced the circuit with three saves.

No secret to each other from their first successful pro performances, both pitchers were fierce competitors. Various later chroniclers speculated about a rivalry between the two men, writing of "brushback" pitches when facing each other and of similar endearments that supposedly occurred during the relatively brief period they both played regularly in the National League.

Did Ward know about Richmond's five-day-old feat? He never said, nor did Richmond comment about it directly.

"There was no indication that I could find that Ward knew of Richmond's game," says Bryan Di Salvatore, author of *A Clever Base-Ballist*, the well-received 1999 biography of Ward. "I would be extremely surprised if Ward had any awareness of it."

The nearness of the towns (40 or so miles separate Worcester, Massachusetts, and Providence, Rhode Island) suggests that the news of the event might have reached Ward in the days following Richmond's success. But daily box scores were rare, and he wasn't exactly tuning in to *SportsCenter*. But even had Ward known, he couldn't have simply arranged to match the feat; in fact, Ward pitched Providence to a 5–2 victory the day before his perfect game, against the same Buffalo team; if he could just pull such a perfect game out of his hat, why didn't he do it then? But of course, he couldn't do any such thing. It's still fun to think about, though.

The two players were also among the few pros who had played a lot of college ball. Richmond, however, was a graduate by the time of his perfect game, while Ward was four years past getting kicked out of Penn State (at 16, he was caught stealing chickens and expelled). Before he had turned to poultry purloining, Ward had played for the Penn State team.

After turning pro, he later became the essentially volunteer coach of Dartmouth in 1879, his first season with Providence. That season, he actually coached the Big Green to an upset win over Richmond and Brown. Di Salvatore forwarded a 1925 obituary of Ward from the Dartmouth newspaper essentially crediting Ward with legitimizing Dartmouth as a college baseball program. Richmond, of course, for his part remained an elder statesman of Brown athletics.

(Parenthetically, another Ward biographer, David Stevens, notes that both Richmond and Ward were two of the few clean-shaven players in a league rich with thick mustaches. Ward, however, later grew a 'stache typical of the times.)

––––––––––

Another comparison for Ward?

How about to Cy Young and Sandy Koufax? Ward joins those two players not only as members of the Hall of Fame but also as the only perfect-game pitchers who would have justifiably become baseball legends even without their perfect games. Young's 511 wins and Koufax's incredible skein of seasons in the 1960s are easy to call legendary, but Ward's career on and off the field combined to make him one of the most fascinating and successful baseball men ever. His perfect game was, as it was for Young and Koufax, icing on the cake. For some pitchers, their perfect game was the entire cake, including the icing, the cherry, and those cool roses made of frosting that the kids fight over.

"I didn't see every paper, of course, but I never saw another mention of the perfect game by him for the rest of his career," Di Salvatore notes, showing that Ward had bigger things in mind when reflecting on his many baseball accomplishments than one shining afternoon.

The comparisons go on. Another perfect-game pitcher, Jim Bunning, became a leader off the field just as Ward would do. Bunning would serve his constituents in Kentucky as a congressman and senator; Ward became baseball's first labor leader, inspiring the creation of the Brotherhood of Professional Base Ball Players in 1885 and the short-lived Players' League in 1890. Just as Bunning didn't win election for "perfecting" the Mets in 1964, neither did Ward need his perfect game to become a driving force in the early battles between players and owners. Bunning could thank his pro player status for name recognition, but he moved up the political ranks from councilman. Ward brought the value of his name earned on the field to the bargaining table, but it was his skill as a lawyer and negotiator, and not his fastball, that won his points.

Want more? This one is kind of goofy, but fun: 6 of the 16 perfect-game pitchers, of whom Ward was the first example, had one-syllable last names (the solo-sound list: Ward, Young, Joss,

Witt, Wells, Cone). In fact, if you want to pitch a perfect game, make sure your name doesn't have more than two syllables. Only Charley Robertson and Dennis Martinez managed to break the short-name stranglehold on perfect games. But I digress . . .

Yes, in case you were wondering, John Montgomery Ward came from the same family that started the department store chain with which he shared his middle name and surname, but it was a distant relation that he paid little, if any, attention to. (In fact, Di Salvatore points out that Ward hated his middle name and went by John M. Ward for all of his adult life.)

Born in Ohio in 1860, he grew up an athletic kid. Ward enrolled at Penn State at the age of 13, believe it or not—college in those days was not the solid four-year track of today. He began playing baseball there in 1875, the first year the school had a team. But, as noted, he ended his college days when he tried one too many stunts of the sort that today's collegians would hardly even get a ticket for. Fortunately, Ward had a career to fall back on: baseball.

At the time, baseball was not seen as a proper career for a college man. Richmond was, as we've seen, bound for bigger things, and baseball was just a way station. And for players from Ward's Dartmouth team, law school and other professions awaited; several players were offered pro jobs, but turned them down for further schooling or to take a "real" job.

For Ward, however, baseball would become his life. He signed with a small team in Pennsylvania in 1877, officially turning pro. He joined Providence the next season and helped them win the N.L. pennant in 1879.

So it was as a third-year pro that J. M. Ward, only 20 years old, took the hill for the Providence Grays against Buffalo on June 17, 1880. Providence was having trouble repeating its 1879 success, but in Buffalo they faced little challenge and would end their season with a collective .226 batting average.

It was on a lovely Thursday morning in June that nearly two thousand people crowded into two-year-old Messer Field in Providence. Morning? That's right, the game's first pitch was thrown just after 11:00 A.M., more than four hours before the normal 3:30 starting time. Di Salvatore reports that the Hop Bitters Regatta on the nearby Seekonk River was set for that afternoon, and the start of the game was moved forward to allow fans to attend both events.

Ward said thanks, and Buffalo hitters said, "raw deal."

Historian Frederick Ivor-Campbell first located the site of the field several years ago.

"We knew it was on Messer Street," he says. "There are photos of the team at the ballpark that show a building in the background with a very distinctive pattern of windows. Turns out that building is still there, a grammar school, I think, built not long before the grounds. So I took Bryan [Di Salvatore] to visit that site, which is now filled with multifamily homes.

"As best we can figure, the batter faced south or nearly so. At the time of the game, then, the sun would be still slightly on the third-base side, but by noon, it was directly over head and moving toward right field."

Had the game kicked off at the proper time, the sun would have passed overhead and begun its afternoon journey behind the right-field stands. As it was, at not-yet-noon, the sun was beaming happily right into the batters' eyes. And because the game took only an hour and 40 minutes to play, it was a problem from first pitch to last. Did that make it easier for Ward? Let's put it this way—it sure didn't hurt.

Though they were the home team, Providence batted first. Home-field advantage in those days often meant who was luckier in the pregame coin flip (or, more likely, whose fans were more distracting to the visiting team); it didn't mean that you automatically batted first. Facing future Hall of Fame pitcher Pud Galvin, the Grays got the first run of the game in the top of the second. Second sacker John Farrell lined a double to left, but Buffalo's left fielder Oscar Walker sailed the throw back in, and Farrell came all the way around. Ward got the only run he would need in a perfect game on an error.

However, the Grays did add single runs in the fourth, seventh, eighth, and ninth. Farrell again reached base in the fourth and moved to third on errors. Ward himself hit a sac fly to score the run. Third baseman George Bradley tripled in the seventh and later scored. With his third hit of the game, Farrell put himself on base in the eighth and later scored his third run. First baseman Joe Start also had a triple and scored in the ninth for Providence's fifth and final run.

As to Ward's defensive support, we are unfortunately cursed by limited reporting. A note in one description talks about a "fine catch" by Providence center fielder Paul Hines, but no other defensive gems are noticed. Bradley and shortstop John Peters (who actually led the N.L. with a .900 fielding average for the season) combined for ten assists, while Farrell had two more. Only five balls were hit to the outfield by Buffalo in the game.

Ward, for his part, induced grounder after grounder with an array of tricky pitches, while also recording six strikeouts. He would write later in an instructional book that speed was not always the answer for a pitcher, but rather he should "use his brain as well as his muscle" to succeed. Cruising along with a nice lead and an apparently charmed defense behind him, Ward wrapped up the second perfect game ever pitched with a 5–0 victory.

Along with the fact that it happened only five days after Richmond's game, perhaps the most surprising fact about Ward's triumph was the work of that defense. Earlier in the season, Providence had managed to string together 11 errors in a 7–1 loss to Chicago. So the *New York Clipper* was justifiably large when it praised the "perfect play" of the Providence defense. (Note that the *Clipper* almost nailed down the name of the game, but no one caught on.) Providence posted a .910 fielding average, fourth-worst in the league, and averaged more than two-and-a-half errors per game. But on June 17, they were, well, perfect.

For Ward, like Richmond, there was no postgame hulla-baloo to live down, no early morning talk shows to appear on. Neither man would have to ask teammates, as Kenny Rogers would more than a century later, "Leno or Letterman?" A hearty handshake, a "job well done," and on to the next game.

"What's interesting to me about the early perfect game is how little they were recognized for what they were," notes Ivor-Campbell, a vice president of SABR. "Pitching was probably recognized as more important that batting. But the pitchers didn't keep as many statistics. Pitching wins were rarely talked about or listed in terms of the pitcher winning the game. It was seen as much more of a team victory, rather than a pitcher's win."

About six weeks later, though, Ward once again made a bid for headlines and immortality, both for himself and Providence. On July 23, again facing Buffalo, he gave up a leadoff single, and then allowed no base runners for the rest of the game.

While Ward's pitching career would have been considered remarkable—he finished with a 164–103 record and a career 2.10 ERA, fourth-best of all time—Ward is not a unique part of baseball history just for his work on the mound. Amazingly, in 1884, his second year with the New York Giants, he threw out his pitching arm and moved to shortstop (and later to second base), playing for most of 11 more seasons while also becoming one of the top base stealers in the majors. He stole a league-leading 111 in 1887 and led again in 1892 with 88 SBs while with Brooklyn. He also occasionally gave his sore arm a rest by playing some outfield . . . and throwing left-handed! He finished his remarkable playing years back with the Giants in 1894 with a career total 2,151 hits. Ward's double-duty performances on the mound and as an everyday player are surpassed perhaps only by Babe Ruth.

Amid all this whirlwind diamond activity, Ward also was busy in the classroom. He returned to college at Columbia in New York, first receiving his undergrad degree and then working for and earning a law degree, becoming perhaps the first pro player to earn a graduate degree while playing. Here is not the place to go into great detail about his many other accomplishments, whether helping players battle against skinflint owners, becoming a top lawyer in New York, or continuing his athletic successes on the golf course. Instead, let us just note that John Montgomery "Monte" Ward was one of the most fascinating, versatile, intelligent, and all-around successful players in baseball history.

And, oh, yes, he also pitched a perfect game.

Boston's team was called the Americans
and the American League itself was only
three years old when Cy Young dropped a
perfecto on the Philadelphia Athletics.
Photo courtesy of AP/Wide World Photos.

CHAPTER 3

Cy Young

May 5, 1904

You might be thinking, oh sure, give a guy an all-time
record 815 chances (the most career starts) to fire a perfect
game, and he'll eventually get one, right? What's that old joke
about a thousand monkeys and a thousand typewriters?

But you have to move down another 19 notches on the
list of career starts to find another pitcher with a perfect
game (Dennis Martinez, with 562). Throwing a perfect game
has nothing to do with how many chances you get to throw
one; witness Charley Robertson throwing one in only his third
start. For Young, it was career victory number 380 on the way
to 511. He certainly was a dominant pitcher, and he did put
together the longest, most successful—in terms of wins—
mound career ever. But he got his perfect game, a 3–0 victory
over the Philadelphia Athletics on May 5, 1904, not by dint of

longevity but just as the other perfect pitchers did: with great pitching, timely fielding, and a little bit of luck.

———————

Baseball in 1904 had changed quite a bit from the days when Ward and Richmond played. Young began his career in 1890, as the overhand pitching style finally was becoming legitimate. Over the first 10 years of his career, the rules changed in several important ways. The pitching area was moved back to 60'6" in 1893, while the number of balls and strikes necessary for walks and strikeouts slowly decreased to their current levels of four and three. Perhaps the key change was finally put into place in the American League in 1903, when all foul balls were counted as strikes (the National League had made this the case in 1901). Previously, a foul ball on a bunt was a strike, but a foul on a full swing was not. Expert batters, such as Willie Keeler, could foul off pitch after pitch with no effect on the count but a mighty effect on the pitcher's stamina.

Unlike Richmond and Ward, Young did start his career after the underhand pitching style had evolved into a more typical pitching motion.

Finally, the ball was less than ideal from a hitter's perspective, being a cotton-and-wool-stuffed, leather-covered thing that by the end of the game could be a contorted, squishy mass. Young was pitching long before the days of umpires providing brand-new pearls for nearly every pitch. While Young's feats were tremendous, it's important to understand the context in which they were accomplished.

Young and the Red Sox entered the 1904 season as defending world champions, having defeated Pittsburg (they spelled it without the *h* in those days) in the first "World's Series" the previous October. Young had two of Boston's five victories in the best-of-nine Series and finished with a 1.59 ERA. He also had led the league with 28 wins, 7 shutouts, and 341 innings pitched. Oh, yes, he also found time to notch a league-leading two saves as well.

Young's victory total of 378 entering the season was already the most in history, and he would just continue adding to that total until he retired. The big farm boy from Gilmore, Ohio, was surely among baseball's elite pitchers of the day, a feared fireballer with an array of tricky off-speed and breaking pitches. Denton True Young had broken in with Cleveland in 1890, a $250 "bonus baby" who earned his famous nickname from one of two sources: the somewhat legendary story of him breaking boards in the side of a barn with his pitching, leading someone to remark that a "cyclone" had been through; or else from his rural roots, which had earned him the popular sobriquet "Cy," given to many farmyard rubes in the big city.

A big man at 6'2" and more than 200 pounds, the Young of 1904 was not yet the rather inflated figure of later years. He was no lean, mean, pitching machine, as he was in the first part of his career, but the most-published photographs of him do not do justice to his image during his prime.

"Cy was a big, burly fellow and he could hide the ball better than anyone else I ever saw," Ty Cobb said in a 1945 interview. "He would turn his back to you in the windup and suddenly the ball would be coming in to you. He had great control, too; he could pitch into a tin cup."

Young himself, in *My Greatest Day in Baseball*, ran down his list of attributes: "I was real fast in those days, but what very few batters knew was that I had two curves. One of them sailed in there as hard as my fastball and broke in reverse. It broke away from the batter. The other was a wide break."

Young was famous for his durability, and he rarely warmed up very long before games. In later years, he claimed never to have had the arm rubbed up by a trainer or treated in any special way. He credited genes for some of that. "All us Youngs could throw," he told Arthur Daley in *The New York Times* in 1945. "I used to kill squirrels with a stone, and my granddad once killed a turkey buzzard on the fly with a rock."

Family members, squirrels, and opponents knew that the ace Boston pitcher had greatness in him; they just hadn't ever seen perfection from him before.

The story of Young's path to perfection actually can begin several days earlier, on April 25, also against the Athletics. Young lost 2–0, but he held Philadelphia scoreless for the final seven innings. He added seven more shutout innings in a relief stint on April 30 in Washington. So even though his 1904 record to that point was only 2–2, he was on quite a roll heading into the game against Philadelphia, played on a sunny Thursday afternoon in Boston.

The opposing pitcher was Rube Waddell, the original pitcher with a "million-dollar arm and a 10-cent head." Mercurial, odd, distracted, yet awesomely talented, Waddell was one of baseball's stars. The man who would go on to set a record that season with 349 strikeouts (a record that would last until Sandy Koufax broke it in 1965), he had beaten Young 2–0 in the April 25 game, and then had thrown a one-hit shutout at Boston on May 2, defeating Boston's Jesse Tannehill. Pregame comments, whether actually uttered by Waddell or "written" by fan-baiting journalists, had Waddell claiming that he planned to "give the same to [Young] as I gave to Tannehill."

The pregame hype, the matchup of two great pitchers, and the ongoing success (they entered the game in first place with a 12–3 record) of Young's Boston Americans, as they were known that season, combined to attract a crowd of 10,267 fans into Boston's Huntington Avenue Grounds. It was the largest regular-season crowd in the club's history at that point. The fans filled the left-field bleachers, which were perhaps 25 rows deep and had been added after the 1903 Series, as well as the wide V-shaped grandstand that stretched from outfield corner to outfield corner. A flat veranda was built above the main stands, allowing a small group of fans to enjoy "upper-deck" views, and nicely presaging the rooftop boxes that would eventually be installed in Fenway Park.

The historic game began unremarkably. After Boston went down in the top of the first, Young took the mound. Pitching to catcher Lou Criger, Young fanned Athletics left fielder Topsy Hartsel to begin his perfect streak. He then induced center fielder Ollie Pickering to pop out to his opposite number, Chick Stahl, who made the catch after a short run. The third out was another whiff, this time off first baseman Harry Davis. Young would end the day with eight strikeouts.

In the second, Young helped his own cause by throwing out Philadelphia third baseman Lave Cross. (Young, like many pitchers of the day, was a pretty good fielder. Ironically, years later, he claimed that fielding hastened his retirement; in the final stages of his career, slowness of foot and wideness of gut made it hard for him to get off the mound quickly. So opposing teams essentially bunted Cy Young out of baseball.) The beautifully nicknamed Ralph "Socks" Seybold, the A's right fielder, also went down on strikes. Second baseman Danny Murphy popped out to Jimmy Collins at third. Collins was also the Boston manager at the time, a man Young called the "greatest of all third basemen."

The first real scare of the game came when shortstop Monte Cross led off the third against Young by popping a ball in back of second base. Right fielder Buck Freeman had a long run, but "tearing in from right like a deer," said Young, he made the play for the first out of the inning. Ground-outs retired catcher Ossie Schreckengost and Waddell.

To start the fourth, Philadelphia manager Connie Mack sent up Danny Hoffman to pinch hit for Hartsel, who had taken ill. Hoffman fared no better, however, and flew out to Stahl. Pickering hit a grounder that second baseman Hobe Ferris fielded and threw to first. Davis then lofted a foul pop that drifted toward the third-base stands. Criger leaped up and gave chase, finally tracking it down just before he would have run smack into the Boston bench, which was level with the playing field at the Huntington Grounds.

In the book *Red Sox Century*, Glenn Stout and Richard Johnson report that at the beginning of the fifth, several fans "paying close attention" began to cheer even harder for Young and his ongoing perfection. Were ten thousand people on their feet screaming after every pitch? Probably not. No-hitters were still rare, but even when they happened, they didn't get the intense coverage of today's games. But the buzz in the stadium had started . . . and it would only increase as the innings, and zeros, added up. People knew then that something special was happening.

In the fifth, Cross and Seybold grounded out and Murphy popped to short. Young followed it up in the top of the sixth by striking out Cross, getting former Cleveland batterymate Schreckengost to pop out, and then striking out Waddell.

However, while Young had set down 18 Athletics (or "Mackmen," in the vernacular of the time) to that point, Boston still had not scored against Waddell, although they had touched him up for several hits. Then Stahl led off the bottom of the sixth with a triple to right field. Freeman matched the feat, and Young had the run he needed.

Leading 1–0 in the top of the seventh, Young allowed the hardest-hit ball of the day so far. The left-handed-hitting Hoffman drove a ball high to left that Pat Dougherty had to chase down into the corner of the field. He and the ball reached the fencing in foul territory at the same time. He leaped to make the catch. It would have been foul and surely no error had he missed. But it was apparently a great play nonetheless. Pickering followed with a slow roller that shortstop Freddie Parent had to charge. Throwing on the run, Parent nipped the Athletics' center fielder.

(As the parade of perfect games plays out, we'll see over and over how defense played a huge part. Of course, that seems obvious; an error ruins a perfect game, so the defense must be equally perfect. But it is the fielders' attitude that is so interesting. Teammates play extra hard when they sense history on the line. Over and over, I spoke to fielders prepared to go to any lengths, to dive, smash into walls, do whatever it might take, to keep the perfect game alive. Dougherty's play appears to be one such in this game. It is not recorded what he thought of the play, but one assumes that in another, similar situation that was not perfect, he might not have made the play or given it the same amount of effort. The same might be true for Parent on the slow roller.)

Dougherty's exciting play, combined with the Boston lead and Young's now-very-apparent no-hitter, had whipped the crowd into an even bigger frenzy. To add to their joy, in the bottom of the inning, Ferris got Boston's third triple of the day and then scored on Criger's double. Boston added an unearned run when Young grounded to short and Davis couldn't handle the throw.

The first two batters in eighth went quietly by baseball standards, but noisily thanks to the roaring crowd. Fans by now were cheering on every pitch, their voices rising up in the other kind of pitch on every out. Cross flew to right; Seybold grounded out to Young.

Shortstop Danny Murphy came up batting right-handed. He couldn't quite get around on a Young fastball and pushed a high fly toward the right-field line. Freeman wasn't going to get there in time, and the fans and the Americans waited while it drifted and finally fell foul. Young, as if angered, then fanned Murphy.

No one paid attention to what Boston did at the plate in the ninth; they were just waiting for Young to finish his feat. One wonders, however: What were they waiting for? Did the crowd in fact know they were watching a perfect game? Or were they just aware of the no-hitter? It had been 24 years since Ward and Richmond's feats. In fact, there was not even a term for what Young was about to accomplish. No one called it a "perfect" game until 1922. The very concept of a game in which no opponent reached base was nearly unheard of. Yes, Ward and Richmond had done it, but that was nearly ancient history, in another time, another place, with different rules. The *Boston Post* called Young's game "the most wonderful game of ball in the annals of America's national sport." Those earlier games counted, sure, but one can assume that fans at the Huntington Grounds—and even the worthy scribes in the press box—were not calling the Elias Sports Bureau on their cell phones to find out the last time this had occurred. Consider, then, that fans were watching history in the making . . . but that they didn't really know just how historic an event it was.

The ninth inning opened with shortstop Monte Cross. After fouling off a couple of pitches (and remember, those now counted as strikes), he took strike three. Schreckengost grounded easily to Parent. And then, with ten thousand fans screaming encouragement, Waddell stepped to the plate.

Some fans near the Athletics' bench reportedly yelled at Mack to pinch hit for his pitcher. For whatever reasons, Mack stood pat and Waddell came up.

"I never worked harder in my life than I did for those last three outs," Young said after the game. "After Parent helped me out by getting Schreck's grounder, it was up to me to go for earnest, and Waddell was the man. I sized him and let go."

Young dug in and then delivered a ball outside.

Waddell swung and missed for strike one.

On the third pitch, he lofted an easy fly ball to center field. The crowd, according to the *Post* the next day, went silent.

"I thought that ball would never come down," Stahl said.

"Never did a ball seem so slow in dropping," Young said.

Young watched, along with his teammates. Stahl drifted back a step or two, and then he made the catch.

Let the heralds of the times (or should I say, the *Post*) record the moment: "As it dropped into Stahl's glove, a roar as if a hundred cannon had belched forth rocked the stands and bleachers; staid professional and business men fell over each other to congratulate Young and the Boston players."

First baseman Candy LaChance was the first to reach Young, and he was soon joined by the entire Boston team and hundreds of fans, who spilled out of the seats to add their congratulations. Young later told a famous story of one man who pressed a five-dollar bill into his hand on the field.

For the first time since pitchers threw overhand, since pitchers were moved back to 60'6", since there were two "major leagues," since ball-and-strike counts were recognizable to today's baseball fan, a pitcher had set down an entire team in order in a game.

"I am proud to have been defeated by such pitching," said Mack.

"I wouldn't have missed that for a hundred dollars," said Waddell.

"It is hard for me to tell how I did it," Young said afterward. "I never felt better in my life. I kept mixing the balls. Criger says I didn't throw two balls alike, and I guess I'll take his word for it.

"The day was perfect."

But did he know the game was "perfect"? Young biographer Reed Browning speculates that he didn't really know until informed after the game, because there was no scoreboard at the Grounds. Also, the very rarity of the event and its singularity in the "modern" game might have made it incomprehensible in the achieving, but certainly recognizable in the aftermath. "Not a Quaker Reached First Base," read one headline.

But although the feat did not yet have the famous name, Young must have realized something. The *Boston Post* quotes him as saying, proudly if incorrectly, after the game, "I am as proud as any man could be to be the first to pitch such a game."

Years later, Young would call the game "my biggest thrill in baseball," but it's worth wondering whether that was so because of the attention paid the feat in the intervening years, rather than the particular emotions of the moment. He did end up with three no-hitters, of course, and again, at the time, this one was lauded and praised highly, but not separated from other no-nos.

Remarkably, Young, who was then 37, at that time the oldest pitcher to throw a perfect game, continued his success in the games following the perfecto. Six days later, he faced Detroit and threw a 15-inning shutout that ended just as the umpire was about to call the game due to darkness. On May 17, he faced his former teammates on Cleveland and kept them from scoring for 7⅔ innings before giving up three runs to lose.

Including his nine perfect innings at Boston, Young had put together a record scoreless-innings streak of 45 innings.

Several other pitchers have since put together longer streaks—including Walter Johnson, several relief pitchers, and the current record-holder, Orel Hershiser at 59 innings—but none of them can say that they included a perfect game in their streaks. Plus, of Young's 45 innings, 24 of them in a row were hitless. No starting pitcher since, including "Double No-Hit" Johnny Vander Meer, has matched that mark, though several relief pitchers have strung together longer hitless skeins. In a career of continuing brilliance—15 20-win seasons, 11 seasons with an ERA under 3.00—Young's 1904 streak was his finest sustained performance.

Young pitched another four seasons for Boston after 1904. Among the highlights was another duel with Waddell, this one a 20-inning marathon in which Young allowed no walks, but which Waddell finally won 4–2. Young also added his third career no-hitter in 1908, at the age of 41; only Nolan Ryan has thrown one at an older age (44 in 1991). Amazingly, in that game, Young walked the game's leadoff hitter, Harry Niles of the Yankees, who was then caught stealing. Young retired the next 26 batters and won 8–0. He was a walk away from another perfect game. Only J. Montgomery Ward, Addie Joss, and Sandy Koufax, who allowed only a single walk in one of his no-hitters, has come as close to two perfect games.

Young returned to Cleveland in 1909 and pitched his last game in 1911. In 1936, he was one of the first five players elected to the Baseball Hall of Fame. Of all the pitchers to have thrown a perfect game, Young and Koufax (and probably Ward) are the only players who would have been assured of baseball immortality even if lightning had not struck them in those games.

Was it, as Young called it, the best game he ever pitched? He had more of those to choose from then nearly any other pitcher, which makes the choice more difficult, and his World Series wins were more meaningful. But we'll just agree with him on this one. After all, he does have that award named after him, so he must know something about pitching, right?

One of early baseball's most tragic figures, Addie Joss was perfect for one day in 1908—and dead of a rare disease three years later. *Photo courtesy of the National Baseball Hall of Fame and Library, Cooperstown, New York.*

CHAPTER 4

Addie Joss

October 2, 1908

T he stories in this book are all ones of triumph, of victory, of feats forever placed on the positive side of the baseball memory ledger. But the story of Addie Joss' perfect game on October 2, 1908, is tinged with the tragedy of his all-too-short life and career.

Adrian "Addie" Joss grew up in Ohio and was considered as a teenager the best amateur pitcher in the state. His debut in the pros was an auspicious one, and it nearly earned him a special double chapter in this book. On April 26, 1902, he took on the St. Louis Browns and allowed only one base runner, that being Jesse Burkett, who hit a pop fly to shallow right. Joss' right fielder, Erwin Harvey, claimed that he had made a clean catch at his shoetops, but the umpires ruled differently and a hit was awarded. That was it; otherwise, Joss put up a clean slate in his first major league game. Not bad, rook.

Tall and slender (6'3", 185 pounds), Joss was a handsome fellow, very laid-back and calm, and quite intelligent. He had the remarkable distinction of being not only a top pitcher but also a well-regarded sportswriter. The *Cleveland Press* hired him to cover games and write about players and drummed up interest in his column by writing that, "Of all the baseball players in the land, Addie Joss is far and away the best qualified for this work. A scholarly man, an entertaining writer, an impartial observer of the game."

After covering several World Series and seeing his dispatches, "the writer was becoming as well known as the ballplayer," according to Joss biographer Scott Longert (*Addie Joss: King of the Pitchers*).

He soon also became the Cleveland ace and one of the best pitchers in the A.L.; he led the league with a 1.59 ERA in 1904 and had 20 and 21 wins in 1905 and 1906, respectively. He then led the league with 27 wins in 1907. His finest season, however, was 1908, when he put up numbers only rarely duplicated before or since. Along with leading the league with a 1.16 ERA, he also exhibited remarkable control; in 325 innings that season, he walked only 30. His average of 7.31 base runners per game trails only Walter Johnson's 7.26 mark of five years later and Pedro Martinez's 7.22 in 2000.

That season, Joss led the Cleveland team—known in those days as the Naps, in honor of star second baseman and manager Napoleon Lajoie—into the thick of one of the closest pennant races in baseball history. With four games to play, four teams were within two games of the lead. Detroit led by percentage points, followed by Cleveland. One-half game behind the Naps came the Chicago White Sox, who arrived on October 2, 1908, for the first of two games at Cleveland's League Park.

Ed Walsh was slated to oppose Joss in the all-important game. Given the two pitchers' great control and quality, team owners feared extra innings and moved the start time to 2:30 in the afternoon. That didn't keep more than ten thousand people from filling the ballpark.

According to Longert, the Cleveland pitcher had finished warming up and found Walsh sitting alone on a bench. He sat down beside his mound opponent; there is a famous photo of the two, allegedly from that moment. Joss looks off to the left, young, strong, his white socks visible nearly to the knee, above which are his dark blue uniform pants. A cowlick of hair dangles down from beneath his cap, and the thick wool warm-up sweater is buttoned up to his neck. Oddly, both men are holding bats and neither has a glove in evidence. Their calm, almost zoned-out appearance gives no hint of the events to follow.

Walsh came into the game with a stunning record for the season, having won 39 games against 15 losses, with a dozen shutouts. His ERA for the season ended up at a minuscule 1.42, a season that greatly helped him eventually claim the all-time career ERA record with a 1.82. It's important to note, of course, that Joss himself trails only Walsh on that same all-time list with a career ERA of 1.89. Thus in this one game, the top two ERA men of all time faced off.

Here's a tip: take the under.

(The *Cleveland Leader* also noted, "Walsh was primed for the game after a two days' rest." Wow, two whole days? What a lazy bum!)

Joss had no trouble in the first inning, getting right fielder Edgar Hahn to dump a ball in front of the plate; catcher Nig Clarke threw him out easily. Chicago's player/manager Fielder

Jones, playing in center, batted second and popped to short-stop. First baseman Frank Isbell flew out to left, one of only four balls hit to Cleveland outfielders in the game.

In the second inning, Joss fielded a grounder by left fielder Pat Dougherty and made the play (not surprising, as Joss is the all-time leader among pitchers in assists per game, with an average of 2.96). Second baseman George Davis flew out to left field.

The third batter of the inning, shortstop Freddie Parent, grounded hard at his opposing number, George Perring. The throw over to first baseman George Stovall nearly pulled him off the bag, but the big (6'2") first sacker stretched up to snag it and end the inning.

After the second inning, and well before anyone was paying attention to perfection, Naps' third-base coach Jim McGuire returned to the dugout carrying a horseshoe; it's not recorded whether someone tossed it to him or whether he had it all along. The superstitious might say that it didn't matter . . . so long as he had it. Also, it may have been that horseshoe that fans of the White Sox were quoted as referring to later in the game. Of course, the cry of "Horseshoes" might also have been the newspapers' family-friendly way of quoting what the fans were really saying.

Chicago catcher Ossie Schreckengost flew out to center to open the third. Third baseman Lee Tannehill grounded out to Lajoie, the first of eight assists the Cleveland player-manager would make in the game. Walsh himself came to bat with two outs; he hit a grounder just to the right of the pitcher's mound that Joss stabbed at. He missed, however, and fell flat on his face. He lay there and watched as Lajoie calmly swooped in and threw out the pitcher at first.

On the first pitch of the Cleveland third, center fielder Joe Birmingham lined a single to right field, breaking up the string of zeros in the hit column. He soon would break up another string.

Dancing off first, Birmingham induced a pickoff throw by Walsh, but he mistimed his lead and was heading for second when Walsh threw over. First baseman Isbell fired to second, but the throw hit the Naps runner in the back and bounded into left-center field. Birmingham easily made it to third, and the Naps had the go-ahead run there with no outs.

They almost didn't get him home. Perring grounded out to short for the first out. Batting next, Joss attempted what sounds like a squeeze of some sort that was evidently not "suicide."

"I tried to bunt and actually could not get the bat out in time," said Joss, praising his fellow pitcher's stuff. He ended up striking out while "Birmy" cooled his heels. Right fielder Billy Goode, who would strike out four times in the game, was up next. With two strikes, Walsh uncorked a pitch that eluded catcher Schreckengost while Birmingham came home. It was called a wild pitch, though Walsh would later dispute the ruling. In any case, it meant a run for Cleveland, unearned due to the error on Isbell. As happened to Lee Richmond in 1880, and would happen years later to Koufax, Barker, Witt, and Martinez, the only runs scored to help their perfect cause were thanks to the mistakes of the other team, rather than the safe-hit efforts of his teammates.

The White Sox' fourth time at bat turned into the Napoleon Lajoie show. Hahn grounded to the second baseman, with Nap racing in to catch the slow roller. Jones then hit "a terrific grasser," which Nap grabbed behind second before throwing out to first. Finally, Isbell ended the inning by flying out to Lajoie in short right field.

The White Sox were hitting nothing hard against Joss, though they had seen his odd delivery before. When no one was on base, Joss made almost a complete half-turn at the top of his windup, with his back nearly facing home. He then delivered the ball with a nasty whipping motion that made it hard for batters to pick up a release point. He "pitched out of his hip pocket," it was said, and his varying arm angles exacerbated the breaks on his curveball. He also threw what sounds like a split-fingered fastball, a speed pitch that allegedly dropped as it reached the batter.

In the fifth, with two outs, Parent dropped a slow roller toward third base. Joss pounced off the mound and threw to first to nail the runner, again showing off his fine fielding.

Lajoie recorded another assist to open the sixth, and Joss then threw out third baseman Tannehill. Finally, Walsh made the third out on a fly ball to right.

Following the Walsh fly-out, which completed Joss' second tour around the Chicago lineup, the righty started figuring out what was going on.

"About the seventh inning I began to realize that not one of the Sox had reached first base," Joss said after the game. "No one on the bench dared breathe a word to that effect. Had he done so, he would have been chased to the clubhouse. Even I rapped on wood when I thought of it."

Joss wasn't alone. By this time, according to the Cleveland papers, a crowd that had been raucous and loud early on had turned eerily quiet. "They soon realized it would be rather sacrilegious to stir the air with horns, cow bells, and the like, and while there were hundreds of noisemakers in the crowd, they were left unsounded."

The paper also noted a detail that would be impossible to find at today's smoke-free stadia: "So intent were the fans upon the game that many a cigar went out and remained unlighted."

The *Cleveland Leader* also tossed in this locals-only reference: "The rooters were well organized and tried hard to keep the White Sox on the anxious seat, but the players paid no attention to the noise. They were there to play baseball."

Amid the silence enjoyed by Joss while pitching, Hahn grounded to Joss to open the seventh for Chicago, then Fielder Jones nearly "coaxed a pass." At 3–1, Jones was up there to walk and took the next two pitches without flinching, but both were over the plate. Protesting the second of these strike calls, Jones returned to the bench. Parent flew out, and Joss was three outs away from perfection.

In the eighth inning, amid the silence of League Park, Lajoie again rose up to help his pitcher. Leading off, Dougherty hit a "red-hot grounder" that apparently took a bad bounce on the edge of the infield grass. But Lajoie stayed with it, grabbed it about eye level, and threw to first for the out. He made the next out, too, catching a pop-up hit by Davis.

Walsh also was getting some love from the crowd, receiving an ovation after each of the last three innings he pitched. "Walsh pitched a most phenomenal game," the *Plain Dealer* reported. "And the rooters wanted to let him know that they thought so and were not bashful about it either."

In the Naps' eighth, Birmingham got his second hit of the game and Perring followed with a single. The players then executed a successful double steal, but the play also cost the White Sox and Walsh their catcher. Schreckengost broke the first finger on his throwing hand trying to catch Walsh's pitch too quickly and get a throw off to second. The injury to "Schreck" was a pretty bad one. The *Plain Dealer* described it gruesomely as "the bone of the forefinger of his right hand snapped in two, only the skin preventing it from dropping off entirely." The hard-luck Ossie, who had lost to Young's perfecto, too, never played in the majors again.

But with men on second and third, Joss and Goode became Walsh strikeout victims, and Bill Bradley grounded out to end the inning.

As the ninth inning began, from the reports in the Cleveland papers, the fans at League Park had gone to see a baseball game and a golf match had broken out. The accounts make the scene one of almost churchlike silence, instead of the raucous "go for it"–type of yelling you might expect. A reporter noted that at one point early in the ninth, the only thing he could hear was the clicking of the telegraph operator sending news of the game to the world.

Still nursing only a 1–0 lead and knowing that the Naps needed a victory at this point more than he needed a perfect game, Joss took the mound for that final inning.

Leading off for Chicago was the first of three pinch-hitters that Fielder Jones sent to face the side-arming right hander. Batting for the catcher Al Shaw, who had replaced the injured Schreckengost, was Doc White, who actually was more of a pitcher than a hitter for the ChiSox and would win 18 games that season. But he proved no match for Joss, either, and grounded out to Lajoie for the Cleveland leader's eighth and final assist.

Batting in place of third baseman Lee Tannehill was first baseman Jiggs Donahue. Befitting his 1908 average of .204 rather than his World Series heroics of 1906, when he batted .333 in Chicago's championship run, Donahue swung "feebly," according to one account, and became only the third strikeout victim on the day for Joss, swinging "his head off," according to the *Plain Dealer.*

Finally, batting for Walsh came John Anderson, who was among team leaders with a .262 average on the season. The silence was mouselike, according to one hyperbolic reporter. On the first pitch, Joss left it a bit high, and Anderson slashed a line drive toward left that slowly curved and landed foul by inches.

Joss fired in pitch No. 2, and Anderson swung and missed.

Now just one strike away, Joss did his pirouette, whirled, and zinged in a fastball. Anderson turned on the pitch and hit a hard ground ball toward Bill Bradley at third base. Bradley, surprisingly, had not had a chance in the game before Anderson's grounder. The White Sox to their credit—and because Bradley was regarded as a very good fielder—had chosen not to bunt to break up Joss' perfecto. But Bradley was still in the game, as he recounted many years later.

"I knew something about Anderson. He was a powerful man, and was a pull hitter, so when he came up, I moved closer to the base. He hit the grounder rather sharply over the bag. I was playing deep and I took the ball in back of the cushion. I threw to Stovall, but the throw was low."

Ten thousand mouselike people sucked in their collective breath as Stovall reached out to try to dig out the low toss. The ball hit his glove, and he appeared to have it for a split-second, but then, stunningly, he dropped the ball. But Anderson was not yet at the bag, so Stovall quickly picked up the baseball again; umpire Silk O'Loughlin shot his arm up, and the game was over.

As O'Loughlin's arm rose into the sky, the once-silent crowd erupted. And Joss turned and sprinted for center field.

Meanwhile, at first, Anderson protested immediately, and from the descriptions in several papers, he may have had a case. But the fans pouring onto the field in pursuit of Joss muted any debate.

"I am taking no chances," Joss said afterward about the fans who had chased him across the diamond in an effort to congratulate him, presumably by hoisting him onto their shoulders. "Suppose they had let me drop. The season is not done yet."

So as Joss and his teammates celebrated in the safety of the locker room, the fans filled the field and enjoyed their own celebration, which soon spread into the streets beyond. Wrote the *Cleveland Plain Dealer* in an early nod to all-inclusive political correctness, "All the people who lived within a 10-block radius of E. 66th St. and Lexington Ave. knew that Cleveland had won and ran out—nursemaids, janitors, grocers, housewives, saloonkeepers, doctors, lawyers, ministers, children—all ran out to ask the score from the first man who passed with a smile."

"I am sorry we lost, of course," Walsh said afterward. "But seeing that we did have to lose, I am glad that Addie took down a record that goes to so few. I guess way down in my heart I was sort of glad when Silk called Anderson out in the ninth. It would have made no difference anyway."

"I didn't try for the record," Joss said. "All I was trying to do was beat Chicago, for the game meant so much to us and Walsh was pitching the game of his life. I never saw him have so much."

Lajoie also basked in the glow of the victory. He was suffering from a cold that one account claimed "should have had him under a doctor's care, but he came out and played anyway."

"Such a game as we won today almost cured my cold," said the future Hall of Famer. "It was the best game I ever saw and the best game I ever took part in. Joss pitched a grand game and so did Walsh. Addie had to pitch a no-hit game against such pitching as Walsh handed us. They certainly don't make any better pitchers than Addie."

According to *In the Shadows of the Diamond*, by Michael Santa Maria and James Costello, Joss boarded a train soon after to travel to the Naps' next game. And he fainted. No cause was determined, but it would presage the tragic end of his life.

But while Joss' perfect game placed him forever in the record books, the victory it symbolized went for naught, in a championship sense. Less than a week later, the great pennant race of 1908—highlighted in the American League by this perfect game and in the National League by the infamous Merkle's-Boner-caused playoff game—was over, and the Naps were on the sidelines. Joss had done his part, however. Along with his perfect game, he threw four other shutouts as part of a 7–1 record in September and October, along with a long scoreless relief appearance in a loss on October 4. Cleveland in the end finished only a half-game behind Detroit, who had played one fewer game. Henceforth, following an off-season ruling that came too late to help Cleveland, the pennant would not be decided in such a manner; games would all be played as needed.

Unlike his teammates, Joss did end up taking part in every game of the World Series while covering them as a reporter for the *Toledo News Bee*. He was the paper's assistant sports editor by title and was about equal to the task, given the style of the times. His insights into the two teams' strategies and into the personalities of the champion Tigers, against whom he had pitched, made his reports more authentic.

An amusing footnote to Joss' story first came to light via Lee Allen, the late longtime historian at the Baseball Hall of Fame. In a 1963 column about Joss, he interviewed the pitcher's son, Norman.

"It's a funny thing," Norman Joss said. "There have been so few perfect games. John [sic] Lee Richmond ended up as a mathematics teacher at Scott High School in Toledo. I was in his plane geometry class and a nice old man he was. But on the first day of school, he said to me, 'Now, look. Your father pitched a perfect game. Well, so did I. And it doesn't mean anything here. The fact that your father did the same thing isn't going to help you with plane geometry.'"

Norman's memory might have had a little help, because he says Richmond called it a "perfect" game in what was probably sometime during World War I, years before the term came into regular use. However, the story remains as yet another nice connection between members of baseball's most exclusive pitching fraternity.

In 1909, Joss had his worst season as a pro, partly due to an arm injury, which caused him to miss much of the 1910 season as well, although he did have another no-hitter that year, also a 1–0 victory over the White Sox. He showed up for spring training before the 1911 season ready to put his arm problems behind him. He worked hard and was rounding into shape when the team went north to start the season. Joss stayed behind for extra work.

On April 3, he fainted again at the Chattanooga train station while coming to meet the team. Rushed to the hospital, he seemed fine at first, but the fainting spells returned, and he went home to Toledo. Doctors there discovered the cause of the spells, and it wasn't good news. There was almost nothing they could do.

Eleven agonizing days later, Addie Joss was dead of tubercular meningitis two days after his 31st birthday.

The baseball world turned out to honor and remember him as few before or since. A tribute game was held on April 24 at League Park that was essentially an all-star game; nine players from the game would end up in the Hall of Fame, including Ty Cobb, Cy Young, Eddie Collins, and Lajoie. Proceeds went to Joss' widow and their two children. Norman Joss was eight years old at the time.

Addie Joss did not make the Hall of Fame until 1978, owing as much to short memories as to his short career. In fact, that short career fell one year short of the 10-season minimum requirement, which was waived especially for Joss' case.

A final footnote: in describing Joss' feat the next morning, the *Cleveland Plain Dealer* marched another step toward finally naming this pitching success: "When he did accomplish the desire of every pitcher, it came to him in perfect form. No hits, no passes, no errors—not a man reached first. There is nothing better in baseball."

You could make a good argument that the same could have been said for Joss himself, had he remained healthy—perfectly healthy, that is.

Charley Robertson, who threw a perfect game in his fourth big-league start, was far and away the most obscure pitcher ever to do so. *Photo courtesy of the National Baseball Hall of Fame and Library, Cooperstown, New York.*

CHAPTER 5

Charley Robertson

April 30, 1922

Was Charley Robertson's 1922 perfect game just what the "doctor" ordered? Or was it just another example of the truly fluky nature of baseball's rarest pitching feat?

Robertson is without much question the most obscure, most surprising, and least known perfect-game pitcher. A 26-year-old rookie and former divinity student who would end his career only a few years later with but 49 wins, Robertson somehow managed to completely blank the Ty Cobb–led Detroit Tigers. Cobb's team had the highest team average (.305) of any team that has been "perfected" or even no-hit, thus leading historian John Thorn to call Robertson's feat "perhaps the most perfect game ever pitched."

Hollywood wouldn't buy this script. (Oh, wait . . . maybe they would. Kevin Costner's character pitched a perfect game in *For Love of the Game,* or did I spoil the ending for you?) Robertson's gem was really, pardon the pun, out of left field.

Along with its sheer improbability, Robertson's is the only perfect game marked by any significant controversy. Detroit player-manager Ty Cobb insisted "to his deathbed," according to one biographer, that Robertson had applied grease or oil to the ball, and this two years after such pitches were declared illegal. As we'll see, the allegations were never proved, but they remain like a small cloud on an otherwise-sunny day.

Another interesting note is that Robertson's was the first perfect game to be called one in print at the time it was thrown. It was not always the lead, and many stories still relied on the "no-hit, no-man-reached-first" sobriquet. One game story notes in a few inches that the White Sox, "according to captain Eddie Collins, had not let the thought of a hit, to say nothing of a perfect game, dawn on them until just three men stood between Robertson and the rarest of baseball glory."

Other stories surrounding the game do not make use of the term, so one gathers that it was not yet in general use. In the clips of intervening years, however, "perfect game" became solidly set as the term for the feat.

Not surprisingly, Robertson's game had the least effect on his life—less than any of the other perfectos had on their pitchers. In his later years, he as much as said that he'd just as soon not have played baseball, let alone pitched a perfect game.

"If I'd known back then what I know now," he said in 1956, "it would never have happened to me. I wouldn't have been in baseball." But he was and it did, and here's the story.

———

Robertson grew up in Texas, eventually attending Austin College in Sherman, Texas, where he studied for the ministry.

He managed to play a few sports in the meantime, starring for the school baseball, basketball, and football teams. (He would later return to coach hoops and football at the school in the off-season, including after his perfect-game season.) He graduated in 1918 and was signed by the White Sox, spending spring training with them.

After a year in the nascent Army Air Corps, Robertson returned to pro ball, enjoying a single cup-of-coffee start in 1919, which he lost. It was three years before the White Sox rotation opened up enough to give him a spot, and he traveled north with the team for the 1922 season.

The young pitcher was described by one writer soon after the game as being as "modest as one of his intellect and soundness of reasoning could possibly be."

His talents were apparently just as modest. He started three games in April, winning one. On April 30, he and the White Sox faced Detroit in Navin Field (later Tiger Stadium) before a surprisingly large crowd of 25,000. The game was played on a sunny Sunday afternoon, and the fans were so numerous, they spilled onto the field, "standing on a fringe around the whole inclosure [sic]."

Robertson's fastball was particularly live that day, nailing the corners. One paper called his control "uncanny." But years later, Robertson remembered his stuff as being "nothing more than usual. I just caught a bunch of ballplayers with the blind staggers."

The staggers started in the first, as Robertson mowed down the first three Tigers, including getting Cobb to ground out to third base.

In the top of the second, Chicago helped Robertson at the plate. Former Red Sox star Harry Hooper drew a leadoff walk. Left fielder Johnny Mostil laid down a perfect bunt along the third-base line, and everyone was safe. Center fielder Amos Strunk sacrificed the two runners over, and then first baseman Earl Sheely slammed a "hard bounder" to the left side. Detroit third baseman Bobby Jones got a glove on it, but it bounced through for a hit, and both White Sox scored.

Now trailing by two runs, Detroit sent Bobby Veach up to lead off the second inning. He hit a drive to left that Johnny Mostil tracked back to the scoreboard. Amazingly, he had to have the help of the crowd that had spilled onto the field and was covering the warning track. One clipping reported that the "crowd in that sector spread out to make his feat easier to perform." He caught it just inside the ropes separating the crowd from the players.

Harry Heilman, another future Hall of Famer on Detroit that day, flied to right. Then third baseman Bobby Jones slugged one to right that Harry Hooper reportedly "caught on the dead run."

The three long outs would be as close to a hit as anything the Tigers hit all day. The *Chicago Daily Tribune* said that Robertson's "mates were not called upon to perform hair raising feats to keep the Tygers [sic, probably a play on Cobb] away from first base. Robby was so good that ordinary fielding was all that he needed."

An interesting note in the fourth is that Sheely's long drive to left landed among the spectators for an unusual ground-rule double. It was not over the fence, so he didn't get a homer, but it was something that you'd simply never see in today's baseball. Chicago shortstop Eddie Mulligan did the same thing in the seventh.

The game had progressed without anything else unusual until the fifth inning.

Leading off was cleanup hitter Bobby Veach.

"I had a 3–2 count on him," Robertson said, noting the only time he fell behind a hitter all day. "And I threw a fastball that didn't even come close, but Bobby bit on it and popped it up [to Hooper in right]. The rest was like batting practice."

For Robertson it might have been like BP; for Cobb and the Tigers it was torture. Maybe Cobb finally noticed something, or maybe he thought it was a good time to try a little rookie hazing. For whatever reason, with one out in the bottom of the fifth, Heilman made the first claims of something fishy. Cobb then insisted that umpire Dick Nallin inspect the rookie for grease or oil, which Cobb said was being put on the ball. Nothing was found at that time, though Nallin did remove several balls from play after the complaints started. Cobb even had Nallin check the glove of White Sox first baseman Earl Sheely. From the fifth inning onward, Cobb continually railed at the rookie and at the umpire about the greaseballs he said Robertson was throwing.

The *Chicago American* reported the next day that the Tigers' team doctor—a more-honest-seeming observer, I guess—said that the balls had been discolored by crude oil. But again, Nallin did nothing other than toss out a couple of baseballs.

In the seventh, Cobb was up third and again started a mouth-foaming argument about the doctored balls. Angry, he struck out.

In the eighth, Robertson struck out Veach, got Heilman to foul to first, and induced Jones to ground out to second. By this time, reported the Chicago papers, the Tigers crowd had turned on their home team and were openly rooting for the rookie to give them a memory for a lifetime.

In the ninth, Cobb played the greaseball card one more time, insisting that Nallin inspect Robertson himself. Again, the rookie passed inspection, and Cobb reportedly railed all the way to the dugout, tossing bats and continuing his game-long invective. We'll never really know if Robertson put some schmutz on the ball or not; Cobb certainly thought so, insisting in many later interviews that his Tigers had been jobbed.

But a reporter at the game wrote that Cobb's protests "sounded like the squawk of a trimmed sucker."

Robertson shook off the delaying tactics and kept at it.

Danny Clark, batting for shortstop Topper Rigney, swung "viciously" at the first pitch and missed, then took two strikes for the first out.

Catcher Clyde Manion lunged at an outside pitch and popped up to second.

Cobb tried a final pinch-hitter, sending up regular catcher Johnny Bassler, who had been given the day off, to bat for pitcher Herman Pillette, who had done a pretty fair job himself, allowing only seven hits, two walks, and the two runs. Bassler would end the season batting .323, so here was a real challenge to Robertson.

"I didn't really believe I was confronted by the chance to win a no-hit game until [Bassler] batted for the pitcher," Robertson said later. "I walked out of the box and said to [shortstop Eddie] Mulligan, 'That little fat fellow stands between me and a no-hit game.'"

Not surprisingly, Mulligan was reportedly stunned at this breach of baseball etiquette and flaunting of superstition. But what the hell, this was so unlikely in the first place that a little rule-breaking couldn't hurt.

And, of course, it didn't.

After taking a couple of pitches, Bassler himself tried a little trick, halting play to go get a new bat from the dugout. The crowd actually booed their own player as they realized his tactics; they wanted to see a perfect game as much as the White Sox did.

New bat or old, he was helpless against Robertson. Bassler sent an easy fly to left that drifted into foul territory, but not far enough to keep Johnny Mostil from grabbing it easily. The Detroit crowd, stunned but elated, swarmed onto the field and carried Robertson off on their shoulders. What must this kid have been thinking at that moment? You wonder how his thoughts as a young pitcher with his career ahead of him might compare to those of Dennis Martinez, finally perfect in his 15th season in 1991. Could Robertson have really comprehended what he'd just done?

Or, sinisterly, did he rise above the crowd knowing that he'd done so in a, well, slippery fashion? (Tellingly, a 1917 note in a Texas paper called him "a shine ball expert." Of course, it was legal back then. . . .)

Robertson, against pretty much all odds you can think of, had joined a list that includes Young, Koufax, Hunter, and Cone but doesn't include Mathewson, Spahn, Gibson, Maddux, or Clemens. Simply amazing. He had thrown 92 pitches, struck out six, and allowed only five balls hit to the outfield. It was a masterful performance.

Cobb, however, couldn't let the matter rest. Three days later, newspapers reported that the Georgia Peach had impeached Robertson and forced A.L. president Ban Johnson to investigate Cobb's protest of the game based on "doctored" baseballs.

According to Rich Westcott in *No-Hitters: The 225 Games*, Johnson did indeed find traces of oil on the balls submitted by the Tigers. But he explained that the traces had come from "the wire screen in the back of the plate." Huh? How many oil-covered wire screens have you ever seen? So

Cobb was disproved, Robertson was cleared, and the perfect game entered the book unblemished by oil, whether from hands, caps, or screens.

Robertson continued pitching pretty well that season, though never really again approaching the dominance he had that day in April. After the season, he expected a nice raise for his 14 wins and season-highlight game. He got one: $100, or the grand total of $15 a month. He was a bit peeved, apparently, but ended up signing on again with the ChiSox.

Robertson left baseball in 1928 with a less-than-sterling 49–80 record. And then, unlike most of the other perfect-game pitchers, he essentially disappeared. His name would come up in reports every time a pitcher nearly matched his feat or on the anniversary of his sole success. But the seasons went on and on without another perfect game, 34 in all, the longest stretch between such games. Columnists like Joe Williams of the *New York World-Telegram* occasionally would wonder in print where Robertson was and ask for readers' help. On the 30th anniversary of the game in 1952, the *New York Herald Tribune* made some attempts, but they, too, were unsuccessful. In 1955, a reader finally reported to Williams that Robertson had not disappeared.

He had just been busy growing pecans.

In 1956, Don Larsen reignited interest in the perfect game, thrusting it once and for all to the top of baseball's list of individual achievements. In the aftermath of the hullabaloo about Larsen, reporters naturally tried once again to track down the previous perfect pitcher, Robertson.

It proved surprisingly easy. UPI, AP, and several local reporters all called Robertson, and he was apparently pretty ready to talk. It sounded as if he wasn't exactly hiding out; he was just not the sort of guy who wanted to trumpet his baseball life.

He had apparently also been one of the few people who wasn't aware of Larsen's game. He said he had been out in the pecan fields. "In this business, I don't have much time for anything else," he said.

He went on to say that his attitude toward the game and his part in it "was not sour grapes or anything like that. Baseball didn't give me a particularly bad break. But I went through it and found out too late that it is ridiculous for any young man with qualifications to make good in another profession to waste time in professional athletics. There's nothing wrong with them, but by the time you're through with athletics, you have to start over, and at an age when it's the wrong time to be starting."

Sounding more disappointed than bitter, Robertson suffered the questions about his perfect game politely and then, once the din had died down, he faded away again.

Apparently some people remembered him, however. When he died in Fort Worth in 1984, his niece reported that he still "gets fan mail from all over the world," including three letters the week he died.

Charley may not have remembered his perfect game with any special fondness, but baseball history won't let him off that easy.

Yogi Berra leaps into Don Larsen's arms after the Yankee pitcher forever changed the meaning of the perfect game by throwing one in the 1956 World Series. *Photo courtesy of AP/Wide World Photos.*

CHAPTER 6

Don Larsen

October 8, 1956

"The million-to-one shot came in. Hell froze over. A month of Sundays hit the calendar. Don Larsen today pitched a no-hitter, no-run, no-man-reach-first game in a World Series."

—SHIRLEY POVICH

When counting years, we divide all of time into two eras: B.C. and A.D.

When looking at perfect games, the division is thus: B.L. and A.L. (and we don't mean American League).

Before Don Larsen threw his perfect game in the fifth game of the 1956 World Series, perfect games were, well, not that big a deal. They were an odd anomaly, briefly celebrated and then glossed over. Those were the bad old days B.L.— Before Larsen.

After Larsen did what many thought impossible (and, in fact, no one has repeated such a feat in a Series since), perfect games leapt light-years ahead in their appeal, estimation, and interest among baseball fans and players. Welcome to A.L.— After Larsen. The impact on Larsen has been well documented;

the performance simply changed his life forever (though it didn't help him finish his career with a winning record). The impact on the importance and relevance of perfect games was even more spectacular.

Midseason perfectos from Hunter to Barker to Rogers became national cause célèbres. The label of perfect-game pitcher forever affixed itself, in varying degrees, to every pitcher who has thrown one since Larsen. The sudden appearance of such a game on the baseball radar is cause for scrambling the media jets, with breathless pitch-by-pitch reporting on radio, TV, and the Internet, until the rocket either lifts off into the heavens or fizzles on the pad.

Witness, too, the national acclaim afforded recent perfect-game pitchers such as David Wells and David Cone, their feats, of course, magnified by the multiple points of coincidence between their games and Larsen's. Witness the attention given the "near-misses" such as those of Mike Mussina and Curt Schilling in 2001. Witness even the media frenzy over young Danny Almonte in 2001, when the lefty from the Bronx pitched a (six-inning) perfect game at the Little League World Series. He became a national hero for being perfect amid the imperfections of little boys. His status as a perfect-game pitcher made the media firestorm over his eventual ejection from the record book for being overage that much farther reaching. Had Almonte merely done well, as opposed to perfectly, his transgression might never have been found out. But in the age of A.L., a perfect game earns you intense scrutiny, whether you like it or not.

As season after season goes by, and no one even approaches a no-hitter in the postseason, let alone a perfecto,

Larsen's feat—and with it, the feat of perfection—simply rises in appeal.

If it were not for Don Larsen's one-in-a-million game (OK, not that many . . . there have been only about six hundred World Series games), would Koufax's perfect game in 1965 have vaulted this rare feat to the top of the charts? I think probably not. It was the timing, of course—along with its stunning improbability, given Larsen's spotty pitching history— that made his 2–0 victory over Brooklyn so remarkable and era setting. October 8, 1956, was like Christmas Day in Bethlehem . . . it changed the calendar.

So, thanks, Don. Without you, I might not have a book to write.

Of course, writing about Larsen's perfect game is like writing about the sunset: everyone has seen one and everyone knows what happens, it's just a matter of your point of view. We've got a variety of those points in here, from a variety of sources. Like a game of baseball "telephone," some of the stories have been told and retold many, many times, with their details blurring and fuzzing as time goes by. It's really a case of hit or myth.

Also, Larsen's game is perhaps the most written-about and most described game in baseball history. There are some incidents that are endlessly reminisced about—homers by Bill Mazeroski, Carlton Fisk, Henry Aaron, and others, for instance—but no single game, I think, has been as thoroughly discussed and dissected. The game took two hours and nine minutes to play, but it has taken almost 50 years to talk about.

We'll add our few thoughts to this canon, calling on many of those usual sources as well as some new voices. (To be fair, here's a special credit for some of this story to Mark Shaw, whose book with Larsen, *The Perfect Yankee*, is the most recent and among the most personal of the many memoirs Larsen has participated in. We've got one chapter for Donald J. Larsen; they have a whole book.)

So, gather 'round the marble temple, kids, and let the myth making begin.

One of the themes we've seen, and will see again, is how pitchers who were not thought to have perfect stuff threw perfect games. The poster boy for this theme is Larsen. He grew up in Indiana but finished school in San Diego, attending Point Loma High School 40 years before David Wells would stride its halls (occasionally). Tall (6'4") and strong, Larsen was thought to be a pretty fair prospect, and scouts and coaches loved his stuff at various times throughout his career. The rap was that he didn't apply himself and that his well-documented love of nightlife and fun detracted from getting the most out of his gifts. Larsen has admitted that he was a bit of a "free spirit," and who's to say what he could have done with, say, some modern training methods or a better sleep-to-party ratio.

His size and gifts got him signed by the St. Louis Browns in 1947, but he didn't make the big club after four minor league seasons, and then he lost two years to military service. He didn't lose much time off the ballfield in the army, however, spending a lot of his service in Hawaii playing ball for the base team.

In 1953 he made the Show and was 7–12 for the Browns. In 1954 he led the American League in losses with 21, against only three victories. Yes, the Browns were awful in those days (or should I say Orioles, because 1954 was their first season in Baltimore?), but Larsen was not exactly showing perfect-game material. Following that very underwhelming season, Larsen was included in the biggest player trade ever: 17 players changing teams between the O's and the Yankees. Future ace Bob Turley was the linchpin pickup for New York; volume was the Browns' aim. After the dust cleared, Larsen ended up in New York. In a movie, this would be the point where we'd see a foreshadowing visit to Yankee Stadium by the big kid from Indiana.

The change did him some good; Larsen was 18–3 in 1955 between the Bronx and their Denver farm club, with half of his victories coming in the majors. Heading into the 1956 season, Yankees manager Casey Stengel famously said of Larsen, "That big feller . . . can be a big man in this business—any time he puts his mind to it."

A spring training car accident—at 5:00 A.M., in which a telephone pole and Larsen's vow to settle down took the brunt of the damage—soured the beginning of his 1956 season with the Yankees, and his performance on the hill didn't improve matters. Heading into September, Larsen was 7–5 on a team headed to the World Series, the number four (usually) starter on a team that needed only three.

But in September, the man they called "Gooneybird," after some big, awkward cranes seen on the team's off-season trip to Japan, started to develop an odd "no-windup" delivery.

He heard that opponents were reading his pitches when he used a full windup and rather than adjust it, he got rid of it. It wasn't really pitching from a set; it was an odd hybrid. He reduced his leg kick to a pump-and-stride, and his glove hand never went above his shoulders. It was quick, and it proved to be effective. He won four straight games in September, never allowing more than four hits in any of them. Heading into October, he was on a hot streak.

He cooled off considerably after Stengel gave him the ball to start Game 2 of the World Series against Brooklyn. Staked to a 6–0 lead, Larsen didn't finish two innings, giving up four runs (though unearned) and four walks in a game the Dodgers came back to win, 13–8.

"When Casey came out to take the ball away from me, he was mad," Larsen said later. "That made two of us because I was mad, too. I was mad at myself, Casey, the Dodgers, everybody in the world. I was boiling in the clubhouse. I was sure I'd never get another chance to pitch in that Series."

Guess again.

Trailing two games to none, the Yankees rallied to take the next two contests, tying the Series and making Game 5 at Yankee Stadium pivotal. Because both teams were in New York, there were no travel days. After Game 1 was played on October 5, the clubs took Thursday off and then played in Series games for the next six consecutive days (wonder what the Players' Association would say about that today?).

Among the many issues about Game 5 that create discussion and debate is just exactly what time Larsen got in the night before. There have been several stories printed, each a little different. Author Roger Kahn quoted Yankees outfielder Bob Cerv as saying, "I left him at 4:00 A.M." Yankees traveling secretary and former sportswriter Arthur Richman may have been toeing a company line when he spoke of leaving Larsen at the pitcher's hotel at midnight, somewhere far short of soused.

Mickey Mantle has Larsen drinking ginger ale (!) in his book *My Favorite Summer: 1956*, but Larsen disputes Mantle's version of events. Restaurateur Toots Shor famously recalled introducing Larsen to Chief Justice Earl Warren amid his (Shor's, that is, not the former California governor) and Larsen's booze-filled evening.

In his book with Shaw, Larsen, who has also described various versions of the evening, comes clean most recently (and most truthfully? We'll never know . . .).

"One thing is certain," he writes. "I did return to my hotel before midnight."

That might seem like revisionist history to some who believe the other stories, but one fact leads me to believe Larsen: he didn't know that he'd be starting in Game 5 the next day. Believe it or not, Casey Stengel not only had not announced his starter to the press, but he hadn't even told the team or the pitcher. In a game that today sees managers laying out starting rotations weeks in advance sometimes, and with day-before pitching matchups distributed religiously, the baseball world—including Larsen—went to sleep Sunday night, October 7, not knowing who would pitch in the World Series the next afternoon (ah, afternoon Series games . . . the good old days). This uncertainty (though perhaps colored in

Larsen's mind by his inept Game 2 performance) leads me to believe that he wouldn't stay out all night because of the off chance he'd be needed the next day. Had he known for sure that he was not going to pitch, I could see him living the high life. But he didn't know.

In the book he adds, "I would never have gotten myself out of top physical and mental condition on the eve of such an important game."

Again, maybe it's a bit of belated image polishing, but there are so many conflicting stories about his exploits that I'm going with the simple story. He went to dinner, went home, and went to sleep.

The way that Larsen finally did find out on Monday morning that he'd take the hill is a very interesting one. Stengel never did speak to him about it. Rather, Larsen found out his role when he arrived in the clubhouse.

"Frankie Crosetti, the third-base coach, placed the pregame warm-up ball in the shoe of the starting pitcher before game time. For me to see that ball there in the shoe probably made my heart stop," Larsen goes on to write.

That's right. The biggest game of Don Larsen's life, and he didn't know he'd be pitching it until two or three hours prior. Can you imagine that happening today? Pitchers are so schedule-conscious these days that many of them, such as Roger Clemens or Greg Maddux, have three or four days of routine they go through before a start. And a manager pulling such a stunt today would be thought insane. And forget the physical side of arranging workouts to peak at game time, there's the mental side of things: charting batters, making a game plan, going through the opposing lineup, all stuff that now happens much earlier. But that's how the Old Perfesser played it, and danged if it didn't work out.

"Don had a look of disbelief on his face," remembered Hank Bauer. "He saw that ball in the shoe and he took a big gulp."

He had good reason to. The lineup Larsen was facing was the most star-studded lineup that anyone ever beat in a perfect game. It included future Hall of Famers Pee Wee Reese, Duke Snider, Jackie Robinson, and Roy Campanella. Gil Hodges was one of those on-the-cusp-of-fame players, and Carl Furillo was a very good hitter. The Dodgers had won their second straight National League pennant and were hoping to make it two in a row in October, too, having defeated the Yankees in the "wait 'til next year" Series of 1955.

Unlike in Game 2, Larsen started out well. He struck out second baseman Jim Gilliam to open the first. He went 3-and-2 on Reese before getting another strikeout. It was the last 3-ball count Larsen reached the rest of the afternoon.

In the second inning, Larsen got a little lucky, as perfect-game pitchers are wont to do. Jackie Robinson, leading off, smashed a hard hopper toward third baseman Andy Carey. Carey reached out for the pea, but it glanced off his glove. If the rebound had not gone right to shortstop Gil McDougald, then the speedy Robinson would have made it. As it was, McDougald's throw nipped Jackie.

Larsen cruised through the rest of the second and the third as well. Again, as we've seen in so many perfect games, the opposing pitcher also threw brilliantly. The Dodgers' Sal "the Barber" Maglie matched Larsen out for out through three and two-thirds. In the end, the Yanks would manage only five hits and two runs against the veteran, normally a performance that should have earned a win. But this was far from a normal game.

With two outs in the bottom of the fourth and Maglie one strike from closing out the inning, Mickey Mantle came through for Larsen and the 64,519 fans packing Yankee Stadium (the largest crowd ever to see a perfect game . . . in person, of course). The 1956 Triple Crown winner and eventual American League MVP pulled a Maglie fastball into the right-field seats. Good-bye perfect game, no-hitter, shutout, and lead.

Maglie got the Yanks again in the fifth, and in the bottom of the frame, Larsen faced Gil Hodges with one out. The future Mets manager hit a line drive that looked to split the gap between Mantle in center and Enos Slaughter in left. No way old man Enos was going to get it, but the Commerce Comet sprinted over and made the grab on the run.

On the MSG Network show *A Perfect Night*, Larsen remembered, "That was a long drive. But I could see I had that deer out there, and I knew he had it."

He wasn't the only one who thought that, but the catch has over the years attained the gloss of myth. Every perfect game needs, or should we say, wants, a game-saving defensive play. If none are obvious, then also-rans attain higher status; fly balls to a player's left become diving, snow-cone grabs, and nice backhand pickups become desperate lunges. Mantle's was a good play, certainly, but one that he should have made in any game, perfect or not.

Historian John Thorn has this opinion. "I actually saw that game on TV and remember it, and, of course, have seen it since. The mythologizing that has surrounded it is incredible.

The Mantle catch was called a game-saver. But he had it all the way. He glided after it and made the catch. It wasn't very challenging at all."

Sandy Amoros followed Hodges to the plate and then to the bench, and Larsen was perfect through five.

Sitting on the Brooklyn bench, in uniform but not on the active roster, was infielder Don Zimmer, who would go on to become the only person to be in uniform for all three Yankees perfect games, although this, his first such experience, wasn't a happy one. "You never think too much about it until you get past five or six innings," he recalls. "[On the winning side], as you get past the sixth, it gets very quiet. No one wants to jinx it. I don't believe in that anyhow, but that's the way it goes. On the losing side, it wasn't too much fun. We're in the World Series, for goodness' sakes. We wanted to get a walk or a base hit or something to get back in the game. People were talking, 'Let's break up this no-hitter.' No one was saying much else, but there wasn't much to say; he was mowing us down one after the other."

Behind the plate, umpire Babe Pinelli, calling his last game behind a mask, also knew what was going on. He'd called four no-hitters already.

"The atmosphere carries you right along," he told writer Glenn Dickey. "You can tell by the ways the players act and the noises from the fans.

"Larsen was a master of control that day. His change of pace was great, curving away from right-handed batters, but the biggest thing was that he was pinpointing his pitches."

The realization of Larsen's feat began to spread through the stadium, into the dugouts, and into the radio and TV broadcasts, all to varying degrees.

Larsen cleaned the slate in the sixth, getting Furillo, Campanella, and Maglie with no trouble.

The bottom of the sixth became the All-State inning for Larsen, when he got an insurance run. Andy Carey led off with a single, only the second hit off the Barber. Larsen sacrificed him to second. Hank Bauer's single to left scored Carey to make the score 2–0.

After a visit from Walter Alston, the Dodgers' third-year manager, Maglie induced Joe Collins to ground into a double play, the second out of which was Bauer in a rundown. The inning was over, but Larsen had a bit of a cushion to work with.

In the seventh, Gilliam grounded to short, Reese flied to Mantle, and Snider flied to Slaughter. (Larsen would later wonder why the veteran Slaughter had not been pulled for a younger, faster player, but the pitcher chalked it up to Stengel's hunches, or perhaps superstition about not wanting to change anything.)

It was going quickly, routinely, with little trouble for Larsen, but with a growing buzz in the stands about what was going on. Larsen was buzzing a bit, too.

"After the seventh, I went back in the tunnel to have a cigarette," Larsen said. "And I spoke to Mickey about the game, asked him if he thought I'd get a no-hitter. He just walked away. After that, the dugout was like a morgue."

"By then we were all talking about it, just not to him," said Yogi Berra on the MSG show.

Also dodging the issue were the radio and TV broadcasters.

"On television, they were talking around it," remembers Thorn. "They were being evasive. It was a jinx [for even a broadcaster] to mention that a no-hitter was in progress. They would flash to the scoreboard and if you could read that, you'd get it."

In the eighth, Robinson grounded out to Collins on an 0–2 count. Larsen was still throwing strikes, hitting any spot he wanted.

"I never had control like that in my life," he said. Obviously.

Hodges again created some quick drama in his at-bat. He smacked a low line drive that Carey caught to his left at dirt level. Thinking that the ump might rule a trap, he fired to Collins at first, but the throw was unnecessary. (Reading about this play, I imagined the controversy if he had thrown it away and then the ump had indeed ruled it a trap. Good-bye, storybook ending, hello goat horns.) Amoros flew out to Mantle, and now Larsen was three outs away.

While no one in the dugout or on the airwaves was talking about it, everyone in the park knew what was going on, and when Larsen led off the bottom of the eighth, he received a tremendous standing ovation.

And thus the myth comes down to the ninth. The hero needs one more sword-blow to fell the monster. Ulysses is stepping off the boat. There's only one more Billy Goat Gruff.

Some words from observers:

"I was there as a Dodger fan," remembered Yankees manager Joe Torre, who would later witness perfect games by Wells and Cone. "But by the time the ninth inning came around, I was rooting for Larsen like everybody else in the park. It is quite a coincidence, isn't it [about Wells]? Both guys free spirits. You don't check their rooms at night.

"One other thing: I did about as much managing in [Larsen's] game as I did in [Wells']." That is, none, except of the encouraging variety.

"I watched that game standing on a sidewalk in Cambridge, Massachusetts," remembers baseball historian Frederick Ivor-Campbell. "I was wandering the streets on the day before my 21st birthday. The game was on in a TV store with speakers out onto the street. And I stood there and watched it. And as it went on, the announcers were being very evasive about it. They were not mentioning no-hitter or perfect game, so you just had to figure that out through their references and from shots of the scoreboard. But I finally caught on, and so I watched to the end."

"Sure, I'm sorry that I didn't play in the game, but he didn't get me out!" Zimmer laughs. "My bat wasn't long enough to try for a hit from where I was sitting."

Santa Barbara, California, history teacher Steve Siegel was 11 years old and sitting in choice seats along third base with his parents and older brother. "I got to miss school that day for the game, even though I had just missed a month of school with a broken ankle. And in my family, you never missed school.

"I sat next to my father, who was an old Giants fan from the John McGraw days, while the rest of us were Brooklyn fans, mostly because of Jackie Robinson. And we're all sad because we're losing. But everyone was whispering about the no-hitter, everyone was on the same page in the stands.

"In the eighth, my father started pounding me in the shoulder, yelling 'History in the making, history in the making.

Stevie boy, Stosh, you're seeing history in the making.' I must have listened, because I became a history teacher."

Sportswriter Dave Kindred, writing in *The Sporting News*, remembered that he stayed home from school "with the World Series flu" to watch the game.

Arthur Daley of *The New York Times* summed up the mood of the fans in the stadium in this colorful passage:

"Somewhere in the middle of the game the crowd seemed to get a mass realization of the wonders that were being unfolded. Tension kept mounting until it was as brittle as an electric light bulb. The slightest jounce and the dang thing might explode.

"Or perhaps it was more like a guy blowing air into a toy balloon. He keeps blowing and blowing with red-faced enthusiasm. But every puff might be the last. Larger and larger grew Larsen's balloon. It was of giant size at the start of the ninth."

No one was immune.

"I never was as nervous as I was in the ninth inning of that game," wrote Mickey Mantle in *My Favorite Summer*. "I was afraid I would do something to mess up Larsen's perfect game. If I dropped a fly ball, it wouldn't stop his no-hitter, but it would end his perfect game, and that added to my nervousness."

Finally—deep breath, everybody—here we go.

As Carl Furillo stepped to the plate amid the din of Yankee Stadium, Berra spoke to him. "This guy's got good stuff, huh?" Berra, according to *SI*'s Robert Creamer, said.

"Yeah, not bad," Furillo replied in the understatement of the year.

In his book with Shaw, Larsen recalls his thoughts facing the "Reading Rifle."

"I wanted to establish myself with a good first pitch that would let him and the Dodger hitters know I was still on track. While most reporters wrote that I threw a curve or two in the ninth, the truth is that they were all hard sliders. I think Yogi believed that my fastballs were my best pitches, and that we'd go with them until the Dodgers showed us otherwise."

Furillo fouled off Larsen's first two pitches, putting him in a hole.

"Should I waste a pitch or go right after Furillo?" writes Larsen/Shaw. "I think my brain may have told me to throw one away, but my arm was almost on remote and I was just throwing as hard as I could to somewhere near the center of the plate. If I got too cute, I'd make a mistake. Yogi had confidence in the hard slider and so did I. Give 'em your best and make them hit it, was my creed.

"I threw the pitch, but it was high from 10 feet out. Pinelli called it a ball, and Furillo backed away for a few seconds. The fact that it was high might have been a blessing. Calling that slider a curve was a misnomer, because it certainly didn't move much."

After that pitch, Furillo fouled off two more. He got a good hold of the sixth pitch, but his long fly ball died short of the wall in right field in Hank Bauer's glove.

One down.

Two to go.

Next up, oh, sure, no problem, Roy Campanella. Three-time MVP. Best-hitting catcher in baseball until Mike Piazza came along . . . 40 years later! Four home runs in four previous Series appearances. Sure, piece of cake.

"Our strategy with Campy was to pitch him inside, even though I had retired him on two outside pitches in both the third and sixth innings," writes Larsen. "This time around, I was determined to throw the pitches inside and keep the ball away from Campanella's power zone. My first pitch was a good fastball in close. The crack of the bat scared me, but Campanella came around too soon and fouled it into the left-field stands for strike one."

Campanella then took ball one. He got the next pitch in on his hands and pushed the ball weakly to Billy Martin at second, who had urged his teammates entering the final inning to "not let anything get through." He took his own advice and threw Campanella out.

Two outs.

One to go.

Maglie was due up, but of course Alston sent in a pinch-hitter, Dale Mitchell, a little-used but quality outfielder. Mitchell had led the American League in hits in 1949 with Cleveland and would end up a .312 lifetime hitter. He had come over from the Indians in midseason and, like Pinelli, was playing out his string. A Game 7 pinch-hitting appearance in this Series would be his last big-league at-bat. This one, however, would be his most memorable, or should we say, most famous.

"I was so weak in the knees out there, I thought I was going to faint," Larsen recalled. "When Mitchell came up, I was so nervous, I almost fell down. My legs felt rubbery, and my fingers didn't feel like they were on my hand. I said to myself, 'Please help me out, somebody.'"

"I was just looking for a good pitch to hit," Mitchell said after the game, matter-of-factly.

With all the people in the stadium on their feet and every voice exhorting him onward, Larsen fired in ball one to Mitchell, outside.

He threw a slider on the next pitch, and it crossed the plate for strike one.

Mitchell swung and missed at Larsen's third pitch, as 64,000-plus sucked in their breath. They exhaled when the ball plopped into Berra's glove.

The unadorned prose of Robert Creamer in *Sports Illustrated* makes the penultimate moment seem more real by its simplicity.

"Larsen turned his back to the plate, took off his hat and rubbed his brow, picked up the resin bag, rubbed his hand on his thigh. He pitched—and it was fouled back."

Again, a stadium- and audience-wide "whew!" of relief.

And then, pitch number 97 of the day from Larsen headed toward home plate.

"I remember watching the ball turn over and over and head on a direct line with Mitchell's uniform letters," Larsen writes. "I saw Dale commit himself and make a futile half swing. He didn't connect and then I saw the ball pop squarely into Yogi's mitt.

"Instantly, Dale looked back at Pinelli. I watched the umpire's mouth open, and he said something I couldn't understand. A second later, Pinelli's right arm pointed upward toward the sky."

And that was it. Don Larsen had changed history. He had moved the baseball calendar from B.L. to A.L. The noise was thunderous. On TV, Bob Wolff could finally say the words "perfect game."

Larsen's reactions were almost robotic. Instead of collapsing, Cone-like, or exulting like Wells, he simply walked off the mound, as if unsure of what he had done.

"I saw Yogi come out as I walked off the mound toward the dugout," Larsen recalled on MSG. "Out of the corner of my eye, I saw Dale turn to argue the call with Pinelli, but no one was there. Babe had left right away and here was Yogi. It was kind of funny to see Mitchell up there all alone.

"I certainly was glad it was over."

Berra met Larsen before he could get to the first-base line and leaped into his arms, forming one of the most famous baseball scenes of all time, the joyous catcher climbing all over the improbable perfect-game pitcher. That only a select few of us remember this scene in color makes it that much more historic, I think. It's easier to think of epoch-changing events if you don't see it the way your eyes see today.

Larsen's teammates crowded in, some random rooters sprinted into the scrum, and in what seemed but a moment, he was gone, into the clubhouse, leaving the stadium to cheer itself hoarse, and then wander, dazed but happy, joined in a unique fraternity, to the exits.

"I remember being amazed to find a new edition of the *Daily News* for sale on the street right after the game, with the story of the game already in it," says Steve Siegel.

In the madhouse that was the clubhouse, Larsen was besieged with well-wishers, including Maglie and Jackie

Robinson, Commissioner Ford Frick, and Yankees owners Dan Topping and Del Webb. A telegram arrived later from President Dwight Eisenhower, who pointed out that the last time there'd been any perfect games was when he was still a bit of a ballplayer himself.

No one really believed it, in some ways. Had Whitey Ford or Don Newcombe done it, sure, maybe. But not only had a nobody like Larsen done it, he had done it on the biggest stage in baseball, the World Series, in the sport's championship home.

"I've said this before, and no one believes me, but I didn't know it was a perfect game until they told me in the clubhouse," he told MSG. "I knew it was a no-hitter, of course, and that we won the game, that was most important. But I didn't know it was perfect."

It was, Don, it was, and in many ways, even more than that. Life in A.L. had begun, long-shot bettors danced to the pay windows, chilly devils chattered their teeth, and children celebrated four weeks of weekends.

The Yankees went on to win the Series in seven games, with Larsen being named MVP. He appeared on the Bob Hope show after Game 7; he was in commercials, on TV, on radio, and in print ads for months.

"If you think I'm not enjoying this," he once said "you're crazy."

Maybe we only get one moment like that. Maybe that's the limit. For Larsen, it certainly was, on the ballfield, at least.

He was with the Yanks for three more seasons, never winning more than 10 games.

From 1960 to 1967, he played for (deep breath) the Kansas City Athletics, Chicago White Sox, San Francisco Giants (for whom he won a nonperfect Series game in 1962), Houston Colt .45s (now there's a name you won't see on a team anymore), Baltimore Orioles, and Chicago Cubs, starting only 30 games in that time, while also working as a long reliever. Whew.

He retired and got into the paper business, as well as continued the business of being Don Larsen, which took him in 1999 to Yankee Stadium to see David Cone match his feat in pinstripes (if not in the Series).

On the MSG show *A Perfect Night*, Larsen was asked by host Michael Kay, "What was the longest time that has gone by without you thinking of that game?"

Larsen laughed.

"Probably a couple of hours."

And baseball will be talking about it for probably a couple of centuries.

The New York Mets would have been happy to vote future Senator Jim Bunning off the mound when he "perfected" them in 1964. *Photo courtesy of AP/Wide World Photos.*

CHAPTER 7

Jim Bunning

June 21, 1964

"Hey, Jim Bunning! You've just pitched the first perfect game in the National League in 84 years! And you've just become the first pitcher ever to win no-hitters in each league! Now what are you going to do?"

"I'm going to HoJo's!"

Yes, that's right. After setting down 27 New York Mets on June 21, 1964, for a 6–0 Philadelphia Phillies victory, Jim Bunning enjoyed a sumptuous congratulatory feast at a one-star Howard Johnson's on the Jersey Turnpike. Pitch a perfect game and pass the paper napkins, please. Since Larsen made the perfect game famous, perhaps no other pitcher has enjoyed so plebeian a postgame feast. Of course, this being 1964, Bunning did get to go on *The Ed Sullivan Show*, the era's equivalent of doing the rounds of all the network morning shows at once and in the evening.

Much has also been made of the fact that Bunning, then the father of seven and eventually the father of nine (hey, he could field his own team!), pitched his perfect game on Father's Day. His daughter Barbara, accompanied by his wife Mary, was the only one of the then-septet at the game, but all of the Bunning kids shared in the joy of their dad's amazing accomplishment.

Not since John Ward, throwing underhand from 45 feet, had a National League pitcher gone 27-for-27. So one could argue that under current rules, Bunning was the very first National Leaguer to toss a perfecto. That Bunning created his gem against the Mets matters not; that was the major league team he was faced with, and he mowed them down like traffic cones at a driving school for the blind.

Bunning was in his first season with Philly in 1964, having been traded from the Detroit Tigers the previous off-season. He arrived as a pitcher coming off a down year, having gone 12–13 in his final season with Detroit after several much more successful campaigns, including 1957, when he won 20 games. In 1958, Bunning had thrown his first no-hitter when he blanked Boston in Fenway Park, 3–0. And in 1959 and 1960, he led the A.L. with, in a nice bit of statistical synchronicity, exactly 201 strikeouts each year. Heading into 1964, Bunning wanted to prove that he was not the losing pitcher of 1963 but rather the big (6'3"), hard-throwing, innings-eater who had starred for the Tigers over the previous half-dozen seasons.

Helped by Bunning's 6–2 record through June 20, the mighty bats of Dick Allen and Johnny Callison, and solid defense, the Phillies found themselves unexpectedly in first place in late June. Bunning's performance on Father's Day took them one giant step further down the road to what every Phillies' fan still recalls as the team's darkest hour. But let's not dwell on that now. Let's share the moment.

On June 21, the sun was shining brightly, the Phils were riding high, and Bunning was in a groove early.

In front of a boisterous Sunday-afternoon Shea Stadium crowd of 32,026, Bunning and the Phils were up 1–0 as he took the mound in the bottom of the first. Johnny Briggs had led off the game with a walk, gone to second on John Herrnstein's sac bunt, and scored on Allen's single.

"It was a nice, hot day," Bunning remembers. He's on the phone from his office in Washington, D.C. After his Hall of Fame pitching career, he became a Republican congressman from his native Kentucky and was elected a U.S. senator in 2000. "It was one of those wonderful starts to a game. I got away with some pitches early. Against Jim Hickman leading off the game for the Mets, I got away with some pitches that should have been hit. But he fouled them back."

"He threw me two good pitches in the first, good pitches to hit and I fouled them off," Hickman said after the game. "Then he stood out there on the mound and laughed at me! After that, I didn't see a good pitch to hit all day."

Few Mets did, and Bunning thought from the start that that would be the case.

"As the game went on, all the pitches were working well," he says. "The slider, curve, and fastball all got thrown to the areas I was trying to throw them to. I was ahead of all the hitters, which also made it much easier."

Also making it easier was the Phillies' offense, which added another run in the top of the second. Tony Taylor led off with a walk against eventual losing pitcher Tracy Stallard. (On the Philadelphia radio broadcast, Richie Ashburn pointed out that Stallard was single and childless, putting him at what you might call a karmic disadvantage to Bunning on Dad's Day.) Cookie Rojas sacrificed Taylor to second (ah, the sacrifice bunt . . . I look forward to telling my grandkids about those), from where he scored on catcher Gus Triandos' double to left field.

The Mets were flailing at Bunning's pitches from the get-go. There wasn't a hard hit ball until the fifth, with the possible exception of a third-inning at-em liner hit by New York's Amado Samuel right at Rojas' shins at third.

But in the fifth, Bunning tried to slip one by Mets' catcher Jesse Gonder.

"I threw him the only change-up I threw all game, and he almost got a base hit," Bunning says. "I didn't throw any more of those!"

The left-handed-hitting Gonder got around on the change-of-pace and drove a hard ground ball between first and second. Taylor ranged to his left and dove to the grass. He managed to knock it down with his glove, but it bounced a few feet away. Hopping quickly up, he grabbed the ball, made a nice pirouette, and fired to first to nip Gonder.

"Taylor made an unbelievable play," Bunning remembers. "If it weren't Jesse Gonder running, he wouldn't have thrown him out. When he did that, I thought I might have something special going. But looking back, man, that was the play."

As happened in several perfect games, a play in the early or middle innings that would have barely been noticed in a 6–3 game suddenly loomed large in the postgame discussion. The play is another chapter in the "razor-thin" story of perfect games. So many things had to go just right on that play, any one of which would have changed the outcome, ended the perfect game, and sent the play and the game into baseball obscurity.

But Taylor's glove was long enough, the grass was dry enough to let him bounce up quickly, he didn't drop the ball when he picked it up to throw, and Gonder was a tugboat in spikes. And boom, Bunning was through five unscathed.

"Immediately after the fifth inning, I became aware of what we were doing," Bunning says.

One of the "we" was Triandos, Bunning's former teammate from Detroit who had been traded to Philly with him. They were working well together on Father's Day.

"Gus and I disagreed on maybe five, ten pitches in the whole game," Bunning says. Bunning then laughs when asked about their game plan for the Mets.

"There weren't any game plans then! This was 1964! I was the only one that kept a book on hitters back then. But there was no game plan. I talked with the catcher, and then I'd move infielders around when I knew where I was going to pitch the hitter. If I was going to go inside on a left-handed hitter, for instance, I'd move the second baseman toward the hole and so forth."

Philadelphia manager Gene Mauch noticed Bunning doing just that early in the game. "He acted like he knew something was up. He was moving infielders all over the place."

Buoyed by his realization of the special outing he was having, Bunning "helped his own cause," as they say, in the top of the sixth. After Callison homered, Bobby Wine walked with two outs, advanced on a single by Taylor, then scored on Triandos' single. That brought up Bunning with two outs and two on.

"And I hit a double to left-center!" he says, still obviously excited more than 35 years later. "Not too bad."

The cat was out of the bag now, and Bunning, going against every "rule" in the book, was letting everyone know about it. Unlike every other perfect-game pitcher that we know about, Bunning was obviously and verbally encouraging his teammates.

"I really didn't care about the superstitions," he says. "I had been through one where I almost had total collapse [the Boston no-hitter]. So it was important to me to relax. Having gone through that game in Fenway really helped me in the perfect game. No one said anything then, and when it was over with, it was total bedlam. I didn't want that to happen again, so I tried to talk about it during the game in Shea."

"He was jabbering like a magpie," Triandos said after the game.

"He was coming back to the dugout yelling at the guys, and counting down the outs," Mauch said later. "Nine more, six more . . ."

"As the game progressed, in the seventh, eighth, and ninth, I kept urging my teammates that we had a perfect game going," Bunning says. "I told them that this was the time to start diving at balls."

But Bunning not only ignored the baseball gods by talking about his perfect-game-in-progress, he also made it easy on his teammates, striking out six of the final nine hitters (he had a total of 10 Ks in the game). In the eighth, though, he had one scare against Mets left fielder Bob Taylor. With two outs, the count went to 3–2. The next pitch was a called strike three, but Triandos dropped the ball. The crowd, which had by now been roaring for Bunning for the past several batters, went quiet before Triandos threw to Herrnstein to retire Taylor. No error, no passed ball, just another K.

"It was unusual to have everyone there rooting for me," Bunning remembers of the Shea faithful who switched sides as they realized what was going on. "It was kind of strange. Everyone stood up. You don't expect the whole crowd to stand up during a game. But they all stood up. It was a little distracting to start with. But I was pretty intent on getting it done, so it didn't distract me but for a second. Yelling on every pitch was also unusual, too."

The only thing left was for Bunning to close it out. In the bottom of the ninth, shortstop Charlie Smith came first, and he popped out weakly to Rojas in foul territory.

With his wool jersey clinging to his sweat-soaked frame, Bunning then prepared to face what he knew would be Mets pinch-hitters.

"I knew that [Mets manager] Casey Stengel had two pinch-hitters, John Stephenson and George Altman, that he'd use for Samuel and the pitcher's spot," Bunning says. "But I didn't know which way he'd use them. I was hoping that Altman would come first, because I knew Stephenson was a little easier for me to get out than Altman. And Casey used them in that order, and I was very happy that he did."

Altman was not a complete pushover. He had some .300 seasons in his past. But that didn't matter to Bunning. Altman fouled off two pitches, then Bunning threw him a low, outside pitch that was swung on and missed.

Then the lip-flapping Phillies pitcher, who had been cheerleading his team for four innings, needed a little pep talk himself. Pausing behind the mound to wipe off his face as he prepared to face Stephenson, Bunning motioned for Triandos to come out.

"He wanted me to tell him a joke," Triandos said. "But I couldn't think of anything! I just told him to go get this guy, and that was it."

"I just wanted to relax a bit," Bunning remembers.

Stephenson was batting a sub-Mendoza .074, but he could have been Ty Cobb for the stuff that Bunning had.

"I knew that if I threw three curveballs over the plate I was going to strike him out," Bunning says. "So it was just a matter of hitting the spots."

Bunning got ahead 0–2, then threw two pitches out of the strike zone, one low and one high, both outside. Then came curveball-to-a-spot number three. It broke like a jet fighter going into a dive, and Stephenson swung over the top.

Shea erupted, knowing that witnessing baseball history was worth more than a Mets victory (though in that 53-win season, wins were almost as rare as perfectos). The Phillies ran onto the field and surrounded Bunning, the proud father who had just given birth to a perfect, two-hour, 19-minute, 90-pitch baby.

"I wasn't aware, really, of the historic nature," he says now. "I knew it was anticipated, but I didn't know all the details of past ones. I never thought about even pitching a no-hitter, and I managed to do one in both leagues. You don't think about those kinds of things while you're doing them. It's afterward that you can put it in perspective."

He quickly was filled in on the history part, eight decades–plus having passed since Ward's. Bunning's was also the first one in the regular season since Robertson in 1922. In a way, the future senator actually started a perfect game skein that saw two more in the 1960s, three in the 1980s, and four in the 1990s.

Mary and Barbara came out of the stands to greet husband, dad, and winner.

"It was great to have them there, of course," he says. "We did all the interviews, including one on the field with Ralph Kiner that I remember. And then we wanted to go to Toots Shor's for dinner to celebrate. But it was closed. So HoJo's was it.

"I was also on the Sullivan show that night. I knocked Ken Venturi off the show. He had won the U.S. Open in Washington that day and almost died in the heat. We've been friends ever since, but I don't think he's ever forgiven me for that.

"It was obviously the best game as far as results that I've ever pitched. I've had better stuff, though, just not as good control. I mean, to pitch a no-hitter against the Red Sox, with the hitters they had, was a tougher feat, I think, than the Mets. I'm not knocking the Mets, but the Red Sox had Ted Williams and Jackie Jensen and Pete Runnels and a lot of other good hitters."

Bunning went on to win 19 games that year, but he'll always have mixed feelings about 1964. With the Phillies up by 6½ games and 12 games to play, they managed to blow the pennant in one of the most stunning collapses in baseball history. It would be 16 years before they had another shot, when they finally won the World Series in 1980.

Bunning continued pitching well for the Phillies, with two more 19-win seasons followed by 17 wins in 1967. "The perfect game wasn't the last good game I pitched; sometimes that's the case," he says. "I was able to maintain my stuff for five or six more years."

He retired in 1971 with 224 career wins and was third all time in strikeouts at the time. He was elected to the Baseball Hall of Fame in 1996.

"The [perfect] game continued to follow me in that people kept reminding me of it," he says. "I didn't have to remind myself or stop to think about it because enough people were always asking about it."

To top it all off, on June 21, 1997, the 33rd anniversary of the Father's Day perfect game, the Bunnings welcomed a new grandson, James Lewis Bunning. Another perfect day for Dad, or should we say, Granddad.

Today, as Bunning works in an imperfect city, does he have any perfect days on Capitol Hill? Ever the politician, he answers, "Sure, I have a lot of perfect days up here."

If only the Democrats were more like the Mets.

CHAPTER 8

Sandy Koufax

September 9, 1965

O K, all together now:

"If there was ever a pitcher who might have thrown a perfect game every time out, it was Sandy Koufax."

Few, if any, pitchers enjoy the immense reputation that Koufax earned with a stunning string of five seasons in the early 1960s during which he won five ERA titles, three Cy Young Awards, and an MVP trophy; set a single-season strike-out record; threw a no-hitter each year from 1962 to 1965 (that last, of course, his perfecto against the Chicago Cubs on September 9, 1965); and helped the Dodgers win three N.L. pennants and two World Series championships. No pitcher has ever had as remarkable, as memorable, or as dominating a five-season run.

"There were days that Koufax would pace the dugout before games and just tell his teammates, 'Give me one run, that's all I need,'" says Ed Gruver, author of the 1999 biography *Koufax*. "That's the kind of confidence he had that he could shut the other team down when he had his really good stuff."

And playing for the Dodgers in those days, one run was often all he got. Los Angeles lived and died with speed, defense, and pitching.

"That was the year [1965] we hit .245 [seventh in the N.L.] as a team and won the championship," says Montreal manager Jeff Torborg, then a second-year catcher. "Our leading hitter was [pitcher Don] Drysdale, who was often our right-handed pinch-hitter. In fact, in 1964, when Sandy pitched his third no-hitter, Drysdale was not at the park. When someone called him that night to tell him that Sandy had pitched a no-hitter, Drysdale asked, 'Did he win?' That gives you an indication of how much confidence we had in our offense."

Along with worrying about his offense, Koufax worried about his left arm, his elbow to be precise. The same wondrous appendage that carried him to stardom would be the anchor that would eventually drag him down and out of baseball. By this point in his career, arthritis was causing him daily pain. There had been talk of him missing more of the season, but he soldiered on with a little medical help. Gruver writes that Koufax took phenylbutazone to reduce inflammation. The pitcher smeared on Capsolin, an ointment that helped him loosen up his muscles. Postgame, he dunked the elbow for up to 30 minutes in an ice bath wearing a protective rubber sleeve devised by the Dodgers trainers.

Koufax kept going out there, however, with an intensity that belied his quiet demeanor. Few pitchers in history had Koufax's skills; fewer still had his drive to win. He was satisfied with nothing less than victory.

The fans around the National League responded to his talent and his grit, turning out in droves every night he pitched. *The New York Times'* Leonard Koppett did a little figuring and noted that Koufax's appearances in 1965 averaged more than thirty-six thousand fans; the N.L. average for all games was just over fifteen thousand. "His 'personal attendance,' in his 40 starts," wrote Koppett, "[will] exceed the total of the Yankees and a majority of the other teams for their 81-game home schedules."

More than twenty-nine thousand of those fans were in attendance on a slightly damp, coolish evening in Chavez Ravine for an odd one-game "series" with the Cubs on September 9. ("It was hardly worth the trip," Koufax wrote in his 1967 autobiography.) The Dodgers trailed the first-place San Francisco Giants by a game; the Giants had put together a 15-game winning streak to catch and pass L.A., so the Dodgers were eager to climb back into first place.

Torborg, who caught for Koufax that night, remembers nothing remarkable about Koufax or the team before this game, though he did delight in pointing out that in those days, the starters warmed on of a mound located in front of the dugouts "so that fans can see the pitchers getting ready up close."

As the L.A. crowd filtered in, Cubs center fielder Don Young stepped to the plate to lead off. Koufax wound up and delivered the first pitch of what would become a historic night . . . and bounced a curveball three feet in front of home plate. Not exactly an auspicious beginning, but he wound up getting Young to pop to second base.

The second batter, second baseman Glenn Beckert, then hit a liner that was "about this much foul," remembers Torborg, who held his fingers an inch apart as he recounted the event. Beckert then struck out, as did Billy Williams, beginning Koufax's game-long string of at least one strikeout per frame.

"Sandy didn't have a real good curveball early in the game, kind of rolling," Torborg says. "He did have his live fast-ball, but he didn't have his real good stuff early. Of course, that was great stuff for everyone else, but not for him."

In the second, future Hall of Famer Ernie Banks was Koufax's next strikeout victim, going down swinging for the second out. Left fielder Pidge Browne then hit a hard liner to center that Willie Davis caught about waist high, the only fair ball that was truly hard-hit against Koufax all night.

Things were going pretty much as planned, at least according to Sandy's plan, that is.

"I didn't talk to Sandy during that game, but that wasn't unusual," says Torborg. "I stayed away from him. I was in awe of him anyway, so that wasn't unusual. Later on, though, I sure wasn't going to be the one who said anything [about the perfect game].

"He knew what he wanted to do. I just asked him what he wanted to do before the game. Nowadays, we have meetings with the whole staff. Used to be that before the first game of a series, we'd meet just in general. We didn't go over how we'd pitch every guy. Sandy let me know how he wanted to pitch them."

And when the 800-pound gorilla talks to a second-year catcher, the kid listens.

In the third inning, Koufax finally, tentatively, tried a few fastballs as his arm slowly loosened up.

"It took him a while," Torborg remembers. "He stuck with almost all curveballs for almost all of the first three innings. He started to get the fastball over then and that was his strikeout pitch."

Opposing pitcher Bob Hendley K'd to end the third, and Koufax was through the order perfectly for the first time. Unfortunately, the same was true for the banjo-hitting Trolley Dodgers. In fact, while Koufax kept the Cubs from the bases through five innings, Hendley didn't allow a base runner either until left fielder Lou Johnson opened the bottom of the fifth with a walk.

That season, the Dodgers manufactured so many runs they should have painted their batting helmets yellow. The only run they would provide for Koufax on this night was a typical "Dodger home run."

With Johnson at first, Ron Fairly laid down a perfect sac-rifice bunt and Johnson was on second with one out. Early in Jim Lefebrve's at-bat, Johnson broke for third, but Cubs catcher Chris Krug threw the ball into left field, and Johnson scored an easy unearned run. (If you're scoring at home, that's yet another perfect game saved by an opponent's mis-cue: see Richmond, Joss, Witt, and Browning.)

Ironically, it was a throw that Krug probably shouldn't have made.

"I had third stolen easy," Johnson said afterward. "Krug told me that the next time I came up to bat."

Now Hendley, who retired Lefebrve and Wes Parker to end the fifth, was pitching a no-hitter . . . and losing to a perfect game.

Koufax commented after the game on the effect of the close score.

"Naturally a pitcher would rather have four or five runs, especially in the last couple of innings. Early on, a tight score might help you pitch better. You have to bear down on every pitch. With an eight- or nine-run lead, it would have been a very different game."

Once again, the formula for perfection included a solid job by both pitchers. There is no telling how many potential no-hitters or perfect games disappear in the fourth or fifth inning as a pitcher works with a multirun pad. It is just so much easier to go after a hitter when you've got crooked numbers on your side. One hit or one walk won't make a difference in a six-run game; it will in a one-run game, and thus pitchers aiming for perfection invariably benefit from the tightness of the score.

In the sixth inning, Krug led off and slapped a ground ball to Dodgers shortstop Maury Wills, who threw low to Wes Parker at first. But Parker dug it out and recorded the out. Third baseman Jim Gilliam threw out Don Kessinger, and Hendley was once again helpless at the plate.

By this time, players and fans were well aware of the unique pitching duel they were either taking part in or witnessing. Torborg claims some level of ignorance while also admitting to the pressure he was facing.

"I didn't think about the crowd at all," he says. "I was so involved in the game. They might have been cheering every pitch, I don't remember that at all.

"You could be hearing your own heartbeat. You want to do everything right. Your heart's pounding. You look up to see a no-hitter, but I don't remember when I thought of a perfect game."

"Around the seventh inning, we knew Sandy wasn't going to give us a hit," said Hendley. "He was just unbelievably fast."

"Around the seventh, I thought a no-hitter was in reach," said Koufax. "And believe me, I really wanted it. I didn't think too much about the perfect game. No one said a word to me about what was going on, but I knew and so did everyone else."

With two outs in the seventh, Koufax reached the only 3–0 count of the evening, to Billy Williams, the only lefty in the Cubs' lineup. But then he grooved two strikes past a frozen Williams, who hit the sixth pitch to Johnson in left for the third out.

In the bottom of that inning, Hendley finally cracked, but just barely. He had been matching Koufax zero for zero, with only the walk to Johnson marring his record. Johnson came up again with two outs in the bottom of the seventh and lifted a soft fly ball behind first base. Former standout shortstop Ernie Banks was playing first, and he gave chase. The ball flopped to the ground just beyond his outstretched mitt, and the speedy Johnson made it to second. Johnson was actually the only player to reach base in the game for either team.

When writing about this point in the game in his 1967 autobiography, written with Ed Linn, Koufax actually made a joke.

"I, of course, sympathized with Hendley mightily. Since we already had the run, I, needless to say, rooted for him to get his no-hitter so that we could walk into the record books hand in hand.

"Like heck I did. I was sitting there rooting for us to score six more times and knock him out of the box."

That didn't happen, but as he had promised in other instances, one run was all Koufax would need. In fact, for the rest of the game, a catcher was really all he would need. The other Dodgers were just as much spectators as the fans in the stands during the eighth and ninth innings as Koufax put on a masterful display of strikeout pitching.

"In the eighth, Ron Santo led off and went up 2–0 before Sandy hooked him three straight times," Torborg remembers. "Santo walked back to the dugout, and he knew, it's over, boys. 'Oh, boy, here we go,' he seemed to say."

"I've never seen Sandy throw as hard as he did when he struck me out in the eighth," Santo says. "He threw one fastball right by and I was waiting for it. He seemed to get a burst of energy in the last innings."

Banks went down swinging, thus making his night a perfect 3-for-3—strikeouts, that is.

Browne also went down swinging. Koufax seemed to grow stronger and stronger as the night went on. Meanwhile, his catcher was still trying to help him out.

"My last at-bat [in the bottom of the eighth] I really crushed one," says Torborg with a big smile. "And as I rounded first, I thought, wow, I hit a homer on the night he did something special. But it was kind of a heavy, humid, damp night, and the ball didn't carry and it got caught at the fence."

Again, Hendley shut down the Dodgers. A harder-luck pitching story has never been written. A player so anonymous that he could have had "journeyman" written on the back of his uniform had come into Dodger Stadium, held the eventual world champs to a walk, a hit, and a measly unearned run, and he would leave that night with nothing but a bagel for his trouble.

And so, on to the ninth.

"Krug threw the ball away to let in our only run, and he led off the ninth inning," notes Torborg. "I remember thinking, if anyone wants to redeem himself, it's Krug."

Up in the press box, Vin Scully continued his remarkable call of the game to the Dodger radio audience. Scully had been on Armed Forces Radio for Larsen's game, and he would go on to call Martinez's . . . an amazing three perfect performances at the mike.

At 0–2 to Krug, Scully said, "You can almost taste the pressure now. Koufax lifts his cap, runs his fingers through his black hair, then pulls the cap back down low, fussing at the bill."

The drama continued as Krug took a ball outside, fouled off two pitches, then took ball two.

"There are twenty-nine thousand people here tonight," said Scully, "and a million butterflies."

Krug swung and missed at yet another fastball, and Koufax was two outs away.

Pinch hitting for shortstop Don Kessinger was Joe Amalfitano, a light-hitting utility player.

"I only called one curveball in the last three innings," says Torborg. "That was to the second hitter, Amalfitano. He'd already gotten big pinch hits off fastballs on us earlier in the season. So I didn't want to give him a fastball. We called a curve on the second pitch and he fouled it off. I was so gunned up I got it before it went anywhere."

After that foul ball, Scully noted that Koufax had taken a walk behind the mound, and the Hall of Fame announcer said, "I would think that the mound at Dodger Stadium is the loneliest place in the world."

Koufax came back from his lonely place with another stunning fastball, and Amalfitano was out hacking.

On the way back to the dugout, Amalfitano reportedly looked at pinch-hitter Harvey Kuenn and said, "Harvey, you might as well not even bother coming to the plate."

Kuenn bothered anyway. He was batting for the hard-luck Hendley, who had stilled the Dodgers' bats nearly as well as Koufax had blanked the Cubs. Koufax prepared to face Kuenn, and we can only imagine what was going through his head. Biographer Ed Gruver imagines something like this: "Players like Koufax have the zone, tunnel vision, where they can block out things. From people I spoke to, Koufax was a guy who did pitch inside. He wasn't a headhunter. But he said, show me a guy who won't pitch inside, and I'll show you a loser. Pitching is the art of making a man flinch, he said. He wasn't above using his fastball as intimidation. He didn't throw at people, but he was willing to come inside. He had the attitude of all great pitchers . . . he wasn't going to back down."

And he didn't back down from former batting champion Kuenn, who must have been experiencing an unpleasant sense of déjà vu. Two years earlier, Kuenn, then with the Giants, had bounced out to end Koufax's second no-hitter.

Kuenn took the first fastball for a strike and watched the next two go by high and tight for balls; on the first of those, Koufax threw so hard that he lost his hat on the follow-through. Scully noted that the hat went so far that Torborg actually got up and retrieved it.

A mighty swing by Kuenn on a high hard one hit nothing but air, and the count moved to 2–2. The Dodger Stadium crowd, already screaming at top voice, reached a crescendo as Koufax went into his familiar kick with the right leg before flinging his arm and body plateward. With velocity that barely wavered from earlier innings, Koufax zinged a fastball that Kuenn barely saw, let alone hit, and it was over.

Koufax had done it, not only pitching a perfect game, but becoming the first pitcher ever with four no-hitters. He had struck out the last six hitters he faced, and seven of the last nine. His 14 strikeouts were the most ever in a perfect game.

Koufax was surrounded by teammates, a big grin plastered on his face. They corralled him into the dugout as he waved to the crowd. No one thought of arthritis or inflammation or pain, they just reveled in the stunning beauty and awesome power of his performance, and indeed of the remarkable rarity of the event they had just witnessed.

A "cleaner" game has never been played in the history of the major leagues. There has never been a complete-game double no-hitter, and so this game set a record that can only be beaten by one: Fewest hits, both teams, one game. Johnson was the only player to safely reach base, on a walk and his double. The Cubs' 27 plate appearances joined the Dodgers' 26 to exceed the minimum for the game (with the home team coming up only eight times) by only two, a stunning accomplishment for the pitchers and defenses, and a stirring display of ineptitude by the hitters. Talk about a pitcher's duel . . . this was perhaps the ultimate such duel, as proven by the record.

In the crowded, happy locker room, Torborg was enough of a kid to make sure that he got an autographed ball from Koufax ("I still have a picture of him signing that ball for me"), but enough of a teammate that he teased veteran John Roseboro. "I said, 'Hey, John, you might have two no-hitters, but I've got a perfect game.'"

(Torborg also notes that he is one of only three catchers to catch a no-hitter in each league, and that surprisingly, all three of them have a perfect game as one of their unusual double plays. "Gus Triandos caught Jim Bunning's perfect game and a no-hitter by Hoyt Wilhelm. Ron Hassey caught the two perfect games, one in each league [Barker and Martinez], and me, with Koufax and Nolan Ryan for the Angels." Torborg also caught a Bill Singer no-no in 1970.)

In the Cubs' locker room, the veterans could only shake their heads in wonder.

"That man could drive you to drink," said a grumbling Ron Santo.

Banks asked a couple of younger players, "Are you sure you want to play in the National League?"

Backup catcher Ed Bailey, who had just witnessed his fifth no-hitter as a player, was the calmest of the bunch.

"He didn't bother me any." Of course, Bailey didn't play.

"I've seen all the no-hitters he's pitched," Dodgers manager Walter Alston said, "and I'd have to say that he had his greatest stuff in this one."

Koufax was exuberant afterward, but in the somewhat subdued way that he had. Here was no David Wells, after all, but a somewhat shy and reserved man who kept his focus where it mattered: on the field. Dodgers owner Walter O'Malley sent champagne to the locker room, but Koufax had a beer instead.

"What struck me about that game was his postgame quote about Hendley," says Ed Gruver. "He talked about how tough it was for the other guy. That was indicative of the kind of character that he has, even at the moment of his greatest triumph to be talking more about the other guy than about himself."

Koufax also thought of his teammates.

"As much as I wanted that no-hitter and the perfect game," Koufax told reporters, "I was just as pleased that I won my 22nd game. I had five starts at it before getting that win and the guys were beginning to think there was something wrong with me."

Nothing was further from the truth. Torborg spoke for all the Dodgers when he said that he felt "not as much awe as immense respect. They were so good, he and Don [Drysdale], they made you feel comfortable that they'd do the job."

Not surprisingly, the arm ailment that would end Koufax's career came up not long after the game. "He has not had a normal arm at any time this year," said Dr. Robert Kerlan, the Dodgers team doctor. "And I'm sure he did not have one last night. It just proves that you can pitch a perfect game with an arthritic elbow."

Koufax and the Dodgers soon did another amazing job, starting almost with this game. Less than a week after trailing

San Francisco by a game following Koufax's perfecto (the Giants and Juan Marichal had also won on September 9), the Dodgers reeled off a stunning 13-game win streak that left the Giants in the dust and the N.L. pennant in Chavez Ravine.

In September, Koufax was his normal brilliant self. Along with the whitewash of the Cubs, he was 4–0 from September 18, allowing only one run while also pitching three shutouts. His 3–1, 13-K victory over Milwaukee on October 3, on only two days' rest, clinched the pennant for the Dodgers.

He wrapped up another ERA title and set a new major league record with 382 strikeouts (later broken by one by Nolan Ryan). To top off yet another remarkable season, he shut out the Twins in Game 7 of the 1965 World Series to help the Dodgers capture another title.

"There should be one Cy Young Award for him and one for the rest of us to shoot at," said Twins pitcher Mudcat Grant.

Today, Koufax lives quietly in Florida, occasionally helping out the Dodgers at spring training and appearing in charity golf tournaments. But he doesn't spend his days reliving his baseball greatness, nor does he spend his time trading on his celebrity status. He lives his life today as simply as he threw his fastball hard. And he seems to do both with equal, effortless ease.

Torborg became the manager of the Chicago White Sox, was a TV analyst, and took over the Expos in the summer of 2001. That perfect game still comes up in his own travels through baseball. In the summer of 2001, he sat in the visiting dugout at Dodger Stadium and reminisced about catching Koufax's gem, as well as the other two no-hitters he caught.

"In fact, last night I thought about that perfect game, first because I caught the foul pop to end the game for Singer right there in front of the dugout." He pointed to a spot 10 yards from the dugout bench. "And then when you see a game like last night [in which the Dodgers' Chan Ho Park went six no-hit innings], you start to go back to those games in your mind. And since I caught Sandy's right here, I wondered if we'd see another one."

No, Jeff, we won't.

Equaled? Perhaps. Surpassed? I don't think so.

Years before he became a feare[d] starter for the Yankees, youn[g] "Catfish" Hunter was surprisingl[y] perfect when he iced the Twins i[n] 1968. *Photo courtesy of AP/Wid[e] World Photos*

CHAPTER 9

Jim "Catfish" Hunter

May 8, 1968

To Athletics fans beguiled by team owner Charlie Finley's fiction, he was Catfish. To all the folks back home in North Carolina, he was just Jimmy, the good old boy who surely did like to catch catfish, but weren't never called that 'round the farm. To American League hitters, he was a bewildering mix of precision and guile. To every major leaguer who has ever signed a free-agent contract that could pay the freight for a small island nation, he was a trailblazer. And to every sports fan—heck, every person—who witnessed the tough, sad end of his days, he was a hero in every sense of the word.

On top of all that, on May 8, 1968, James Augustus "Catfish" Hunter was perfect.

Hunter was born in Hertford, North Carolina, in 1946 and grew up a country kid who loved to play country hardball. He played basketball and football, too, but after leading Perquimans County High School to a state title in 1964, he was drafted by the Kansas City Athletics. Finley gave the country boy a $75,000 bonus, a ticket directly to the bigs, and a nickname.

After hearing the kid, who was then called Jim, talk about a boyhood fishing trip, Finley weaved a tale about the youngster skipping school one day and coming home with a string of catfish. The nickname stuck whether Hunter liked it or not. (And the fiction stuck firmly enough that, in those innocent, precynicism days, even *Sports Illustrated* quoted the tale as gospel three years later when recounting the events of Hunter's perfect game.)

Catfish was the bonus baby expected to help the young Athletics into the promised land. In three seasons in Kansas City, Hunter didn't have a winning season, but he did make two A.L. All-Star teams and post a 2.81 ERA in 1967. While not exactly failing in his early promise, Hunter was struggling to succeed as he began his fourth pro season in 1968.

"From an ability standpoint, from a pitching standpoint, he was there already. He just hadn't had the numbers yet," says former teammate Rick Monday. "He never threw exceptionally hard. The best way to describe it was that he did surgery from 60 feet, six inches. He was like a surgeon trying to dissect each hitter's strike zone. At times you got the impression that he was toying with people. At that point in his career, I don't think he knew just how good he was."

Ron Fimrite was a columnist for the *San Francisco Chronicle* and later a longtime baseball writer for *SI*. He was at Hunter's perfect game.

"Hunter hadn't had a winning season and he wouldn't end up having one that year," Fimrite says. "At 22, he was sort of an unknown quantity."

That season was also the Athletics first in Oakland; Finley had pulled up the team's roots after 12 years in the Fountain City and headed west.

The Athletics of 1968 were only four years from beginning a three-year romp through baseball and the World Series. But in the summer of '68, they were just kids.

"That team, when it first moved out there, was very young," Monday says. "Most of us on that team had our baptism in the pros in the majors. There wasn't a lot of minor league experience on that team."

Hunter, in fact, was one of them, having jumped right from Perquimans H.S. to the A's.

"The nucleus of some great teams were there," adds Fimrite. "But at the time, no one expected them to do anything. Also, they had those wild uniforms. I wrote at the time that they looked like softball uniforms, plus they had those damned white shoes."

The shoes were white and the stadium was new. Hunter pitched (and lost) on Opening Day, 1968, in the new Oakland Coliseum; California governor Ronald Reagan threw out the first pitch. But pretty soon, the glamour of the new park wore off, and its nickname of "Oakland Mausoleum" was born.

"The small crowds were one thing that wasn't perfect about Oakland," Hunter wrote in his autobiography (*Catfish: My Life in Baseball*, written with Armen Keteyian). "For the first three or four years we played pretty much to ourselves. Heck, we got outdrawn by World Team Tennis one night."

"It was a very forbidding ballpark," Fimrite remembers. "It certainly earned its nickname. And Finley did nothing to beautify the ballpark. It was ugly and spare. It wasn't a good place for baseball, especially on nights like [May 8]."

Catfish, however, had found a home.

"I always loved pitching there," Hunter wrote of the park that would have only 837,000-plus fans that season. "The foul areas were the biggest in baseball, eating up one would-be souvenir after another. Plus, the ball never carried at night."

He got the chance to test that theory in the 12th game played at the Mausoleum, a May 8 contest against the Minnesota Twins that started at the unusual time of 6:00 P.M. that Wednesday.

"I remember it was a cold night in Oakland," Fimrite adds with a laugh. "The press box was not enclosed, either."

Down on the field, the Athletics were getting ready to play, and Hunter had a pregame run-in with manager Bob Kennedy that was oddly prescient of the night's events.

"We were taking batting practice," Hunter told writer Glenn Dickey. "Everyone was supposed to take six swings and a bunt. Well, the pitcher threw ten pitches to me and eight of them were balls. Heck, one of them almost hit me. Then Kennedy came around and told me to get out of the cage. He said my time was up and I was fouling up the hitters."

In his own book, Hunter added his thoughts on Kennedy's micromanagement. "[It was] horseshit. I'd proved I can hit; I'd always taken great pride in my hitting. In high school I was one of the best hitters on the team. So I grabbed my bat, whipped it against the cage, and walked out. I was pissed off, and I left in a huff."

Ninety minutes later, Hunter huffed to the mound to face a Twins lineup that included future Hall of Famers Rod Carew and Harmon Killebrew, perennial batting champ Tony Oliva, and slugging outfielder Bob Allison. They weren't the 1927 Yankees, but they were no slouches, and in fact many of the Twins were only two seasons removed from the World Series.

Cesar Tovar, Carew, and Killebrew went 1–2–3 to open the game, with the Killer going down on strikes, the first of three times he would do so and the first of 11 punch-outs Hunter had in the game.

In the second, Hunter went 3–0 on Oliva, but then burned him with three straight strikes. The third was a clean slate, too, with no trouble.

The fourth inning saw the first time that Hunter's teammates helped him out with a difficult play. And ironically, it was a player in his first major league game who came up with it.

Called up from Vancouver only a day before, Joe Rudi put on the green and gold for the first time on May 8 and took his place in left. Rudi had been a special project for new A's minor-league instructor Joe DiMaggio, hired by Finley to give the new Bay Area team its own local hero.

Now all of Joltin' Joe's work paid off. Tovar led off the fourth with a low, sinking liner.

"I stood out in left, nervous as hell," Rudi said. "I had to make a tough catch, a sinking, slicing line drive. Got it about knee high."

In the next inning, another future World Series hero made the second key defensive play of the game. Playing right field and incongruously batting second was a kid named Reginald Martinez Jackson. With one out in the fifth, Reggie raced back to the wall to snag a long drive by Minnesota's Ted Uhleander. "That was a great defensive team, those A's, all good defensive players," says Fimrite. "Even Jackson in those days, who was very fast with a great arm. Rudi was a terrific outfielder, Bando, Campy, and Green on the infield. Hunter had a strong defense behind him."

That defense made another sparkling play on the next batter, Bob Allison. Sal Bando, playing third, snagged the hard one-hopper that bounced up near his face at the last moment, and fired to first to record the third out of the inning.

While only a few of the fans were beginning to take some notice of Hunter's perfection, there was one group in the stadium that knew exactly what was going on. "In the press box in those days, they always had a no-hitter pool," Fimrite says. "If a pitcher went the first three innings without a hit, you'd pick the player who would break it up and toss in a buck. So there was no question what was going on if for no other reason than that. I don't think I was in the pool, it was mostly for the beat guys. But I know it was floating around."

———————

After getting the Twins out in the sixth, Hunter retired to the bench, which was fast becoming a very quiet place. Behind him as he got a drink, however, Hunter heard backup outfielder Mike Hershberger ask, "Didn't someone get on in the early innings?" The answer came back no, but Hunter wasn't sure himself, and he quickly headed back to his own corner.

"I didn't want to hear any of that conversation. I knew I was pitching a no-hitter. Beyond that, I wasn't sure. I thought maybe I'd walked somebody somewhere."

In the stands, however, another member of the Hunter family was quite sure what was going on.

"I knew all about it," remembered Catfish's high school sweetheart and wife, Helen Hunter. "I was sitting with some of the other wives, who were trying to console me. I started to cry at the start of the seventh. I was crying in the eighth and ninth. I was really excited."

Hunter and Keteyian also recounted the scenes back in hometown Hertford as Hunter's parents, brother, and cousins smashed their ears to radios to catch the crackling late-night broadcast.

With one out in the seventh, Carew hit a long drive to left, and once again Rudi came through.

"There were only four balls hit hard that night," Hunter would later write. "But that was the only one that worried me."

"I was hoping the ball wouldn't be hit to me, I was so nervous," Rudi told Glenn Dickey. "When the ball was hit my way, I thought it was over my head. But I got back in time to get it."

Hunter faced another test in Killebrew, who would go on to have an off year in 1968, but was coming off a typical

44-dinger performance in 1967. Killebrew worked the count to 3–2. Eschewing the usual diet of fastballs and sliders that had gotten him this far, Hunter reached into his bag of tricks and threw an off-speed pitch, a change that had Killebrew so far out in front that the bat slipped out of his hands and helicoptered toward Hunter. The pitcher ducked and the bat landed harmlessly behind the mound, the inning over and the perfect streak intact.

"That was the greatest and guttiest pitch of the game," manager Kennedy said afterward.

"That at-bat made me as nervous as anything else," Hunter said. "I was more worried about him than anyone else all game, anyway. He was the best bet to break up the game with one swing of the bat. I was as worried at that point about getting beaten as I was about getting a no-hitter."

The score stayed tied at 0–0, and the quiet on the bench continued as the Athletics listened to "Take Me Out to the Ballgame" while getting ready to bat in the bottom of the seventh.

"There was a point in time that the pitcher becomes the chief of a leper colony," Monday says. "Jimmy was always loose enough to understand what was going on. At one point, he joked, "'What, does my uniform stink?'"

Adding to the team's nervousness was the fact that Twins starter Dick Boswell had nearly matched Hunter, allowing only a handful of hits and no runs through six innings. The game, as often seems to happen in perfect games, was close. As Hunter noted, he and the A's were in as much danger of losing the lead as the no-hitter, perfect game, or even shutout.

Finally, in the bottom of the seventh, the Athletics broke out.

Monday, the former first-ever overall No. 1 draft pick in 1965, led off the bottom of the seventh with a double. Rudi was up next and struck out, but Monday advanced to third on a wild pitch during the at-bat. Whether manager Bob Kennedy liked it or not, his pitcher was going to hit next, BP or no BP.

Hunter had already gotten a double in the third, but he had been stranded on base. He got the sign for a squeeze bunt and laid it down, well, perfectly. Monday scored easily, and the bunt was so good that Hunter made it to first safely. Jackson and Bert Campaneris stranded Hunter there, but now he had the lead he needed.

"It was all hard stuff now," Hunter writes. "Fastballs and sliders on almost every pitch. Working fast. Painting the black."

Oliva, Uhleander, and Allison went down quietly in the eighth.

In the bottom of the eighth, Hunter relieved some of the tension he was feeling by getting another turn at bat. Bando and first baseman Ramon Webster singled. With two outs, Monday walked, loading the bases. Danny Cater, pinch hitting for pinch-hitter Floyd Robinson, who was batting for Rudi (did you follow that?), walked to force in the Athletics' second run.

That brought up the slugging Jim Hunter, already two for three in the game with an RBI, much to the dismay of the manager who had kicked him out of the cage before the game. Catfish smacked a single to right field that drove in two runs. Thus, in the game he pitched a perfecto and had three

RBI (most ever by a pitcher in such a game, for those of you keeping count).

(After the game, wrote Hunter, he paid a visit to Kennedy in the manager's office. "'Well, Mr. Kennedy, can I hit now?' He smiled. 'Kid, you can do anything you want.'")

As the ninth inning began, the six thousand–plus fans left in the Mausoleum did their best to sound like sixty thousand. Out in right field, Monday also noticed a rather unusual phenomenon.

"Although the stadium was not jammed to the rafters, on that night you could feel them begin to breathe in unison. The breathing pattern was every windup, pitch, and call. With every out, there was a full exhale. Whether it was actual or perceived by us on the field, you could feel that pattern and you could feel it get more and more labored as the game continued."

OK, deep breath, everybody . . . here we go.

Veteran catcher John Roseboro was sent up to hit for shortstop Jackie Hernandez, but he grounded out to second. Catcher Bruce Look then made like his name, gazing longingly at strike three.

The final batter was Rich Reese, pinch hitting for pitcher Ron Perranoski, who had relieved Boswell in the eighth. Hunter writes in his book that he considered Reese one of the premier pinch-hitters in the league; in fact, Reese hit .317 as a pinch-hitter in 1967.

Catfish toed the rubber, faced the little utility man, and threw the first act in one of the most intense at-bats in perfect-game history.

Reese, batting left-handed, screwed down his flapless helmet and stood in. Tellingly, he fouled off the first pitch, a fastball. He took the second pitch low and inside for a ball. Ditto the next pitch. He swung and missed at Hunter's fourth straight fastball.

With the count 2–2, Hunter fired a slider that, he wrote, "knifed through the strike zone, cutting the plate in two."

But the knife wasn't sharp enough, apparently, and the pitch was called ball three. Catcher Jim Pagliaroni started to protest and kept up some chatter as he tossed the ball back to Hunter. Catcher and umpire continued jawing slightly as Reese got ready to hit. Hunter moved around the back of the mound while the fans continued screaming and yelling for all they were worth.

Finally, everyone was set and Hunter fired in another fastball.

Reese fouled the ball back.

The same thing happened on the next pitch.

Monday was doing his own thinking in the outfield as Reese filled the stands with baseballs.

"You're telling yourself, hit the ball to me, hit the ball to me. I dare you to hit the ball to me. I think that you have to have that mentality in every game, magnified in a situation like that. Then [Reese] fouls off all those pitches and you just start thinking forget hitting it . . . just throw a strike, throw a strike."

Hunter kept throwing strikes, and the pesky Reese kept fouling them off, extending the agony of the fans and the announcers, who were trying not to go hoarse as Reese kept Hunter from his goal.

A third fastball came toward the plate . . . and a third baseball headed back toward the seats.

"He never lost his fastball," Pagliaroni said afterward. "He was still firing in the ninth. His control was fantastic."

Another fastball, and then, agonizingly, it happened again, the ball spinning off Reese's bat into foul territory. He wasn't hitting them hard, just peskily getting a piece to keep the at-bat going.

"The tension was really alive at that point," Fimrite remembers.

The count was still 3–2, and Hunter was either one pitch away from perfection or one pitch away from the Appendix, "Nearly Perfect."

The kid from North Carolina went into his windup and hummed in another heater. And, believe it or not, Reese fouled it off. The souvenir count reached five in a row.

"For a while there, I thought I was never going to get him out," Hunter said afterward. "That boy kept fouling off everything I threw up there."

Hunter got a new ball from Pagliaroni and wasted little time. On this cool night in Oakland, Catfish was hot and ready, and on pitch number 107, Reese finally swung and missed.

Rather than imagine what he was thinking at that moment, I'll let Hunter tell us.

"Suddenly here's Bando sprinting over from third. He's screaming, 'Perfect game! Perfect game!' I honestly didn't know at that moment that that is what I had done."

Hunter wrote that he was so surprised that after the game, he wrote "no-hitter" on the winning ball, and not "perfect game."

The fans stayed on their feet, a cheering mass amid the massive emptiness of the park. The players mobbed Hunter on the infield and attempted a short shoulder ride before he came down and was herded into the clubhouse to continue the celebration (something the young A's were well known for, even when they had little more to celebrate than being young and free).

Champagne flowed in the locker room as the young team danced around with joy, not quite believing what had just happened. Hunter wore an enormous smile as he swigged champagne and iced his elbow in a big metal bucket.

A call came to the clubhouse not long after the game. It was Finley, calling from his home in Indiana, for Hunter.

"I'm giving you a bonus of $5,000," said the notoriously skinflint owner. "Call your dad and tell him."

"I happened to be right next to Hunter when he took that call," Fimrite says. "Hunter was like, 'Yes, Mr. Finley. Yes, Mr. Finley. Thank you, Mr. Finley.'"

Back in North Carolina, the Hunters got a call from their happy son at about 2:00 A.M. "The hound started barking as soon as the game ended," Hunter's dad reported. "Congratulations, Jimmy." He also sagely warned Hunter to tell him all about the five grand "when he got it."

"At $5,000 a shot, I'll take all the no-hitters I can get," Hunter laughed.

(A few days later, Finley did the honors in person in a pregame ceremony, signing a new contract with Hunter that included the raise and giving Pagliaroni a $1,000 bump. Hunter then presented Pags with a gold watch inscribed,

"Thanks . . . Catfish." "Catching is 50 percent of the game," he said.)

"He made my job easy," Pagliaroni said in the clubhouse. "He had an outstanding slider and threw only one change-up. The only bad pitch was a hanging slider that Killebrew fouled off."

Years later, Hunter told *The Sporting News*, "I had control on every pitch that night. I felt like I could hit any spot at any time. It was like I could get anyone out."

He didn't just feel like it . . . he went out and did it.

———————

The perfect game didn't exactly help Hunter take off like a rocket. He ended the 1968 season at 13–13 and was under .500 in 1969. But this was a young A's team slowly gelling into a champion. And in Hunter, they had found their ace. By 1970, he was a winning pitcher on a winning team. In 1971, he started a streak of five straight 20-win seasons.

Along with his Hall of Fame credentials as one of the dominant pitchers of the 1970s, Hunter is best remembered in the baseball world for two things: being the first big-money free agent (he signed a five-year, $3.75 million deal with the Yankees in December 1974) and being one of the nicest guys in the game.

As former Yankees teammate and current Seattle manager Lou Piniella said, "If you didn't know he was making that kind of money, you'd never guess it because he was humble, very reserved about being a star-type player. If you didn't like Catfish, you just didn't like people."

Folks back in Perquimans County still knew and loved the old Jimmy who had grown up with them and who hadn't been changed by all the attention and all the money. Catfish was a funny, good-hearted, fun-lovin' country boy with an eerie ability to throw just the right pitch at just the right spot at just the right time.

His skills on the diamond and his popularity among fans and fellow players thus made the announcement in 1998 that he had contracted amyotrophic lateral sclerosis (ALS, Lou Gehrig's disease) that much more painful.

"Last winter, I couldn't lift my shotgun with my right hand," Hunter said when announcing his illness. "It was a little cool that day, and I thought there was something wrong with me that would go away. But it just kept getting worse."

From the retirement comfort of his family farm, Hunter was suddenly thrust back into the spotlight, this time to put his courage on display as he had put his fastball on for show as a player. Fans and teammates poured messages of support onto him, and Hunter was out and about quickly, forming a fund-raising foundation for ALS patients that's still around. An annual old-timers' game at Perquimans High that had first been held in 1980 in honor of Hunter became an ALS fund-raiser. In 1999, that game happened to fall on the 31st anniversary of his perfect game, and a dozen former teammates showed up to take part in support.

His old teams have also honored him with special days at Oakland Coliseum and Yankee Stadium. "I was at that event at Oakland [one of the events honoring Hunter]," Monday says. "And though he couldn't move his arms or get around very well, Catfish was still sharp as a tack."

Such is the tragedy of ALS that a sufferer's mind shines brightly on while his or her body fades out.

Hunter soon lost the use of his arms, the same ones that had wound up and sent fastball after fastball Reese's way more than 30 years before. A marvelous article by Steve Rushin in *Sports Illustrated* helped tell the sports world about Hunter's life and simply cemented his reputation as a good, kind, solid guy who had been dealt a tough break, but who was dealing with it as best he could.

Sadly, in August 1999, Hunter took a bad fall at his house. Unable to use his arms to catch himself, he was seriously hurt and was unconscious for several days. He recovered enough to go home from the hospital, but a week after returning to the family farm where he had been raised, Catfish Hunter died on September 9, 1999.

In an article for *Esquire* magazine, writer Michael Paterniti remembered meeting Hunter during research for an article on Thurman Munson, the late Yankee catcher who was a teammate of Hunter's in New York. I never had the pleasure of meeting the man who was apparently one of baseball's nice guys, so I'll let Paterniti sum up the man who hung in there to make Reese out number 27—and then went on to fashion a Hall of Fame career.

"That comical bushy mustache and his mouth moving beneath it, gritty voice growling and reeling and pitching story after story. Gales of laughter; fits of pleasure. In that [picnic-table candle] light, there was something clean and pure and artful about him, and something mischievous and fun-loving and absolutely, undeniably real. He looked 23 and he looked 53, his real age. And though half of him was already gone, well, wherever he was going next, that's where you wanted to be."

And if we're lucky, we'll all go there someday, too.

The blond head at the center of this celebratory scrum, Cleveland's Len Barker made 27 Blue Jays fly away while throwing a perfect game in 1981. *Photo courtesy of AP/Wide World Photos.*

CHAPTER 10

Len Barker

May 15, 1981

Picture a grungy bar in the Flats in Cleveland, about a dozen years before Jacobs Field (among other things) came along to revitalize the area. An old geezer is watching the late sports news. On the screen, a big, blond Indians pitcher is jumping up and down with his teammates. A second geezer joins the guy at the bar.

First Geezer: Barker pitched a perfect game.

Second Geezer: You're kiddin' me? That wild man? No way.

First Geezer: No, I'm serious, he pitched a perfect game.

Second Geezer: Yeah, right, and monkeys might fly out of my . . .

But he did. Cleveland's Barker, who for a while was the living embodiment of Nuke LaLoosh, became perhaps the second-most unlikely player ever to fashion a perfect game when he set down the Toronto Blue Jays in order on May 15, 1981, winning

3–0. Nothing he had done in his career to that point gave evidence of the possibility of perfection . . . and nothing he would do later would suggest that it had been possible indeed. But Barker, along with Larsen and Robertson, simply proved that the fickle finger of fate often makes a stop in the Twilight Zone of baseball, if you'll pardon me mixing 1960s TV references with baseball.

As we've seen before and we'll see again, the combination of factors that make a perfect game happen are as unpredictable as George Steinbrenner's moods. Some games were pitched in beautiful weather; some, like Barker's, were in the damp and misty air. Some were thrown by Hall of Famers; some, well, some were not. Some were thrown against great teams; some, again like Barker's, against less-than-stellar though still major league lineups.

Is it fair that, among all the fastballin', strike-avoidin', tall drinks of water who ever fired a two-seamer plateward, Len Barker was the one who pitched a perfect game?

Should we have been surprised that it was Barker for whom the Indians' had a special 20th anniversary event in 2001, and not some other "more deserving" pitcher?

"That was great," Barker says. "I threw out the first pitch of the game. Rick Manning, who caught the last out of the perfect game, caught the pitch. They showed the game on the big screen, and there were all sorts of articles about it in the paper. That brought back a lot of good memories."

Why Barker?

Why not?

Kentucky-born Leonard Harold Barker stood 6'5" in his sanitary socks and weighed more than 220 pounds. Blond and sporting a wide, thick mustache, he was the perfect picture of a power pitcher, with a 90-plus fastball that was normally as accurate as an archer with one eye shut.

"He used to throw one out of five pitches back to the screen," Indians manager Dave Garcia said at the time.

"Lenny wasn't the type of pitcher with control," says catcher Ron Hassey, who caught Barker's perfect game (and, 10 years later, became the only man to catch two when he was behind the plate for Dennis Martinez). "Going into a game, you'd expect him to walk a few hitters."

In fact, in 1980, Barker had led the American League with 187 strikeouts, but he also had allowed 92 walks. Not exactly pinpoint control.

Barker spent three undistinguished years in the Texas Rangers bullpen before joining Cleveland in 1979, where he found a spot in the rotation, and, apparently, the plate. In 1980, he had his best season as a pro, winning 19 games to go with his strikeout title.

He was off to a hot start in 1981, entering the game against Toronto with a 2–1 record and a 1.69 ERA. At 25 years old, Barker was the ace of an Indians staff that also featured Bert Blyleven and John Denny. Blyleven, in fact, had taken a no-hitter into the ninth a week and a half earlier, also against the Blue Jays. In its aftermath, Cleveland pitching coach Dave Duncan suggested to reporters that only Blyleven and Barker had no-hitter stuff. Suggesting perfection for a guy—Barker—who averaged more than three walks a game seemed a bit of a stretch.

And, in what was perhaps a bigger surprise, the Indians were in first place. The Blue Jays, who would finish what became a strike-split season with only 37 wins, were not anywhere near first.

The game was played on a Friday evening, with the temperature in the 40s and a misty rain scudding in off Lake Erie. Before the game, Barker was one traffic jam away from missing his spot in history entirely.

"I had to pick up my brother from the airport," Barker says. "And his plane was late because of the weather. I didn't get to the ballpark until about 6:30. By the time I got to the field, it was about 7:10. Normally, I get to the field about 5:00, so that kind of messed up my routine. I warmed up, but it was kind of rushed."

While the weather made him late, it may also have helped him once he took the mound.

"We had played in that kind of weather before; that was sort of typical for early season in Cleveland," Barker says. "But the misty conditions helped me rub the ball up better," he says. "Sometimes you get balls that umps haven't rubbed up enough, and they get kind of slippery. So the water helped me rub them up where I could get a really good grip that wouldn't slip, and that gave me better rotation on the curveball."

Though he didn't know it as he was finishing his warm-up tosses, that better grip would also give Barker a grip on perfection. *Sports Illustrated*'s Bruce Newman called it a "God-given spitter."

"His curveball was the best I'd ever seen him throw," Hassey says. "There were times in other games that he'd try to throw breaking balls and they would end up bouncing in front of home plate. But during that game, the ball was breaking so much that Toronto players kept asking to see the baseball."

"The rotation on the pitch was so tight, it was a perfect curveball," Duncan said after the game.

"Normally, 90 pitches out of every 100 I threw would be fastballs," Barker adds. "But in that game, I ended up throwing about 64 or 65 curveballs. We realized it early and stuck with it. I don't think I shook off Ron more than once or twice. He just kept putting down two fingers.

"Unfortunately, I never found that curveball again after that game. I've been looking for it for 20 years."

It seems appropriate as one looks at the stunning unusualness of Barker's feat that it could be said that on this occasion, the baseball gods literally threw us—and him—a curve.

While Barker was finding his curveball, Cleveland fans were finding their damp seats, along with plenty of room to spread out. The official attendance was 7,290, but in the vast bowl of 80,000-seat Municipal Stadium on a lousy night, it seemed as if Barker and the Jays were playing to an empty lot. The game was also telecast locally on WUAB, Channel 43, so perhaps more than a few fans decided to toast the Tribe in the comfort of their wood-paneled, suburban dens.

Up first for the Blue Jays was shortstop Alfredo Griffin, and he nearly ended this chapter with his first swing. The speedy Griffin hit a slow roller up the middle, just to the left of second base. Cleveland shortstop Tom Veryzer moved far to his left, almost past second base, and threw on the run to get Griffin by a step.

"I had to come in fast, and I almost ended up at first base myself," Veryzer said.

At the time, the play was a good one, a nice, professional play by a veteran infielder. No big deal. He'd made a hundred like it and would make hundreds more. But that was it for Toronto. That was really as close as they came to a base hit for the next two hours and nine minutes.

(A great side note on Griffin: as far as I can tell, Griffin is the only player in baseball history to have played on the losing side in three perfect games. His Blue Jays lost to Barker, then he was with the Dodgers when they were "perfected" by Tom Browning and Dennis Martinez. "If that's how I get into the record books, then I guess I'll have to take it," Griffin, now an Angels coach, says with a smile.)

Lloyd Moseby and Jorge Bell grounded out to end the Toronto first.

That was almost all that Bill Elwell got to hear of the game. Barker's father-in-law was listening to the game in Norristown, Pennsylvania. When a rainstorm garbled the transmission, he hopped in his car and spent the next hour cruising the greater Norristown area looking for clear reception. He finally found it near a golf course and sat in his front seat in the rain, listening as his son-in-law made history.

While Elwell was looking for his car keys, the Indians came to bat in the bottom of the first. Facing Toronto pitcher Luis Leal, center fielder Rick Manning led off with a single, then Mike Hargrove grounded a ball that got by first baseman John Mayberry for an error. With runners on second and third, Andre Thornton hit a sacrifice fly that scored Manning. Hassey followed up with a single that scored Hargrove. No Pedro Martinez–like worries about run support (see page 266) on this misty night; Barker was up 2–0 as he took the mound for the second.

Mayberry and Willie Upshaw went down quickly and quietly. Then Damaso Garcia, a normally light-hitting second baseman, hit a drive to left-center that Manning tracked down. It's interesting to see the various ways the catch is described. If the game had not been a perfect one, the catch would not have even made the game articles. "Manning glided over," according to the AP report. "He made a long run to haul down" the liner, according to *SI*'s Newman. Bob Sudyk in *The Sporting News* also had Manning running a long way, as did Tony Grossi in the *Plain Dealer*, but neither gave it much spectacular flair. However he made the catch, the Blue Jays were done in the second.

By the fourth inning, Barker had gone through the entire Blue Jays lineup flawlessly. It didn't matter to him, nor should it to observers, that Toronto's team batting average coming into the game was .218. Nor should it matter than they hadn't scored in their previous 21 innings as the game began. But when the baseball gods are looking for a miracle, it's easier to mold one with soft clay.

Then again, Barker's was the first perfect game in which a designated hitter was used, Toronto's Willie Upshaw. Unlike previous pitchers who had enjoyed a soft out when the opposing pitcher batted at least a few times against them, Barker faced nothing but hitters. (Though we should also point out that both Hunter and Bunning contributed both hits and RBI to their victories, so the pitcher wasn't always a softy.)

Another of those Toronto hitters was right fielder Lloyd Moseby, who struck out with one out in the fourth, as Barker finally seemed to fully warm up. Moseby was the first of 11 strikeout victims for Barker, tied for the third-most in a perfect game behind Koufax's 14 and Randy Johnson's 13, and all of them came from among the final 17 batters of the night. Amazingly, all 11 strikeouts were swinging.

"Lenny was getting ahead with the fastball, then we followed that with the breaking ball," Hassey remembers. "But then we began starting guys off with the curve, it was so good."

Stunningly off-balance, the Blue Jays hitters flailed. One of them was Upshaw, a lefty who in the fifth inning reached out and popped a foul that was drifting toward the third-base stands. Toby Harrah tracked it all the way.

"I felt if I had to dive, I'd do it," he said after the game. "I got a good jump on the fans. They really didn't see it until it landed there."

Or, to be more precise, until Harrah landed there. The third baseman left his feet, dove for the ball, and caught it two rows back before crashing into the customers and losing his hat. Unlike the diverging opinions of Manning's catch, pretty much everyone agreed that it was a spectacular play; the Blue Jays' Danny Ainge called it "unbelievable." While it would not have spoiled the perfecto had Harrah missed it— it was foul and no sane scorer would have given Harrah an E-5—after the game, it and Veryzer's play—which was actually in the UPI lead that night—were the defensive gems that everyone was talking about.

After the fifth, the superstitions began to emerge. In the Indians' office in the stadium, traveling secretary Mike Seghi was watching the game as he worked. After 15 Blue Jays had gone down, he decided to stay where he was. "Being superstitious, I decided to watch the rest of the game right there. Not that it was going to matter at all if I left the office, but I just didn't want to jinx it."

Up in the press box, Tony Grossi was getting nervous. The *Cleveland Plain Dealer* reporter was only 24 and covering his second game ever as a pinch-writer for beat man Terry Pluto. The paper's sports editor, Harding Christ, even stopped by to watch. Whether it was to check on his young writer or not, he got to see the kid help write history . . . literally.

"My editor said he was going to wait for the first hit," Grossi told the *Plain Dealer* in 2001. "I was worried about a no-hitter, and then all of a sudden, a perfect game broke out. I don't think [Pluto] took a day off for the next 10 years. It was tough to break in on a perfect game. What an awesome responsibility."

Pluto did arrive later and filed an additional reaction story.

In the TV booth, Joe Tait was trying hard to describe what he and viewers were seeing without saying "perfect game" or "no-hitter." (Imagine if I'd tried to do this book that way. . . .)

In the sixth, center fielder Rick Bosetti got a fastball in on the hands and jam-drove it toward second baseman Duane Kuiper. He speared the liner on one hop and threw out Bosetti. A nice play, a good play, but again, inflated in significance by circumstance.

Around this time, Barker's brother Chuck, the one who had made him late to the park, noticed that Bonnie Barker, Len's wife, was quite nervous. "I just wasn't thinking no-hitter," he said. "I knew she was very nervous, but I didn't realize why until the ninth inning."

"I am so superstitious," Bonnie said. "I was thinking about it from the fifth inning on, but I kept trying to blank it out of my mind." To say nothing of not bothering to let her brother-in-law in on it.

Leading off the seventh inning, Griffin sent a grounder to Kuiper's left. He ranged over to get it but had to take a couple of steps before he could set and throw. He just beat Griffin. "I was more worried about Griffin's ball than Bosetti's," Kuiper said. "Because of his speed, I was glad I got off a good throw."

By this time, every time Barker got two strikes on a hitter, the smattering of fans were making as much noise as they could in the old ballpark. As Blue Jay after Blue Jay flapped his wooden wings for outs, the crowd roared as much as seven thousand soggy people could roar.

"I didn't react to the crowd at all," Barker says. "I had total concentration and I didn't even hear them until the end. I had never focused on anything as much as on those last three innings."

If the crowd was urging him on, his teammates were, too, but in a more traditionally baseball way. "I remember Rick and Toby mentioning that they were behind me and that I should just go out and get it. They didn't say the words 'perfect game,' but I knew what they were talking about."

For his part, manager Dave Garcia just kept his distance. "I felt like I had the plague," Barker says. "In the ninth, I sat down next to Dave and he just got up and walked away without saying a word."

Cleveland's automated scoreboard obviously paid no attention to superstition. In the eighth, the preprogrammed trivia question for the night asked which two major league teams had never been no-hit. At the end of the night, of course, it would be only one (then the Seattle Mariners).

In Philadelphia, listening to the game on the radio, one fan was paying special attention. Barker's mother, Emogene McCurry, was tuning in long-distance when all of a sudden she lost the signal. Unlike Bill Elwell, she couldn't get it back.

"It was fading in and out, and it came back in the eighth, but then we lost it in the ninth," she told the AP. She had to wait until the TV sports report came on with news of her son's accomplishment.

If Mrs. McCurry was in the dark as the ninth inning began, Len Barker knew he was in the spotlight.

"I have to admit, I was pretty nervous going out there for the ninth inning," Barker recalls. "I picked up the ball to start my warm-up pitches, and I dropped it, and I almost tripped and fell picking it back up. But after my warm-ups, I felt fine."

The crowd was on its feet as Bosetti led off the ninth, and he came within a seam or two of ruining the night for everyone.

"On the second pitch, Barker gave me a slider [actually a curve, according to Barker] right down the middle," Bosetti said. "I couldn't have asked for it in a better spot. Nuts! I fouled it off the screen. It was the best pitch I saw to hit all night. Then he got me on a good curve."

"It was the one bad pitch I made," Barker said after the game. "But he fouled it back. He could have hit it."

Bosetti, his chance for his own little bit of fame ruined, then popped meekly to Harrah.

Al Woods pinch hit for Ainge and struck out on three pitches. It hardly seemed fair to bring a guy in cold on a lousy night to face a guy with such nasty stuff. It was as if Woods wasn't even there.

Finally, Ernie Whitt, batting for catcher Buck Martinez, stepped up as the last chance to spoil it.

"I was thinking of pointing to center field [like Babe Ruth] to show where I was going to hit it," Whitt told *SI*'s Newman. "I thought it might upset his concentration." He left the joke in his mind, however, and then proceeded to hit it right where he had imagined pointing. Whitt flipped a soft fly ball to Manning, who swooped in on it with his arms spread out wide.

"If I had to run to the pitcher's mound to get it, I would have," said Manning afterward.

He didn't have to go that far, though the pitcher's mound was where he and every other Indians player immediately ran. After congratulating Barker, Manning asked if he could keep the ball. He got it and it sits today in a case on a shelf in his home. "Looks just like it did then, too, all dirty and scuffed up," Manning told the *Plain Dealer* in 2001.

One of the players who joined the mob on the mound was Hassey. Guess what he didn't know?

"To tell you the honest truth, I didn't know it was a perfect game until someone out there told me," he says today. "I knew it was a no-hitter, but I didn't know it was perfect. Lenny was known for walking guys, and I just didn't think he'd gone a whole game without one. I remember saying, 'He didn't walk anybody?' But that can happen if you're really focused on what you're doing."

"That last out is my biggest memory of the game," Barker says. "Watching Rick catch the ball and then jump up and down after he caught it. I felt a big relief when he caught that ball. Then all my teammates just piled into me."

Fans at home and in the stadium watched fireworks explode over Lake Erie for the Tribe's victory and Barker's feat. They also watched the mob scene at home plate, but TV viewers didn't hear Joe Tait for a minute or two. "I remember thinking the fewer words I use, the better it would be," he said.

Barker finally made it to the locker room to find a trail of white towels leading to his locker, where a bucket of iced champagne awaited him, both courtesy of clubhouse man Cy Buynak. "We gave him the white-carpet treatment," Buynak said.

Sitting on Barker's chair was a six-pack of beer arranged to form a big zero. Teammates, media, executives, and pretty much anyone who could get into the room poured congratulations on him. Meanwhile, Barker poured some champagne on Manning, spraying others in the process.

He was surrounded by reporters and tried to put into words what had just happened.

"I knew I had good stuff, maybe awesome stuff," he said. "I just don't know what to say."

All around him, teammates were trying to come up with ways to describe what they'd been a part of. Garcia and Blyleven both called it the greatest game they'd ever seen pitched; that was more than 60 combined years of pro ball talking.

Back in the stands, the amazed Cleveland faithful who had shown up on this moist night stayed for half an hour chanting "Lenny! Lenny!"

Not quite as happy were the Blue Jays, who added another dismal page to what would be a horrible season. Ainge spoke for many Blue Jays. "Everything went his way. The way he pitched tonight, I don't see how you can pitch better."

Barker had thrown 103 pitches, of which 84 were strikes. He had never reached a three-ball count on any hitter. He said afterward that it had been only the season before that he could remember even making it through a game without a walk, and suddenly, he didn't even bother to go to three balls.

Along with the effect the game has had on his life, Barker also remembers the game's effect on Cleveland. "It was the whole town, the whole region, the whole place shared in it. At the time, the city was getting a bad rap for a lot of things. It was a nice boost for everyone."

Harrah agreed, enthusing after the game, "Imagine! A perfect game! And we're all in it, all of us and the entire city of Cleveland! It's so great for everybody."

By the time Bonnie and Lenny got home that night, their neighbors had covered their garage with signs and posters. He didn't get to sleep until six the next morning, but he was up two hours later to field calls. Barker turned down a trip to New York to be on the *Today* show, but other than that he has enjoyed just about every accolade and reward thrown his way for the feat, including the $5,000 bonus that Indians president Gabe Paul gave Barker the day afterward.

"People ask me if I get tired of talking about it," Barker says. "I say whenever someone asks, it's an honor. People are always telling me stories about where they were when it happened. I had one woman tell me she was in labor during the game and told the doctor she wouldn't deliver until the game was over. And even though there were only 7,900 people there, I've probably signed 100,000 autographs for people who were at the game."

Some of us have long, productive lives with a few special moments. Some never do. So Barker realizes how lucky he was to have had his, and to have it so well documented and to have made it so memorable.

"The feeling I had after that game is something I still can't explain," Barker says today. "I was so nervous at the end. My stomach was a wreck. I still think about it often. It was one special night and something very special happened."

Unfortunately, not much else special happened to Cleveland or anyone else in baseball that year, because less than a month after the game, the players went on strike on June 11. Ironically, the All-Star Game was the first game back after the strike, held August 9 in Cleveland, and Barker made his one and only career appearance in the game. The season was split in two, and Cleveland's momentum was lost; the Tribe finished seven games back overall. For his part, Barker finished 8–7 on the year. He did win 15 the following season, but it was his last winning season. Traded to Atlanta in 1983, he was plagued with shoulder and knee problems and his career fizzled out in 1987. His career record: 74–76 . . . but one of those 74 was perfect.

"I'm not bitter at all," he says today. "I had a great time playing in the majors. I had parts of 11 seasons up there and that's a lot more than most guys had."

Barker moved back to Cleveland in 1996, after living in Atlanta for a dozen years following his stint with the Braves. He lives near Cleveland and runs a construction company. You'll love the name: Perfect Pitch Construction.

Just to throw one more curve at you, we'll let Barker's late maternal grandmother, Tokie Lockhart, have the last word. Asked afterward about her grandson's game, Tokie, then 92 years young, told the AP, "Tell Len I'm very proud of him. I hope he does better next time."

As if.

CHAPTER 11

Mike Witt

September 30, 1984

You are getting sleepy. Your eyelids are getting heavy. (And I hope it's not because of what you've read so far in this book . . . bear with me.) You are drifting into a deep, deep sleep.

OK, he's out, anything else you want to tell him?

Tell him to pitch a perfect game.

OK, no problem. Mike? Can you hear me? When I snap my fingers you will awake and remember nothing. But on September 30, 1984, you will pitch a perfect game against the Texas Rangers. Do you understand? He's nodding.

Good. And tell him he owes me money.

Very funny. OK, Mike, time to wake up. (Sound of fingers snapping.)

"Hey, I guess it didn't work, huh? I was never out."

Oh, you were out, Mike, you were out.

And about a year later, so were 27 consecutive Rangers. California Angels pitcher Mike Witt really did use hypnotism to improve his performances on the mound, though those sessions did not, as fancifully described here, include the posthypnotic suggestion to be perfect (or at least, we don't think they did). In late 1983, Witt was a talented but as-of-yet lukewarm pitcher. A hometown boy made good, he had grown up only minutes from Anaheim Stadium. After winning state pitcher of the year honors in 1978 at Servite High School, he signed with his favorite team, swayed by the thought of wearing the Big A and by scout Larry Himes' claim that Witt "would be pitching in Anaheim in two years." Himes was only a year off and Witt joined the big club in 1981.

He had two pretty good seasons as both a starter and long reliever, but in 1983, he regressed, going 7–14 with a 4.91 ERA. Confused, Witt went to winter ball in Venezuela to get sharp, and he went to hypnotists Harvey Misel and Lee Fisher to get focused.

"My mind tended to wander a bit," Witt said at the time. "I know that's not a good thing for pitching success."

OK, who's up? Ripken, right, OK. Keep the ball down and away, don't give him anything to pull . . . Is that a jet going by? . . . Start him off with a curve . . . say, did I leave the oven on?

Witt ended that sort of thinking, bore down, and, in 1984, turned in his best season as a pro. He would finish 15–11 with a 3.47 ERA and 223 strikeouts, third best in the A.L. Sounds like more pitchers should sit down in front of a swinging watch.

Did that ability to concentrate help him in the perfect game? Does Uri Geller bend spoons? That level of confidence was hugely important to Witt and brought him through 1984 with 14 wins and a place among league strikeout leaders heading into the last game of the season on September 30 in Texas' Arlington Stadium.

What might have been a triumphant march through Texas turned into a depressed slog on the way home. Witt and the Angels had been eliminated from the A.L. West race just a few days before. A season that had had a chance for postseason glory was now blowing away in the Texas heat. It was get-away day, and both teams were playing out the string.

"It was as meaningless a game as you ever could imagine, in the state of Texas on a Sunday afternoon when the Cowboys were playing," recalls writer Tim Kurkjian, now of ESPN, but then covering the Rangers for the *Dallas Morning News*. "I'm sure that many people in the stands had their radios tuned to the Cowboys' game."

There weren't that many radios. Only 8,375 people were allegedly in the stands when the game began. "It looked more like about 1,500," Witt says with a laugh.

Angels manager John McNamara did his best to make sure his team didn't just phone it in.

"We had a chance to finish .500 with a win," he said after the game. "Plus a chance to finish second and get more money out of the playoff pool. We have some guys around here who could use that. We went into the game wanting to make it more than just the 162nd game. Mike, of course, went out and made it even more important than we thought it could be."

Johnny Mac must have started his pregame "this-one-counts" cheerleading on Sunday, not Saturday night. The Angels weren't exactly treating that last night on the road as a chance to bone up on Sunday pitcher Charlie Hough's tendencies.

Witt's memories of his perfect day actually begin the night before with noises in the hallway.

"I had my wife, Lisa, on the road with me that particular trip. I remember a lot of guys in the hallway coming back from having a good time. I remember her asking, 'Aren't those guys getting in a little late?' It was the last day, and I was just taking it easy. I woke up relaxed and I knew that everyone else was, too, since they'd had fun the night before."

Witt's calm state of mind, whether induced by hypnotism or a pleasant evening with his wife, continued as he got ready for the game.

"I remember being so relaxed that day. It was perfect weather," he says without realizing the pun. "Seventy-five degrees, no wind, no clouds. A perfect day to play. I was nice and loosey-goosey, no tenseness."

For their part, the Rangers were, well, they were less than enthusiastic.

"I don't want to take anything away from him," Texas' Mickey Rivers said after the game. "But everyone had their bags packed and we were in a rush to get out. For the first five innings, we just wanted to get it over."

That "take a dive" attitude rings slightly false today. There's nothing a ballplayer likes less than losing, and if there is, it's losing and getting embarrassed.

"Ballplayers don't like to lose at tiddlywinks, let alone baseball," says Mike Brown, then the Angels' right fielder and a player who would make a game-saving defensive play. "I had been in some near no-hitters, and I know how hard players try to be the one to break it up."

So, yes, the Rangers may have been a bit lackadaisical in the early going, but by the later innings, they were battling to end Witt's bid (or, as one headline in *The Sporting News* put it, they were at their "Witt's End") to end their season perfectly . . . for him, that is, not for Texas.

Witt took the mound to face Rivers, leading off as the DH, and true to his postgame comments, he went down quickly, becoming the first of Witt's 10 strikeout victims on the afternoon. Wayne Tolleson flew out to left, and Gary Ward grounded to second.

"The first inning was just one, two, three," Witt says. "It felt pretty good, but you never know. I've felt good in the seventh and ended up giving up 10 runs in the eighth."

It kept feeling good for the rest of the day. Witt got the first defensive help he would need against Larry Parrish leading off the second. Parrish topped a swinging bunt toward Doug DeCinces at third, who swooped in and grabbed it and fired to first in one smooth motion.

"At the time, it was a nice play, but no big deal," DeCinces says. "But as you looked back on it, you thought, wow, that could have been the difference."

"If it's in the eighth inning, does he make that play?" Witt wonders. "But I'll take my chance with Doug anytime."

Pete O'Brien and George Wright followed Parrish back to the bench. In the bottom of the second, Texas pitcher Charlie Hough put up another goose egg as well. The wily knuckleballer was going for his 17th win and was certainly not phoning in his performance, no matter what his teammates said after the game. The Angels managed only seven hits off Hough and no earned runs.

In the third, Witt effortlessly struck out Tommy Dunbar and Donnie Scott and then got Curtis Wilkerson to ground to Dick Schofield at shortstop.

"We started thinking about a no-hitter even then," said Texas batting coach Marv Rettenmund after the game. "Charlie was walking through the dugout saying, 'The stuff this guy's got today, he's got a chance to do it.'"

"He was throwing his curveball on either side of the plate whenever he wanted to," Hough said. "His stuff was awesome. I saw Jerry Reuss and John Candaleria pitch no-hitters, but this was by far the most overpowering. I mean, this was no contest."

The fact that the Rangers were talking about it in the dugout that early also helps give the lie to their postgame comments. Again, were they less than 100 percent focused? Maybe early on, but that focus sharpened quickly when they saw what was going on. Of course, by then, it was to prove too late.

For their part, the Angels were taking notice of Witt's excellence early on as well. Brown remembers thinking about it in the fourth inning.

"In 1983, Britt Burns was throwing a perfect game against us," he says. "I overheard Reggie Jackson saying that Rod Carew was our last chance to break it up. I was like, hey, I still get to bat, too. So he got Carew out, then I hit a line drive to left-center to break it up in the eighth inning. The next day, [then–Chicago manager] Tony LaRussa said it wasn't hit that well, but hey, that was a line drive! So that's why on the flip side, I was aware of it so much earlier, probably in the fourth. The Rangers were falling asleep out there. I don't think Texas realized it until the seventh."

In the stands, Lisa Witt was paying attention, but she thought her husband was aiming for a no-hitter. "I had never even heard of a perfect game," she says with a laugh. And this from a woman who met Mike when she was on the Angels marketing staff.

"In Arlington, the stands were very close to the field," DeCinces remembers. "And I could see Lisa real well from my position. She was sitting right at the end of the dugout. And she was totally nervous the whole game."

Like a cha-cha line facing Bugs Bunny in his baseball cartoon, the Rangers marched up to the plate and then marched back. Witt (Mike, that is, not Lisa) mowed them down as easily the second time through as the first.

Soon, others began to pay attention as well, including some who were supposedly being paid to do so.

"It crept up on all of us," says Ross Newhan of the *Los Angeles Times*. Newhan, who was inducted into the Baseball Hall of Fame in 2001, was covering the game with one eye on the field and the other on the future. "We were all packed and ready to go to Kansas City for the opening of the playoffs. I was writing the Angels' season wrap-up and working on a pre-playoff story.

"Then, about the sixth inning, we all realized that he's got this perfect game going. You're thinking, someone's going to get a hit, this can't happen now. I hate to say this, but in some ways you're rooting against him. You don't want to have another story on getaway day."

"I'll be honest with you, I barely even looked at the game for the first six innings," Kurkjian said. "It took about an hour, and we looked up and this guy had not allowed a base runner."

It was even worse for *Orange County* (California) *Register* beat writer Tom Singer, who couldn't have paid attention even if he had wanted to. He had gone ahead to Kansas City, and the paper was using a wire service. Kurkjian took Singer's call and very kindly helped him out with some information so Singer could file from Kansas City for the Monday paper.

While the boys in the press box were scrambling to their scorebooks, the Angels were scrambling to stay away from Witt. Adhering strictly to superstition, the Angels were avoiding Witt the way the Rangers were avoiding getting hits.

"By this time in the game, everyone was 10 feet away from me at least, so I figured out that something else was going on besides a no-hitter," Witt says. "You can see it on the tape. They show me on the bench, and there's this huge space on either side of me.

"For some reason, it didn't make me nervous. I think my relaxed pregame attitude carried through. I knew subconsciously that I had to keep doing exactly what I was doing. I didn't want to screw it up."

One thing that could have screwed it up was if the Angels didn't score. They finally did their part on offense in the bottom of the seventh. DeCinces led off with a single and moved to second when one of Hough's knucklers danced by catcher Donnie Scott. Brian Downing grounded to second to move DeCinces to third, and Reggie Jackson grounded to first. Pete O'Brien threw home to try to get the runner, but DeCinces slid in safe with the unearned run. It could have been more, after Brown doubled Jackson to third.

"And Reggie would have scored if some fan hadn't jumped out of the stands to grab the ball," Brown remembers, still ticked 17 years later.

Dick Schofield walked, but Rob Wilfong grounded out with the bases loaded to end the threat. But still, the Halos had gotten the run Witt needed.

In retrospect, Witt thinks it's probably good that the Angels didn't score more.

"Up until the seventh, the whole consideration was 0–0. I gotta keep guys off base and win the game. Charlie was very capable of throwing a shutout. But after we scored, there came a point that keeping guys off base to keep them from scoring became one and the same with keeping them off base to keep the no-hitter alive. If we score more, or had we scored earlier, maybe I walk somebody, maybe I don't bear down as much on 3–0, or let a pitch get away and before you know it, you give up a single. Having the game 0–0 helped me get the perfect game."

Rivers opened the bottom of the seventh by striking out, bringing the always-dangerous Wayne Tolleson (.213 in 1984) to the plate.

"When Tolleson went 3–0, and I was in right field, I was thinking, 'Not this guy. Parrish, O'Brien, Ward, OK, but not this guy,'" remembers Brown. "Not that he was a bad player, but he just wasn't big time."

Last game or no, Tolleson was up there to break it up. He looked at three balls.

"He was up there to walk, I think. When I had gotten three straight balls to him again, he did a fake bunt on what was strike one," Witt says. Ironically, he says this only a month after Schilling lost his perfect game to Ben Davis' bunt. "But I remember thinking, man, what a terrible way to lose it—on a bunt. I would have been ticked off. Even though it was a close game. It was just that the game meant nothing, except to the starting pitchers."

But Witt then threw strike two, and Tolleson grounded out to second. Ward followed by doing the same, and Witt was clean through seven.

"I think I realized then no one had gotten a hit after the second time through the lineup, probably about the sixth inning. I don't think I realized it was a perfect game, but right after the seventh inning, I realized that I'd just gotten Gary Ward for the third time in the seventh inning. And he was batting third.

"I remember going back to the dugout and thinking, just stay with what's going on. I tried not to shake [catcher Bob] Boone off as we went on. In the seventh and eighth, I realized I had the same stuff I'd had in the first."

"I was thrilled for both Mike and myself to catch this game," Boone said afterward. "It's an exciting thing for a catcher to have a pitcher respond to everything you ask him to do."

So far, no one had made a credible threat to Witt's perfection. His stuff was still as sharp as it had been early on, and it had been ungodly then.

In the bottom of the eighth, perhaps the most dangerous hitter in the Texas lineup, third baseman Parrish, led off. "He had taken some very good swings against me already," Witt says.

One of them came now, as Parrish hit a slicing drive toward right-center. "That ball was hit good," Witt says with a laugh that sounds slightly nervous even 17 years later. "I was going away, away, away on him all game long. And he was a good opposite-field hitter. When he hit it, I thought it was a home run."

Mike Brown, in right field, had other plans.

"I remember it being much more difficult than it looks like on the video that I saw on ESPN Classic not long ago. I had to go a long way, and it was the bottom of the eighth in a perfect game. That made it difficult. I didn't care if I ran into that wall at full speed, I was not pulling away from that ball. I remember thinking that I cannot let a teammate down at a moment like that. Plus, the game was close. You were going to have to stop me with a wall at that point."

"I thought it had home-run possibility," Witt told reporters after the game. "Then I thought it had fence possibility. Then Mike got there and I thought it had glove possibility."

Breathing a sigh of relief, Witt K'd Pete O'Brien and George Wright, the latter for the third time.

"George Wright was a pedestrian center fielder on that team," Kurkjian recalls. "He had had a great 1983 and a poor 1984, and in the perfect game, he struck out three times. Afterward, I asked him what he was planning to do next, and he joked that he was going to change his name and move to Africa."

Witt was three outs away from the sixth perfect game in A.L. history and the first ever for the Angels. A sense of history for his boyhood idol occurred to Witt during the game. "Growing up, I remember watching Nolan Ryan throw no-hitters.

And during this game, I remember thinking, 'Hey, this must be what he felt during those games. And now it's happening to me.'"

The little Angel fan turned Ranger killer went out for the climactic bottom of the ninth. "Going out for the ninth I was as nervous and jittery as I was for my first major league start," Witt says. "It was a relief when I threw that first strike."

Before he got a chance to do that, McNamara made several defensive changes, seemingly flying in the face of superstition. Bobby Grich came into the game to play first base, while the entire outfield changed, with Fred Lynn moving from center to right, Gary Pettis coming in to play center, and veteran Derrel Thomas coming in for Brian Downing in left.

McNamara wanted three vets in the outfield for the final inning of this final game. Brown remembers that he helped start the shuffle by honestly replying to a question from McNamara about a sore throwing arm.

"It wouldn't have mattered on a catch, but I told him it was really bothering me," Brown says. "So they pinch ran Pettis for me after I walked in the eighth. And he tried to steal to build another run but he was thrown out. Then they put him in center and moved Lynn to right. Pettis was a Gold Glover, so I had no problem getting taken out. Besides, that way I got to be in the pileup with Mike after the last out."

"All I remember was Grich going to first," Witt says. "Grich had better hands than [Larry] Sconiers. But until you mentioned it just now, I didn't notice that there were three new outfielders out there." That's what concentration will do for you.

Witt also was buoyed by his swift pace and low pitch count. Like Koufax, he didn't have much time on the bench between innings to get cold. Hough was making short work of the Angels. In fact, the game ended up being played in only one hour and 49 minutes. Witt threw only 94 pitches on the afternoon, 70 of them for strikes.

"Since I averaged 110–120 pitches a game that year, I was pretty fresh," Witt says. "The way they were swinging at some of these pitches, I didn't think they'd be able to hit it. And I knew guys coming off the bench [to pinch hit in the ninth] would have even more trouble. I had a little pattern going against the other guys. So I mouthed some stuff to Boone to make sure we knew what to do to these new guys. But I pretty much just followed him."

Right fielder Tommy Dunbar looked at two curveballs for strikes then fanned on a fastball. One down.

Bobby Jones was brought in to pinch hit for catcher Donnie Scott.

"The cat was dealing," Jones said. "I knew in the eighth that I was going to pinch hit, but it didn't do me any good. I don't know how you get ready for something like that."

On the second pitch, he grounded out, Wilfong to Grich. Two down.

Marv Foley came up to bat for shortstop Curtis Wilkerson. He looked at a strike and then ball one.

"I knew that Mike really had it when he threw a curveball right down Broadway that the ump called a ball," Brown remembers. "I was thinking, you've got a perfect game on the line here and you call that a ball. The strike zone should look like the back end of a truck at this point. But Mike never wavered, he had no expression on his face. And he threw a strike on the next pitch."

Foley swung at the next pitch and hit the Rangers' eighth ground-out to second, and their 27th out overall.

It was the final at-bat of the game, as well as Foley's last at-bat ever.

"Then I knew that something would happen, as far as jumping up and down, but I didn't know who was supposed to start it," Witt says with a smile. "I made sure to turn around and find Bob Boone. He was coming right toward me; he wasn't going to back up first. As soon as it was hit, he headed toward the mound. Then everybody just came out."

What was left of the pro-Cowboys crowd cheered for Witt while his teammates poured out to celebrate with him.

In the Texas locker room, Texas manager Doug Rader made a halfhearted attempt to find a reason for his team's frustration at the plate. "No one could see the son of a bitch," he said. "The glare was rough. The visibility was zero. But I'm not saying that to detract from what the kid did. This was no fluke."

Would that we could have mentioned to Rader that the game was played in his home park, and if anyone was at a disadvantage because of visibility issues, it was the Angels.

"This is not a surprise to me," Boone said afterward amid the Angels' brief locker-room celebration—they had a plane to catch. "I think he's the premier pitcher in the league. When he's on, they're not going to hit him. With his stuff, he has the potential to do this every time out."

"After I'd seen all the teammates, I went to find my wife," Witt says. "And she was just smiling real big. I never saw her the whole game until afterward."

Not many people in the Dallas area saw much about the perfect game, either, remembers Kurkjian. "The next day, the

Dallas Times-Herald, my competitor, ran Mike Witt's perfect game at the bottom left-hand corner of the sports page, in two columns, with the headline 'Witt Flawless.' The same amount of copy was on the opposite side about some player at Texas A&M, and all this was well below the coverage of the Cowboys' game [author's note: a 23–14 victory over the Bears, if you really must know]. [Reporter] Phil Rogers called the *Times-Herald* and complained to his editors, but they told him, 'Yeah, but he did it against the Rangers.' Phil pointed out that the fact that it happened in town was the point, after all."

Coming as it did on the last day of the season, with the NFL season in full swing and the playoffs two days away, Witt's perfect game got perhaps the least publicity of any of the "modern" games. The subdued nature of his feat was symbolized by what became his biggest worry after the game. And no, it wasn't dealing with the "crush" of media.

"I had to get my rental car back to the airport," he says, laughing. "I might have been the only guy who rented a car on that trip, because I had Lisa along with me. So I'm trying to hustle back to get this rental car back, after doing this great thing. I had to get it in and meet our plane. Then some fan, some guy and his wife, said, let us take it back for you. I had no idea who he was or what his name was. But he looked so decent, and my wife just said, trust him. So I gave him the keys, and yes, the car made it back there."

And he gave some anonymous Texan a baseball story he's been telling ever since.

And then, after a paper cup of champagne on the flight home and an appearance on *Good Morning, America* the next day, that was about it.

But while the hoopla died out quickly, the effects of the game on Witt lingered long after, from the next season to today.

"That year was the first year that I won 15, and I was finally beginning to be the ace of the staff. And I remember saying after the game that I always thought no-hitters were for the aces of a staff, the guys who won 20. Then I realized that maybe I should start thinking of myself like that. It kind of gave me a boost the next season, too."

Witt reeled off four more seasons with double-digit win totals, earning two All-Star selections. In 1986, he helped the Angels win their division and get to within one strike of the World Series. But after being traded to the Yankees in 1990, injuries sent him to the D.L. seven times and he was never the same. He retired after the 1993 season.

"I think I was always trying to figure out a way to find what I had that day again," he says thoughtfully. "I was always watching that tape, when I would get in a slump or something, to figure out what I had been doing right. It was like trying to chase a rabbit with a greyhound, you'd never quite catch up to it. I'd get glimpses of it, but I never got that stuff back."

Though that holy grail eluded him, he is perfectly at peace with having held it for only a day. Witt should be a case study for successful, nonsuperstar baseball players on how to plan for the future, and welcome it when it arrives.

Witt has become the exemplar of a successful baseball player in retirement. He and Lisa live in the Orange County house they bought 10 years ago with some of that Yankee money. He calls himself "semiretired" and works only when he wants to, helping out local high schools as a volunteer coach or going to an occasional card show.

"I played at the right time," he said. "I was just at the start of the time that money could set you up pretty well. Plus, I wanted to be around my younger kids. So I didn't want to take a coaching or scouting job that would make me travel."

Still, the perfect game comes up again and again. "It was fun to meet people in Anaheim, who'd come up and say, 'Hey, I was at your perfect game, I got the ticket stub and everything.' I'd say, 'Really, where were you sitting?' and they'd say the club level or something, and I'd say, 'That game was in Texas.' And they'd look at me and say, 'No, it wasn't!'

"If all the people I've talked to about it actually had been there, there would have been forty thousand people there instead of about eight thousand.

"But that game will always be special. It was a once-in-a-lifetime event, and it really catapulted me into some good years."

Watching Witt wave good-bye from the driveway of his big brick house, under clear blue California skies, surrounded by a garage full of kids' toys and a family that knows he's always around, it's nice to think that Mike Witt has lots of good years ahead. And who knows, maybe even some more perfect ones. He's just hoping that he never wakes up to find that it's all been a hypnotic dream. Trust us, Mike. It was—and is—real.

It was worth the wait: Cincinnati's Tom Browning hung around after a 2½-hour rain delay to fire a perfect game at the Dodgers. *Photo courtesy of AP/Wide World Photos.*

CHAPTER 12

Tom Browning

September 16, 1988

Before and after the Cincinnati Reds' 1–0 victory over the Los Angeles Dodgers on September 16, 1988, Tom Browning was all wet.

Before, it was from the rain.

After, it was from the champagne.

After waiting out a two-hour and 27-minute rain delay to start the game, Browning became only the third left-hander ever to throw a perfect game when he blanked L.A. (The Dodgers would go on to win the World Series that year, thus becoming the only team to lose a perfect game and win a championship in the same year.) In a couple of those great perfect-game comparisons we keep seeing, Browning wore Sandy Koufax's 32 and lived at the time in Kentucky as a constituent of then-Congressman Jim Bunning.

Browning was in his fifth big-league season; as a rookie, he won 20 games and finished second in the 1985 rookie-of-the-year voting. But in 1987, only a year before he became perfect, Browning was sent to the minors after seeing his ERA soar above 5.00. The wake-up call must have helped, because he bounced back to have the first of three straight winning seasons in 1988; his perfect game was the 16th of his 18 wins that year.

Coming into the game, the Reds were chasing the Dodgers in the N.L. West. However, there were less than two weeks to go in the season, so the Dodgers were actually approaching magic number territory rather than feeling the Reds breathing down their necks.

"We went into the game seven games ahead in the West," remembers Dodgers broadcaster Ross Porter. "We pretty much had the division clinched, so it wasn't really a pressure game for us."

But as game time approached, a storm lingered over Riverfront Stadium in Cincinnati, drenching the field and driving the (allegedly) 16,591 fans under cover to wait, possibly, for the game to begin.

On the other side of the press box from Porter, veteran Reds play-by-play man Marty Brenneman also awaited the first pitch. "I can remember how bad the weather was," he says. "I find it humorous to talk to people who claim they were there. There were probably some who showed up and left."

For his part, Browning spent a little time in the dugout, just watching the rain . . . and his opposite number, Tim Belcher, who was sitting in the Dodgers dugout.

"I smiled at him and gave him some grief about hitting a home run off me in L.A. [the week before]," Browning told the *L.A. Times.* "I only sat out there for about 15 minutes when the game was supposed to start. I got irritated that it didn't look like it was going to break up."

"I spent the time playing cards in the clubhouse, I think," says Browning's catcher, Jeff Reed. "It wasn't anything out of the ordinary for a rain delay. But once we got started, it was over pretty quickly."

Also waiting out the delay was a man who would become a unique statistic. On that rainy night in Ohio, right fielder Paul O'Neill played for the first time on a team that won a perfect game. He would later do so twice more with the Yankees, thus becoming the only player ever to be on the winning side of three perfect games.

Asked about that fact in the Yankee clubhouse before a game, O'Neill said, "Really? I didn't know that, but obviously that's neat. Those things happen to good teams with good pitching."

Meanwhile, over in the Dodger clubhouse, shortstop Alfredo Griffin awaited his turn at a place in history.

"We weren't thrilled to have to play that game," he says before a game in Anaheim, where he is the Angels' first-base coach. "You get lazy waiting around all that time. If you get in your mind that the game will [not be played], then you don't have the same energy. It was a bit of a down game, but Browning did great."

Griffin, of course, had already lost in a perfect game to Len Barker while with Toronto and would "threepeat" the feat in 1991 against Dennis Martinez, thus setting his own dubious record. In this one game were the two players who own both ends of the obscure "most perfect games played in" record.

That late in the season, umps were eager to get in every game that they could. And unlikely as it might have been at the time, a game between the two division leaders could have meant something at the end of the season. So, the cards kept being dealt, the announcers killed time in their booths, and fans filled up on soggy hot dogs under the stands.

Finally, at 10:02 P.M., eastern time, the game started.

———————

Right away, the Dodgers knew that Browning was on.

"He was a lucky son of a bitch," laughs Mickey Hatcher, playing first for L.A. that night. "Everything that we hit was right at somebody."

Reed knew it, too.

"Tom only shook me off two or three times all night long. When he was pitching well, you tried to keep him in rhythm. He likes to work quick, so we were on the same page all night long. I got the ball back to him as quickly as possible. He kept everything down; his breaking ball was really good. It seemed like anywhere I was, outside, inside, up, or down, the ball was always right where I put the mitt."

The one thing that kept coming up in people's memories of this game was its almost resolute routineness. Reed, Brenneman, Porter, Hatcher, and others echoed each other when describing the game as "being over before we knew it." Browning was methodical, he worked quickly, and there was also not a lot of scoring by the Reds to extend things.

It was, if anything, a workmanlike perfect game.

Perhaps the only defensive play worth mentioning didn't come until the fifth. Mike Marshall hit a high chopper toward third base. Chris Sabo ranged to his right, backhanded the ball, and fired to first. Marshall is not exactly the Flash, and Sabo's throw beat him, with first baseman Nick Esasky making a nice stretch.

Porter must not have thought it was that unusual, though it was the only play mentioned in most game accounts.

"I actually just got out my scorecard for that game to check," he says, prompting a vision of a cluttered home office stacked to the ceiling with programs, media guides, and scorecards. "I always put an exclamation point down on my scorecard for any great defensive plays and there's not one anywhere during that game."

Meanwhile, Belcher was doing pretty well himself. Through five innings, he also had allowed no hits—shades of Koufax/Hendley. In fact, Belcher can blame himself for some of Browning's success. Or at least, Browning did.

"He was pitching a hell of a game," Browning said. "That helped me maintain my intensity, because it was so close."

Once again, as in more than a few perfect games (such as those pitched by Richmond, Joss, Koufax, Martinez, and, to some extent, Larsen), it could be argued that the very fact that the game was close contributed to the perfect-game pitcher's ability to focus and achieve perfection. Yes, David Cone and Jim Bunning did it with lots of run support, but as noted, more than half of the 17 perfect games were either 1–0 or 2–0.

Browning added when praising Belcher, "Any mistakes might have cost us the game."

It turned out that a mistake helped cost the Dodgers the game.

"In about the sixth inning, I became aware of what Tom was doing," Reed remembers. "I started thinking that I don't want to mess this up! We all didn't want to mess it up for him. As I recall there wasn't really a great play behind him. It just seemed like everything went bang-bang and before we knew it, it was over."

But first, the Reds had to give Browning something to work with; otherwise, he'd have been another Harvey Haddix or 1995 Pedro Martinez, perfect but without a little help from his friends. With two outs in the bottom of the sixth, however, shortstop Barry Larkin got the Reds' first hit, a double to the right-field corner. Then Sabo hit a bouncer to third baseman Jeff Hamilton. Trying to distract the fielder, Larkin was running all the way and crossed Hamilton's path just after the ball.

Hamilton's throw was a low one-hopper that Hatcher, playing first, knocked down but couldn't grab. It rolled toward the Reds dugout and Larkin came around to score the game's only run on the E-5. Like Richmond, Joss, Koufax, and, later, Martinez, Browning's only support was unearned.

"For a while there, it was like 'Is anyone going to score?'" Reed says. "Neither team could get anything going that night. We got a gift run, and it was like 'Whew!' That way, if they don't put one across, we can go home. It was a long night with the delay, and it seemed like runs would be hard to come by."

Up in the booth, Brenneman knew what was going on, and so did anyone listening to him on the radio.

"I'm not a superstitious person, so I talk about them all," he says. "I always talk about the no-hitters in progress, and in this case, about Tom's perfect game.

"My recollection is that there weren't enough fans to really generate a lot of excitement. It was a weeknight, with people going to work the next day. It didn't carry any sort of significance in the pennant race. So people weren't going to hang around with that weather during the week for a game that didn't mean anything to the race. So you were not in a position to get caught up in the excitement of the crowd because the crowd wasn't big enough to generate that kind of excitement."

A soon-to-be World Series hero created a little excitement in the top of the seventh. Kirk Gibson, who would hit one of the most famous homers in baseball history just over a month later, was kicked out of the game for arguing a strike-three call that ended the inning.

Not surprisingly, the emotional Gibson was still chafing about it in 2001 when asked about the game.

"It was a huge strike zone, ridiculous," he says. "Not to take anything away from either pitcher, because it was a well-played game. We all argued, and you try to make adjustments, but when the plate gets too big, it's just hard to handle. But you've got to give them credit. The strike zone was established, and they utilized it."

Reaching the eighth affected everyone, it seems.

"From the eighth inning on, I was so nervous, I could hardly keep my own scorebook," Brenneman recalls. "I knew what was going on, of course, and I was selfish enough to feel like I really wanted it. A lot of guys have been [calling base-ball games] for a long time and never had one. I wanted it as much for me as I did for him.

"Once we got to the eighth inning and he was six outs away, then it got rather unsettling for me. Anybody in my business, when you're confronted with something like this, the one thing you don't want is to screw it up."

Browning, too, didn't want to screw it up.

"I started to think about it—no, to realize I could do it— in the eighth inning," he told the *L.A. Times* after the game. "Once I got to the eighth, I started feeling a little antsy. I was feeling the pressure and I had to make sure that I calmed myself. After that, everything just seemed to fall into place."

With a little help from a friend. In *The Sporting News*, Hal McCoy reported that Reds manager Pete Rose instructed Reed to "Slow [Browning] down. He's getting excited; don't let him rush. Sometimes when he is going good, he throws a first-pitch fastball right down Broadway and gets hurt with a home run."

All that positive energy must have helped, because the Dodgers went down meekly—and quickly—in the eighth as well.

Behind the plate, Reed was still amazed by the rapid pace of the game, which would end up taking only one hour and 51 minutes.

"It almost seemed like it was too easy, like someone had something planned," Reed says. "The game went so quick, with Belcher pitching so well, too. Before you knew it, it was the ninth inning.

"In the ninth inning, with everyone on their feet, that's when I felt some pressure," Reed continues. "I didn't want to put down the wrong pitch and allow a hit, or miss the ball or anything. Tom was the type of pitcher who didn't throw all that hard, and his breaking ball wasn't unhittable. It was just that everything was right where it should be. I could be maybe three inches off the plate . . . and the pitch would be three inches off. It was like there was a magnet in my glove and he just threw the ball right there."

Catcher Rick Dempsey led off the ninth inning. Browning and Reed started him with an off-speed pitch that he took, and then a fastball that he also let go by.

"He'd been the only one who gave us trouble all night," Reed says. "He was a first-pitch fastball hitter and he had hit the ball hard his first two times up."

Indeed in the ninth, Dempsey drove Browning's third pitch, a change, to the warning track in right, but O'Neill was there in plenty of time.

One down. Browning had been here before. On June 6, he had taken a no-hitter (not a perfect game, but close) into the ninth before San Diego's Tony Gwynn got a single with one out.

But Browning did not repeat that bit of history, and he induced Steve Sax to hit a grounder that Larkin tracked down and threw easily to first.

Now, with the remaining damp fans really doing their best to sound like a stadium full of people, Browning was one out away.

Sitting in the Reds dugout at that point was a pitcher who could literally say, "Been there, done that." On May 2, 1988, Ron Robinson had become one of only six pitchers to lose a perfect game with two outs in the ninth. Robinson, in fact, had come even closer than that, taking the Expos' Wallace Johnson to a 2–2 count before Johnson lined a clean single, thus costing Robinson his own chapter in this book (though he did make the Appendix; see page 293).

Browning also had come close (with an asterisk) to a perfect game before, when he threw a seven-inning, complete-game no-hitter when in the minors with Wichita. His 2–0 victory over Iowa was spoiled only by one error (and of course, the fact that it was only seven innings long, but still . . .).

Browning ignored both of those historical precedents, but he also took pinch-hitter Tracy Woodson to a Robinsonian 2–2 count.

"Then I threw him a fastball, about forehead high," Browning said. "I was surprised he swung."

But "swung" Woodson did, and it was strike three, ballgame, 27 up, 27 down.

No matter what the weather was or what time of night, at that point the sun was shining on Tom Browning. At just before midnight on a rainy late-summer evening, Tom Browning's glass cleats fit.

Reed led the way to the mound, and the Reds turned into a Little League team, piling on and pounding Browning.

"We just piled on. I remember me and Tom were on the bottom of the pile," Reed says with a laugh. "It was a really special night, and it couldn't have happened to a better guy."

"Hey, we're all little boys at heart," Sabo said later. "This is what dreams are made of."

Browning, who had given a special one to the team, also took one for the team at the bottom of the pile of jerseys.

"I looked at Reed and pumped my fist," Browning said after the game. "And then the dogpile hit. Somebody actually split my lip under there by accident! When they lifted me to their shoulders, I felt a tear come to my eye."

In the locker room later, Sabo exulted like a guy who'd just won the Super Bowl. "Hey," he yelled. "We're all going to Cooperstown!"

Another opinion came from a guy who, unfortunately, would never make it to Cooperstown, though his play on the field certainly earned him a ticket.

"I can't think of a better game I've ever seen pitched," said Rose. "And I've been around no-hitters, both for and against. He was just, um, perfect. What else can I say?"

Browning threw 102 pitches, of which 72 were strikes. To 21 batters, he threw first-pitch strikes, and no batter reached a 3-ball count. He probably wished he could face the Dodgers again. Counting a no-decision a week earlier, he ended up retiring 39 Dodgers in a row.

Even their fellow Los Angelenos were jazzed.

"It was exciting," Porter says. "In the bottom of the eighth inning, I went to the field to get ready to do the postgame interview. And I actually got Tom after the game for a few minutes and could see how excited he was. That game might very well have been rained out. That late in the season, they want to try to get it in. Any other time, they might have called it and it would never have happened.

"As a baseball fan, you get excited about the moment, about watching history, even though your team is on the losing end of this particular one."

"What I remember is that they broadcast my partner Joe Nuxhall's interview with Tom through the sound system to the whole stadium," says Brenneman. "The only other time I remember them doing that after a game was for Pete Rose's record hit.

"For me, this perfect game ranks second only to Pete's record-breaking hit. But we knew that was going to happen, it was just a question of when. But you don't expect a perfect game, you have no reason to. Browning was not the kind of pitcher you'd expect to do this. He didn't have overpowering stuff, but he did have great command of the strike zone on both sides."

Browning admitted as much a few days after the game.

"Sometimes I lose my concentration and make bad pitches. But that night, I never lost it. I was in complete control of the strike zone. They were trying to hit my pitch, but they couldn't."

For the next couple of seasons, Browning's pitches avoided bats a lot more than most pitchers', and he posted three seasons of 14 wins or more. In 1990, he helped the Reds win the World Series, winning a game apiece in the NLCS and the Series. But arm injuries struck, and his career faded to a close in 1995.

Many players keep mementos from their perfect games, but Browning is one who can't enjoy looking at the ball from the game.

"The ball from the game used to sit on my mantel," he said. "Where is it now? I don't know if the kids played with it or not. I think it's in the woods behind our house. It didn't have anything on it, and it was just sitting there. I guess the kids needed a ball to play with."

It seems appropriate that a ball from such a waterlogged game might now be soaked, soggy, and mildewed in some secluded wood. It's probably very happy.

Montreal's veteran right-hander Dennis Martinez thinks that he had someone beside his fielders to thank for his 1991 perfect game, a "fan" with the best seat in every house. *Photo courtesy of AP/Wide World Photos.*

Dennis Martinez

July 28, 1991

Dennis Martinez might have had a little extra help when he pitched a perfect game on a sunny Sunday in 1991. Game time was 1:05 with Martinez and the Expos scheduled to leave the hotel for Dodger Stadium at 10:30. But that was when Martinez had planned to go to Mass, which he did every Sunday. So, his choice: head for the Great Dodger in Chavez Ravine or the Great Dodger (etc.) in the sky?

Martinez chose the latter and went to Mass. As he walked out, the first thing he saw was a cab. (No, it was not being driven by an angel.) He was at the stadium just before noon and headed right out to warm up.

"Maybe if I don't go [to Mass], I would be out by the first inning," Martinez said. "Who knows? To me, that was the key point to the day."

Just getting to that day, arriving at the chance to pitch at all, let alone to pitch a perfect game, was a blessing for Martinez. After nine full seasons with the Baltimore Orioles, including helping them win the 1983 World Series, Martinez developed shoulder trouble. He also began exacerbating a drinking problem, a problem that finally came to a head with a late '83 DWI arrest.

He entered a treatment facility in 1984 and kicked alcohol. What was harder to kick in some ways was the perception big-league teams had of his future in the game. He kicked around with the Orioles for a couple more years, never really regaining his top-starter form, before the O's finally let him go. He caught on with Montreal in 1986 and even spent time in the Expos' minor leagues before finally landing a solid spot in the Expos' rotation. Showing the kind of determination that would become his hallmark, as well as his best tool on the road to recovery, he had an 11–4 record in 1987 that began a string of 10 consecutive seasons with double-digit wins (the last two with Cleveland) that included four All-Star selections and the 1991 N.L. ERA title. (Martinez would win a career total of 245 games before he retired in 1998 as the winningest pitcher ever from Latin America.)

From very, very far down, Martinez had bounced back. He'll be the first to tell you that he had help, just as he credited God with helping him on July 28, 1991. His impressive comeback also added to his remarkable reputation back home in his native Nicaragua. The first player from that nation to star in the majors, Martinez had talent, perseverance, and obvious love for his country that earned him the nickname "El Presidente."

Entering the July 28, 1991, game against the Dodgers, Martinez was 10–6 and led the N.L. with a 2.05 ERA. Two nights before, Mark Gardner had given the Dodgers a taste of what was ahead, pitching nine innings of no-hit ball, but, Harvey Haddix–like, receiving no support. Gardner lost the no-hitter and the game in the tenth inning. Then, on Saturday, the Expos were squished 7–0. After that game, Martinez promised that the 'Spos would bounce back on Sunday.

"[Dennis] comes up to me after that game and says, 'You've got nothing to worry about tomorrow,' because he knows I worry," Montreal pitching coach Larry Bearnarth told *The Sporting News.* "After the perfect game, he came up and reminded me of what he had said."

Welcoming Martinez to the mound as he tried to make good on his promise to Bearnarth, the Dodgers' organist played "El Nandaimeno," a song from the pitcher's hometown of Granada, Nicaragua. (In earlier games, organist Nancy Helfly had played a song called "Managua" in Martinez's honor, but he corrected her not long before the game in July.)

Martinez's control was perfect early on, and the Dodgers knew it.

"You could see it early," said Brett Butler. "I was 1 and 2 in the first inning, and he struck me out on a pitch that was close. I was 3 and 2 [in the fourth], and he threw one away that [I grounded the opposite way to short]."

The sun shining down on the 45,560 fans and the two teams would also play a big role in Martinez's success, players said.

"The first couple of batters came back to the bench and said it was hard to see, and then I knew it would be a long day," said Dodger shortstop Alfredo Griffin. "And with Martinez hiding the ball like he does [during his windup], it was tough to pick up the spin."

The glare worked both ways, however, as both the Dodgers' Mike Morgan and Martinez mowed down batters like a pair of big-league Danny Almontes. Through four innings, the Dodgers had yet to hit a ball out of the infield, but the Expos hadn't done much better, with no base runners either.

With one out in the fourth, Juan Samuel hit a hard grounder that third baseman Tim Wallach fielded on the grass before throwing to first. Most accounts called it the hardest-hit ball of the game.

That inning, while making a pitch to Eddie Murray, Martinez's left, or plant, foot slipped and he felt a twinge in his back. Ironically, the pitcher had complained to stadium workers and the umpires that the mound was slippery before the game. Though he was assured it would dry off, apparently it didn't dry enough.

"Before the game, [umpire Bruce] Froemming said it would dry out in a few innings," Martinez joked later. "I told him I didn't know if I'd be around that long."

Expos trainers visited Martinez on the mound to inspect his back and right hip, but the twinge wasn't serious. He took a couple of warm-up pitches and decided to hang in there.

"What kept me in there was a willingness to stay out there to try to win the ballgame," he told the *L.A. Times'* J. A. Adande later.

Out in center field, Marquis Grissom had one of the best seats in the house.

"After the fifth, I remember him making just the right pitch every time he got in trouble," Grissom says. "He had a good fastball, but it wasn't overpowering. It was just never straight. He'd get to 2–2, 3–2, and then he'd throw so many perfect pitches, right on the black. There were only one or two balls hit hard the whole game. He pitched the ideal perfect game, bouncing back with strike after strike. It was a beautiful thing to watch."

Grissom and his Expos teammates were watching a pretty beautiful thing coming the other way, too. Morgan was just as perfect as Martinez through five innings, setting down 15 straight Dodgers. But Ron Hassey, who would prove such a big help to Martinez behind the plate and who knew a few things about perfect games, broke things up with a leadoff single to center in the sixth. But he was stranded, and the inning ended with the score still tied 0–0.

"It was still a tough situation at that point," Hassey remembers. It would soon get tougher for the Dodgers.

But first, with one out in the bottom of the sixth, Griffin whacked a grounder at Delino DeShields, and the second baseman hurried his throw to first, knowing Griffin's speed. The throw was low, and Larry Walker was nearly pulled off the bag stretching for it, but the out was recorded. Morgan then flied out to Marquis Grissom, the first fair ball hit into the outfield by the Dodgers.

The dam for Morgan finally broke in the seventh.

"Sometimes it's not how you pitch, but when you pitch," said Morgan afterward. He also pointed out that he had previously lost a 1–0 decision to Martinez; add in this one, and one-third of his six losses to that point had been to El Presidente.

As so many perfect-game pitchers have seen, for Martinez, the opposing defense was a big help.

Martinez led off the top of the seventh with a ground ball that was booted by Alfredo Griffin. Two outs later, one of them a sacrifice bunt by Ivan Calderon, right fielder Larry Walker went to 2–2 on Morgan, then took a pitch that generated some postgame discussion.

"Morgan had Walker struck out," said Dodgers manager Tommy Lasorda afterward, commenting on the 2–2 pitch that was called ball three.

"It was a fastball on the outside corner," Morgan added. "I felt like I had him, and then I hung one."

Walker slugged the hanger into right-center field for a triple, and Martinez himself easily scored the go-ahead run. Walker scored right after him when Griffin made his second error of the inning on a grounder by Hassey.

"Once we got those runs, we said 'Thank goodness we aren't going to have another Mark Gardner night,'" said Montreal shortstop Spike Owen. "Those runs took the pressure off of Dennis while the rest of us started thinking about the perfect game."

With one out in the bottom of the seventh, Martinez himself got into the act. With a sore back and on 36-year-old legs, Martinez bounced off the mound to snag a bunt by Juan Samuel (can you say "Ben Davis"?). He made a good throw to first to nail the scrappy (though Arizona manager Bob Brenly might have used another word in 2001) second baseman.

"That was the only play that I have circled and highlighted on my scorecard," says announcer Ross Porter, who called the game for the Dodgers and called up his scorecard from his archives to check.

Next up was Eddie Murray, and for only the first time all night, Martinez went to a 3-ball count, 3–2 in fact.

Adande wrote that Martinez told himself, "I'm gonna go with my best pitch and see if they bite, and not give them something straight that they can hit better."

Murray bit hard and grounded out to DeShields, and Martinez was 7-up, 7-down.

"There was nothing we could do but just sit there and take it," said Murray afterward of Martinez's performance.

Behind the plate, Hassey was starting to experience a serious case of déjà vu, wondering if he'd become the first catcher ever to backstop two perfect games and mentally comparing his two pitchers.

"Dennis was completely different from Lenny [Barker]," says Hassey, now a minor league instructor for Arizona. "Dennis was a pitcher. He had to hit his spots, he had to have his command to get guys out. He was not overpowering like Barker. So you had to be a little more protective. You couldn't get away with pitches. But Dennis had outstanding control, and he knew how to pitch."

The real comparison in his mind began not long after the Expos scored.

"I think it was around the seventh or eighth," Hassey remembers. "I told Larry Bearnarth, don't even worry about this one, we've definitely got a no-hitter. And he laughed. I didn't say it in front of everyone, of course. You don't want that superstition to come back and bite you in the ass. But this time around, I was going to have a good time [catching a perfect game]. I remember looking at Larry in the eighth and ninth. After every out, I looked over at him. Then in the ninth, I said, 'Watch this, it's going to be great.' It was really fun."

Compare that to Hassey's memories of Barker's perfect game, in which he says he was so oblivious that he barely knew it was a no-hitter in Cleveland, let alone a perfecto.

Hassey says now that he wasn't doing anything differently with Martinez, but the pitcher remembered it differently afterward.

"[Ron] would catch the ball and point with his mitt, and then go, 'Yeah! Yeah!' He really was psyching me up out there," said Martinez after the game. "The intensity was really something."

Grissom remembers continuing to be impressed as he stared in from center.

"Looking in from center, I had a chance to see a lot of those pitches. It was like an artist making a painting, and I was out there just watching it be created."

As the ninth inning started, what has been seen at other perfect games happened again: the home crowd started cheering for the opposing pitcher. After all, the Dodgers were up by six games at that point (over Atlanta), and how many times do you get a chance to see something like this?

Sitting in the Dodgers clubhouse in 2001, Grissom said, "I remember the crowd as plain as day. It was so odd to be in a place where the fans are rooting for the other team. Going out there for the ninth, he almost got a standing ovation to go out and shut those guys down.

"He just went out and went to work on those guys. You see a guy three times a game, you usually figure something out. But with that big curveball and his running fastball, he dealt that day."

But while the Dodger Stadium crowd was fully behind the inspirational Martinez, one of his teammates was particularly nervous.

"My hands were clammy, sitting there on the bench," said Mark Gardner, the hard-luck guy who had been in a similar spot days before. "What happened to me, I didn't want to happen to him."

While his teammates sweated on the bench, Martinez's countrymen watched apprehensively as well. Normally, all of his starts were "described" by broadcasters getting a phone feed from the States. But on this day, the state-run television network interrupted programming to show the game live.

Catcher Mike Scoscia led off and flied out to Calderon.

"We might have played 20 innings and not gotten a hit off of him," says Scoscia, now the Angels' manager. "He had great command with great change of speeds."

Stan Javier then pinch hit for the snakebit Griffin (this, of course, would be the third of Alfredo's three losing perfect games, and he had handed the only runs of the game to Martinez with two errors), but Javier fared no better, becoming Martinez's fifth and final strikeout victim.

Finally, Chris Gwynn pinch hit for Morgan.

"I was so overexcited out there," said Grissom. "I was just thinking, please, no line drives, nothing hard. I didn't want to be the one to ruin history."

Grissom got his chance, but Gwynn went up there with little chance, even in his own mind.

"Anybody from the bench or the stands could have seen [Martinez] had it all," Gwynn said. "The only thing I can try to do in that situation is to see the ball."

At 1-and-2, Gwynn saw an outside fastball and hit it toward right-center. The ball rose up quickly, and Martinez felt his heart in his throat.

"It never really looked like it would get over Grissom's head," remembers Ross Porter. "But I remember that Martinez was watching it very carefully."

"I remember that as being one of the best-hit balls of the whole game," Hassey recalls.

"That ball and the '95 World Series ball [which Grissom caught to close out Atlanta's championship] was the longest I've ever seen a ball hang in the air," Grissom says with a smile. "I remember those plays plain as day. I'm just telling the ball, 'Come on down, come on down out of the air!' It finally did. It was a very happy moment not just for me, being a part of history, but for our teammate who just went out there and was an artist."

"It was scary," said Martinez. "I thought it was hit well and might be extra bases."

It was no bases.

It was, instead, the end of the 13th perfect game in baseball history and the first by a pitcher from outside the United States.

"After it was over, my mind went blank," Martinez said. "I didn't know what to do or what to say. So I said nothing. I just cried."

"I guess I'll be on the news all night," Gwynn said, looking for any silver lining.

Teammates mobbed their teary teammate as the crowd continued cheering for their new favorite pitcher. Martinez waved at them, and then he disappeared into the clubhouse.

"I thank God for giving me this so late in my career," Martinez enthused. "I feel joy. Happiness. It was like I was dreaming. It was like it was somebody else down there instead of me."

One teammate who could help attest that it really happened was "Two Perfect" Hassey, who also realized that perfect games have to have a base of support and talent, along with a dose of fortune.

"The biggest satisfaction of catching a perfect game was that after going over every hitter the pitcher is going to face and learning their strengths and weaknesses, and then you get a game like that. Well, then you know you accomplished what you set out to do. All that work on charts and reports paid off. Anytime you win a game, you're doing what you set out to do in working up a game plan, but a perfect game is so very special."

As is usual at these events, champagne corks popped and beer showers were poured. But Martinez kept his mouth shut except to shout with joy.

As he put down a glass of champagne without taking a sip, he told Adande that he "thought about where I had come from and everything I'd been through. Not drinking is tough, but drinking is worse. I told the guys, 'Hey, remember, I don't drink.' But that doesn't mean I don't celebrate."

After dressing and finally escaping the reporters clamoring for details of his every thought, Martinez continued the celebration by signing autographs for excited fans still lingering in the box seats.

They weren't the only ones celebrating. Far to the south in Nicaragua, people were literally dancing in the streets.

"Dennis Martinez was already the most popular man in the country before he pitched a perfect game," said *La Prensa* sports editor Tito Rondon in Managua. "Now he's just more popular."

The connection to his countrymen was one that Martinez felt keenly in the moments after the game, dedicating his victory to them. Congratulatory phone calls from back home helped limit his sleep the night of the game to only two hours. But he didn't mind.

"After all they've been through, the turmoil, the earthquake, the war," Martinez told *The Sporting News* that week, "I think this was the big moment to bring happiness to the Nicaraguan people. I wanted to be there, fly down there. I could hear them in the streets when people called."

A month later, he returned to Nicaragua for a nationwide celebration. Odes were written, speeches made, keys to cities presented, tears shed.

Long after the game, Martinez, who continues to this day to be a tireless supporter, inspiration, and fund-raiser for Nicaragua, much of it through his Miami-based foundation, reflected on the importance of his feat to both him and his country.

"I think there was a purpose to the game," he says. "This time more than any time, the people needed me to help them get back on track physically, spiritually, mentally. It's impossible to fill every heart, but I do what I can. The game gave the people something to cheer, something to celebrate."

Remember—hearkening back to Martinez's first actions on his special Sunday—another word for a Mass is . . . *celebration.*

CHAPTER 14

Kenny Rogers

July 28, 1994

T he screenwriter walks into the producer's office.

"I got a great one for you," he says, beginning to tell his tale. "It's got drama, humor, family, baseball . . . I see Costner in the lead."

The producer takes another puff of his cigar. "Go on," he says from behind the cloud of smoke.

"OK, there's this pitcher, see, only he's not a pitcher when we meet him, he's a skinny little high school outfielder. He doesn't think he has any chance at pro ball, he's just out having fun. He's not going anywhere next except back to work in the strawberry fields in Florida. But he breaks his glove, see . . ."

"He breaks his what?"

"His baseball glove. It breaks. So he's talking to the coach about fixing it, and the coach introduces him to a scout who's actually there to see the player's teammate. Anyway, the scout likes the kid's smile or whatever, so he watches him make some great left-handed throws from the outfield. Bingo, he's drafted and signed. Gets to camp and he's so clueless he doesn't know what the stretch position is. He's never thrown a breaking ball in his life."

"Costner's not left-handed," interjects the producer.

"Then we get one of the kids from *The O.C.* Anyway, the pitcher slugs along for seven years in the minors—I'm thinking montage there, something like that—before he makes the Show. Then he sees the first major league game he's ever been to from the home-team bullpen. Then a couple years later, he becomes the first lefty in American League history to pitch a perfect game!"

"Hold on," the producer says. "You want me to try to sell a story of a strawberry patch kid who throws a perfect game?"

"Hey, yes, that's the title. *The Strawberry Patch Kid.*"

The producer points to the door. "Come back when you've got something I can believe."

Believe it or not, that's the Kenny Rogers story. Swear to God. Rogers really was a left-handed right fielder and occasional shortstop on his high school team in tiny Dover, Florida. He was 5'11" and about 130 pounds, 30 of them teeth from the looks of his smile ("I was so small it was sick," he says). He's at a game one day and a scout is there to see Rogers' teammate Stanley Boderick.

"That's a name I'll never forget," he says with a smile in the Texas locker room.

Rogers' glove comes up a few laces short, and he runs in for a new one. While he's fixing it, his coach says, "Kenny, meet Joe Marchese. He's with the Rangers."

That handshake, though he didn't know it at the time, was the most important moment in Rogers' baseball life, until July 28, 1994.

"If my glove doesn't break, he doesn't watch me. Then, a couple of days later, I pitched for him in a gym, then went outside and hurled against the side of the building because I was sick. I was thinkin', there goes my career. I was brutal and then I throw up."

Marchese, for whatever reason, saw a left-handed pitcher in that vomit-spewing, unschooled Florida prepster, and several months later, Rogers was a 39th-round draft pick literally learning pitching from scratch.

"I can't tell you how little I knew about pitching," Rogers says with a laugh, his Southern accent becoming stronger as he tells his remarkable tale. He had to learn how to pitch from the stretch, and his first attempts at a curve nearly sprained his wrist.

But Marchese must have seen something that even Rogers hadn't known was there. Because after seven years in the minors and another six years bumping around between the bullpen and the rotation, and with but one winning season to his credit, Kenny Rogers pitched a perfect game, defeating the California Angels 4–0 on July 28, 1994.

He just shakes his head at the memory. "I sit here now in my 20th pro season, and I just don't think you can comprehend how many things had to go just right just to get me to pitch in the big leagues, let alone pitch a perfect game."

Rogers' too-wild-for-the-movies saga somewhat mirrors the pursuit of any perfect game. Just as a wondrous confluence of events turned Rogers away from the strawberry fields and into the bigs, so, too, did each pitch in his game, each ball put in play, each call by the umpires. All click into place like the winning reels on a nine-inning-long slot machine. He breaks his glove. Click. He gets a good call on the leadoff hitter. Click. Marchese happens to see him throw a pea from right to home. Click. Rusty Greer makes a diving catch. Click. It all works together in a startling display of synchronicity.

And now the kid from Florida can sit in the big-league clubhouse, wearing his Rangers jersey, shaking his head at the wonder of it all, and be amazed all over again that not only did it happen . . . it happened to him.

———

More than a dozen years after that fateful day in Florida, Kenny Rogers took the hill to face California on a pleasant July evening in Texas. For once, it wasn't steamy hot in Arlington; it was actually kind of nice. Rogers was nursing a sore shoulder, a twinge he'd gotten throwing between starts three days earlier.

The former high school outfielder was 10–6 and the top pitcher on a Rangers team that was leading the division by a game and a half. Some players who have remained stars in the years since were young Texas guns then: Juan Gonzalez, Rusty Greer, Ivan Rodriguez, Dean Palmer. Jose Canseco was on his way back to his slugging best after injuries; Rogers would be glad Jose was feeling good this day.

Also feeling good were Rangers fans, who were enjoying their first season in the brand-new ballpark in Arlington. Among the first of the "new wave" of modern ballparks, it didn't have a roof to keep out the Texas heat, but it had enough charm and amenities to make it a real attraction. A crowd of 46,851 had nearly filled the place, and they would soon become the largest regular-season crowd to that point in history to witness a perfect game in person.

"It was awesome," remembers enthusiastic former Angels utility man Rex Hudler, who played second base for California that day. He said, "It was a new ballpark, and there wasn't an empty seat in the house. It was an atmosphere players love to play in."

One of those 46,000-plus people sticks in Rogers' memory years later.

"I was warming up like normal. But for some reason I noticed someone sitting in the stands behind the catcher, just watching intently everything I did. I can't even remember a face, just that there was someone there. When I threw a pitch, if it was good, he shook his head, yes. If it was bad, he shook his head, no. Pretty soon, after every pitch I was looking at him to see if it was OK. Went on like that the whole warm-up session. After it was done, I threw the ball up toward him to give it to him, but it went over his head and someone else got it. So I'm sure wherever he is out there, he's still a little irritated."

If that fan was ticked off, he was soon drowned out by the rest of the Ranger faithful as Rogers began a systematic creation of a team of fallen Angels.

"I remember the first hitter, Chad Curtis," Rogers says. "I got to 3–2 and threw him a low fastball on the outside corner, a pitcher's pitch. We were watching video of that game not long ago with him [Curtis was Rogers' Texas teammate in 2001], and everyone was like, 'That's a strike!' And Chad took it. The umpire made a little hesitation, and I was holding my breath, and then he called it strike three."

Spike Owen followed with a grounder to short, and Jim Edmonds was also out on strikes.

Rogers, like Len Barker and Jim Bunning, got all the runs he needed right off the bat. With two outs, Canseco went yard deep to left. Will Clark walked, Juan Gonzalez singled, and Palmer singled Clark home with the second run.

Chili Davis, Bo Jackson—on the first of his three strikeouts in the game—and J. T. Snow were Rogers' victims in the second. Rex Hudler, Chris Turner, and Gary DiSarcina followed in the third. After describing DiSarcina grounding out to Palmer at third, Rogers recalls breathing an extra sigh of relief.

"We had a terrible infield that year . . . as in grass and dirt, that is, not the players," Rogers says. He's too nice to mention that Texas, perhaps "helped" by their field, entered the game last in the American League in fielding—so the defense's sterling yet out-of-character performance was just another off-kilter domino that managed to fall in the right place somehow for him.

"Every ground ball was tough, there was a bad hop waiting everywhere," Rogers adds. "Deano got one from DiSarcina that almost spun down under his glove. He had to go down and get it in an awkward motion and come up throwing. And it was bang-bang at first base. If he takes a millisecond longer, he's probably safe."

The Rangers added two more runs in the bottom of the third with back-to-back jacks by Rodriguez and Canseco. Jose's blast would soon earn him a very strange footnote to history, if you'll pardon the pun (you'll see why).

Taking all this in from the bench was Mickey Hatcher, the Rangers' hitting coach in 1994. He had also watched from the bench in 1988 as Tom Browning threw a perfect game against the Dodgers, then joined his L.A. teammates with an oh-fer against Dennis Martinez three years later. Now he had another front-row seat for history.

"By the fifth or sixth inning, Kenny still had some good stuff," Hatcher remembers. "His change-up was good, he was spotting his fastball, getting a lot of ground balls. And by the seventh and eighth, he still had all his pitches. And we felt like he was going to do it. By then, you look to see if a pitcher's best pitch is working. And his were. I think that in a situation like that, a pitcher gets stronger. Kenny did that, turned it up an extra notch. They're looking at every hitter as the guy who could break it up."

For the Angels' part, they were certainly aware of what was going on. "Every out was a big deal," says Hudler. "Guys in our dugout were saying, 'We can't let him do it.'"

(Aware of the Ben Davis/Curt Schilling incident that occurred not long before being interviewed for this book, Rogers made a point of saying, "The Angels, in the later innings, never went up there trying to work a walk or something. They were trying to get a hit. I appreciated that more than anything else. It was nice of them to try to beat it in the right way." However, he did note that he had no problem with Davis' bunt. "Any team can do anything they want to try to win. But I'd have loved it if they bunted them all in those days. I was a lot quicker then!")

Perhaps hoping to keep the spirits alive and on Rogers' side (or perhaps they were just being downright silly), Chris James and Gary Redus set Canseco's shoes on fire in the fifth inning. As the DH, Canseco was on the bench while Rogers was on the mound for the fifth. James and Redus had gotten a pair of Canseco's oldest, smelliest shoes and doused them with alcohol and lit 'em up. Manager Kevin Kennedy joined Canseco and everyone else in dugout-wide laughter, but Rogers didn't know what had happened until after the game.

Will Clark did. "I looked over from first base, and I couldn't see, I was laughing so hard."

Maybe the sacrifice of leather helped, because although Rogers showed the first signs of trouble in the sixth inning, going to a 3–0 count on the pesky Gary DiSarcina, he then induced a ground-out back to the mound.

In the seventh inning, he kept the fans on the edge of their seats by going to a 3-ball count on each hitter. But Curtis grounded out to third, Owen flew out to left, and Edmonds once again struck out, this time on a change-up that Rogers remembered as being one of his best pitches of the day.

"What probably helped me more than anything else was not focusing on [3–0 counts] like that," Rogers says. "I was totally oblivious to the perfect game. I knew I had a no-hitter, but even in the ninth I never thought about 'Did I walk anybody?' I was really focused on each hitter as he came up, even in that last inning. Walking a guy never entered my mind, throwing a bad pitch, nothing negative entered my mind. That was the biggest thing for me all game long."

The huge crowd was really behind Rogers now. Playing center field, Greer remembers, "From the seventh inning on, every ball was a boo and every strike was a cheer. That's when it started sinking in."

In the dugout after retiring Edmonds, Rogers nearly ran afoul of the superstitions surrounding his path to perfection.

"There was a little assistant trainer who ran up and gave me a cup of water after every inning. I remember in the seventh, I sat down and he didn't show up, and I knew I had the no-hitter going by that point, but for some reason he hadn't brought it after a few minutes. I had been lining them up there under the bench, some of them still half full, and I was looking for him to get the next cup. And I couldn't ask him to, either, 'cause that would mess it up. But he finally did come, and I gave him a little look. And he was right on time the next inning. After the game, I did an interview on the bench, and the cups were still lined up there, eight in a row. I looked at them and thought, wow, that's amazing. I'm just glad no one knocked them over."

Fortified once again by water and the continuation of his perfect-cup streak, Rogers struck out Bo Jackson for the second out of the eighth inning.

"I remember he swung at a change-up that was *waaay* off the plate. I'd never had a guy swing at a pitch that far outside. No one could have hit that ball. It would have been behind a left-handed batter. I had him thinking one speed or the other, fastball or change. And he couldn't gauge the speed. But he swung at a ball that was too far outside for him or any human to hit."

As Rogers took the mound for the ninth, the fans took to their feet, where they would stay for the rest of the game.

"I was aware of the fans, but I wasn't focusing on them at all. I just wanted to win the game. That kept it simple and kept me in a positive mind-set, thinking about my job. I never thought one negative thought all day. And that's a rare thing."

Another rare thing was the play that happened next.

"I was leading off the ninth inning, three outs to go in the perfect game," says Hudler. "I'm in the on-deck circle, absorbing all of this. We were cherishing the moment. You don't want to be no-hit, but as long as I was there, I was smelling the roses. I was having fun with the Rangers' fans, who were standing and cheering. I pointed to my chest with my thumb, and told them that I was going to get him, I was going to break it up. The fans in the stands by the on-deck circle were laughing at me. It was a fun thing. You don't like getting your lunch handed to you, but you can have fun with it."

Hudler took a couple of balls, then fouled a pitch off. Then he got a high fastball he liked and took a solid swing.

"I whacked it! I got my top hand on it and I whacked it good," Hudler enthuses, almost jumping through the phone. "It went sailing. It didn't go up, it was a line drive."

"He flared one out there," Rogers says. "His version was a rope, probably."

Greer agrees that the ball was firmly struck but was no line drive/frozen rope.

Whatever it was, "I took off out of the box and I was smiling," Hudler goes on. "I got him, I got him! I was three or four steps from first base when I saw Greer, this rookie who could really run, and I saw him leave his feet, he was flying. It looked like Superman. And it was in front of him, which is a tough play. He leaves his feet and I thought what the heck is he doing? It was magical. As I crossed first base, I was going for a double. But he caught it, and I just kept running in. The roar after he caught it was one of the biggest roars I've ever heard as a player. It was unbelievable."

"It was in the right-center-field gap," Greer says. "As I was going to the ball, I was thinking that I'd better dive for this ball one way or the other. And as I got about halfway to it, I knew I'd have to dive for it. But I had a good feeling that I'd catch it. Then when I left my feet, I knew I was going to catch it. It was just a matter of hanging on to it at that point."

Hang on he did.

"I took my helmet off and flipped it toward the on-deck circle so it spun toward the people I'd been laughing with," Hudler says. "And they were all standing up and pointing at me, saying, ha, you didn't do it."

"I threw it in and went back to my position," Greer says. "I hadn't heard the crowd to that point. But Kenny was taking a little extra time on the mound, and then I heard them. It was a deafening roar."

Greer had earned it. There have been 16 perfect games in history, and many of them had defensive gems turned in at various parts of the game. But the fuzzy-haired Greer is the only player to make a truly perfect-game-saving, diving catch in the ninth inning, when everyone with eyes and ears knew what was going on.

"I never thought he was going to get it," Rogers said after the game. "I thought it was going to drop. Then, I was worried that it would pop out when he fell."

Descriptions of plays like this from other games varied from writer to writer. An easy grounder to one scribe was a sharply hit ground ball to another. A long fly-out to some eyes is a near home run to others. Hudler's line drive was Rogers' flare and Greer's soft liner. But in this case, all accounts agreed that Greer's had been a remarkable play, made even more stunning by its timing.

Chris Turner then grounded uneventfully to shortstop, bringing DiSarcina to the plate as the 27th man.

"I had handled Gary very well in my career, but he's such a good hitter," Rogers recalls. "I was thinking to myself that this is the time he's going to get a hit. I was thinking that he was the last guy I wanted to have up there. He was something like 0 for 20 against me at that point. He's due to get a hit."

Rogers delivered and DiSarcina swung at a high fastball. He lifted the ball to Greer, appropriately, in center.

"I actually misread that ball a little bit and had to jump for it," Greer says with a laugh. "But I played it off good like it was no big deal."

Let the pileup commence.

"Will Clark got there first," Rogers says. "I didn't know how to act at all, or where to look."

So he just looked around and saw nothing but fans on their feet screaming and teammates surrounding him. They lifted him to their shoulders and he waved his cap at the fans and the sky, pumping his mitt over and over as he waved.

"To be honest with you, when I had waved to the crowd and I went to sit down in the dugout to take a breath, [Texas media director] John Blake walked up to me and said, 'Congratulations, that's only the 12th perfect game in major league history.' [Blake meant post-1900, of course].

"I literally went, 'What?' I knew about no-hitters, you hear about them, and I knew they hadn't gotten any hits. But I never looked across all the way, no one on base, no errors. So even during the celebration, I didn't know it was a perfect game."

Everyone in the clubhouse already knew, and Rogers was besieged with congratulations, questions, phone calls, photographers, and more. His wife, Becky, found him in the hallway outside the locker room; there was an AP photo in *Sports Illustrated* the next week of a sweaty and happy Rogers holding up his baby daughter Jessica and kissing her while Becky looks on happily.

"She was only a few months old; she had no clue," Rogers says, referring of course to Jessica. "But we have that photo and she'll be able to look back someday and say she was there."

Interviews went on for a while, his teammates stayed to party with him, and slowly the hullabaloo died down.

And then . . . he didn't sleep all night. "Nope, not a wink," he says with a big grin, going back to the moment. He stayed up with teammates for several hours, then talked all night with his wife, then he was on *Good Morning, America*, then actually played golf ("badly," he says). He was back at the ballpark after his round to do some interviews. In the club-house that afternoon, he asked teammates, "Letterman or Leno?" and the next Monday, he was in New York talking to Dave.

It was perfect.

Two weeks later, on August 12, the season was over.

A labor dispute ended the 1994 season nearly two months early. Here was yet another point of synchronicity for Rogers. If they set that strike date two weeks earlier, he's just another journeyman pitcher with an admittedly great backstory.

Texas actually ended up "winning" the A.L. West that season, but it was a hollow victory. Rogers himself finished the year 11–8, and he was an All-Star the next season while going 17–7.

He traces some of his success since to that magical night in Arlington.

"The game was huge for me. You don't think about it all the time, but it helped. After it, when I would struggle, I would be able to say, I can come out of this. Confidence-wise, my perception of what type of pitcher I could be advanced. The next year, I threw 39 straight scoreless innings."

After stints with Oakland and the Yankees, he came back to Texas in 2000, back to the place he'd made history. It's a historic moment he'd like to repeat, but in a different way.

"I've wished a few times that I could have been outside myself that day for a while and just sat in the stands and watched. While you're doing it, you don't get that chance to sit back and enjoy. You know if you start to do that, there goes your focus and any chance of staying in that zone. I'd love to go back in time and sit and watch and remember what I was thinking, what I was feeling. Then to just look around at the fans and see how they were so excited. It would be great to be able to do that."

There's no going back in time for Rogers, and there will be no going back to the farm either. But if it weren't for a weird set of coincidences, and a gutsiness that he probably didn't know he had, it would have been strawberry fields forever.

Yes! David Wells watches with glee as the last out of his 1998 perfect game falls from the sky at Yankee Stadium. *Photo courtesy of AP/Wide World Photos.*

CHAPTER 15

David Wells

May 17, 1998

What you often hear about David Wells and his gem of a game in 1998 is that "an imperfect man pitched a perfect game." However, Wells was no more imperfect than other perfect-game pitchers . . . he was just more colorful. His off-field demeanor and exploits serve as a frame around the game, but the perfection of the painting within that frame matches up with any of the other 16 gems. You can criticize his weight, his wild lifestyle, his tattoos, or his gruff demeanor, but none of that mattered to the Minnesota Twins on May 17, 1998. The Twins didn't get blanked in every way possible by a "character"; they were perfected by a pitcher.

Now it is true that Wells was almost a walking cartoon, a sitcom in pinstripes. He signed with the Yankees in 1997 after 10 pretty good but not distinguished seasons with Toronto,

Detroit, Cincinnati, and Baltimore. He was a solid pitcher with good control and an ERA that consistently hovered below 4.00. But early on in New York, he found a spot in the tabloid headlines when he broke his pitching hand in a fight in a bar and then missed some spring-training games due to a bout with gout. Yes, gout, believe it or not. Plus, he wasn't exactly Mr. Cliché when it came to his dealings with the media and his manager.

"I'm just the kind of guy who is just going to give the manager crap," Wells said. "Joe [Torre] knows that and he has to deal with it."

Amid all of the distractions, Wells pitched well. The San Diego native had also been a lifelong Yankees fan, a student of the team's history, and his arrival at the House that Ruth Built rejuvenated him tremendously. After being told that No. 3 was unavailable (some former outfielder had claimed it, apparently), Wells decided to take 33. Later in 1997, he wore a Babe Ruth cap to the mound for an inning. Amid his Hell's Angels rap and underneath all the tattoos (son Brandon on right bicep and late mom Eugenia Ann on his chest), it turned out Wells was as much of a baseball history geek as you or me.

But many argued that he wasn't exactly honoring the legacy that he loved with his pub-crawling activities and smart-ass comments. Frankly, he didn't care. That was perhaps Wells' greatest asset: he just didn't give a rat's ass what you thought, or at least that's what he said in public. Nonetheless, he defended teammates with ferocity and heaters and was the first guy off the bench into an on-field scrum.

And yeah, he was big. He was round. He was a bit flabby, compared to the cut, sleek, six-packed guys he showered with. He was listed at 6'4", 225, but no one believed that. Again, Wells just didn't care (although he did get pretty pissed off at *Sports Illustrated* when they made his weight the focus of a piece after he had rejoined Toronto in 1999).

So, was Wells perfect? No. Then again . . . who is?

He grew up in San Diego and, in a wonderful coincidence, attended the same high school, Point Loma, that had produced Don Larsen. (In case you're wondering, yes, that's the only high school to produce two perfect-game pitchers.) Contacted after Wells' perfect game, Point Loma athletic director Lois Craig said that Wells had thrown one in high school. She also praised the former hellion for his largesse.

"He has been very gracious in giving back to the community that helped him grow up," she said, while also remembering her former charge as "a free-spirited, hardheaded youngster."

Point Loma coach and teacher Bennie Edens also remembered Wells, in an article for the *L.A. Times.*

"He once told me he grew up playing catch with Hell's Angels. I don't think you could say that David was particularly motivated toward his studies. He didn't worry too much about getting to class on time, and you never put it past him to cut class and go to the beach.

"Baseball was where he belonged. That was his love."

His other love was his mother, Eugenia Ann.

"This game is dedicated to her," Wells said after his perfecto of his deceased mom and best friend, memorialized on his chest in permanent ink. "And she did have the best seat in the house."

Ironically, his father and son had had to return home that Sunday morning, having come into town for his scheduled start on Saturday that was postponed by rain.

The former San Diego beach-bum-turned-Yankees-ace took the hill on a gray, overcast Sunday afternoon, May 17. (Thus May tied June and July for "month with most perfect games," with three each.) The sky was still gray, and though no rain threatened, it was not a sunny summer day. The lights were on early at the Stadium, and an enormous crowd had assembled. How many were there for actual baseball could be debated because that Sunday was Beanie Baby Day in the Bronx.

A stuffed white bear with a red heart sewn on the chest was given out to kids under 14 (and any adults who paid kids to go to the game for them, this being the middle of the Beanie Baby craze). After the game, not surprisingly, enterprising New Yorkers were standing at the exit gates offering cash for the prized bears, which came complete with an official Yankees bear card.

"It's nice to have [a perfect game come] on a day when there's 50,000 [actually 49,820] people," said Torre afterward. "We'll remember what Beanie Babies mean from now on. Even though Boomer [Wells] is the furthest thing from a Beanie Baby."

"Before I left for the game, my kids made sure I knew to get those bears," remembers Yankees outfielder Paul O'Neill, who that afternoon would take another step on his road to becoming the only player to be on three winning perfect-game teams.

Those thousands of Valentinos proved to be good news bears for Wells, who was 4–1 with an unperfection-like 5.23 ERA entering the game. In fact, he hadn't made it out of the third inning in his previous start.

He buzzed through the Twins in the first with no problem, a quiet start to what would end up a very loud afternoon.

"Early on, you had the feeling he had really good stuff," remembers Yankees broadcaster Michael Kay. "But when you think of perfection, you don't normally think of David Wells. I mean, you don't think that about anybody, really. 'Wow, he has great stuff, he might pitch a perfect game?' You just don't think that. But he had great command right off, he had a great curveball, his fastball seemed pretty live."

Once again, as perfect game tradition almost dictates must happen, the team being blanked helped out by donating a run to their opponents' cause. Yankees center fielder Bernie Williams doubled in the second inning, took third on a passed ball, and scored on a wild pitch by LaTroy Hawkins.

In the top of the third, Wells seemed to kick it up a notch and struck out the side. The second out of the inning was shortstop Javier Valentin, and here Wells came close to losing it, going to three balls in a nine-pitch battle before recording the K and adding to his collection of zeros, a collection noted by someone in the press box.

"The first thing that drew my attention was my scorecard," remembers Yankees play-by-play man John Sterling. "You keep score in your style, everyone's different. But anyone could see that the arithmetic perfection of Wells' game after three innings just looked so good."

Kay noticed something else about the game early on.

"There were a lot of kids in the stands, too, because of the giveaway. I remember a lot of high-pitched squeals. The pitch of the voices was higher than you normally hear at the Stadium. And how great is it that a lot of seven-, eight-, nine-year-olds were there with their moms or dads. I think they're hooked on baseball after being a part of that game."

Up in section 2, longtime Yankee fan and Sunday season-ticket holder David Fischer was noticing the same thing.

"The ballpark was full of families because of the Beanie Baby giveaway, lots of kids in the stadium, and from the outset I noted the game was different because the PA system wasn't blaring rock music. The surrounding sounds were more family-oriented, if not quieter, but it gave the ballpark a really different atmosphere."

Amid the squeals, Wells had no problems through four or five, although he did go to 3–0 on leadoff hitter Matt Lawton before inducing a pop-up to short in the fourth. Again, center fielder Williams helped the cause, this time with a fourth-inning homer that made it 2–0 Yanks.

Slowly, others began to take notice of what was happening. In the dugout, pitching coach Mel Stottlemyre said he and Torre had mentioned the word "no-hitter" as early as the fifth inning.

"We were worried about the pitch count," Stottlemyre said of Wells, who went to 3-ball counts twice early on. "We were concerned he would run out of strength and we'd have to make a tough decision. But he got up on the right side of the bed that day. He just had outstanding stuff, from the moment he threw his first warm-up pitch."

"Obviously, from about the fifth inning on, that's when you start noticing that, wow, he's gone through the lineup untouched," says third baseman Scott Brosius. "And the crowd starts taking notice, and you can kind of feel the electricity build in the air a little bit."

The air kept crackling in the sixth as Wells notched two more strikeouts (he would finish with 11 in the game). Behind the plate, Jorge Posada was starting to realize things were happening, too.

"To tell you the truth, I didn't even know what was going on until the sixth inning," he says, taking a trip down memory lane while in the Yankees clubhouse before a 2001 game. "I knew a no-hitter was going on, but I didn't know he had a perfect game going. And then every out, the fans kept getting louder and louder.

"He had something special going that day. The main thing was throwing strikes. He threw a lot of strikes. Everything he threw, all his pitches were unbelievable. He had everything— down in the zone, throwing strikes, elevating the ball when he needed to."

Fans listening on radio and TV started to hear about it, too, as both broadcasters ignored superstitions and started talking about the progress of Wells' pitching.

"The first time that John and I got excited about it was when we looked at each other after the sixth inning," says Kay. "Then we really got into it after the seventh, and the crowd did, too. He had great stuff and the Twins were not an incredibly great-hitting team. I said on the radio after the seventh, 'If you have a friend who likes baseball, even if he doesn't like baseball, give him a call and tell him to tune in. We might be watching something very special here.'"

In the top of the seventh, the Yankees padded the lead, turning a tight game into an easy W, if they could wrap up the Twins. Williams got his third hit with a double, Darryl Strawberry tripled Williams home, and Chad Curtis singled in Strawberry to make it 4–0. So now, the score became secondary to the drama playing itself out on the mound. The bear-bearing fans, the scorecard-keeping broadcasters, and the feebly swinging Twins were all watching, as were the Yankees, but the latter were not talking, certainly not to Wells and only occasionally with each other.

"[We] hardly spoke the whole game, until the end," Posada remembers. "We talked before the game, and went through the whole [Twins] lineup, but during the game we didn't talk. During the first two innings we talked, but that was it. And I think everybody in the dugout didn't even move from their seats until the game was over. Me and [catcher Joe] Girardi were sitting together, and we were just talking about who's coming up and all that stuff. He was just trying to keep me a little loose. It was fun to see all the teammates doing [superstitious things], you know, staying in the same spot the whole game. It was a lot of fun to catch it."

In the top of the seventh, there was drama and tension to go with the fun. With the pursuit of perfection, or at least a no-no, on everyone's mind, the combative Wells gave every-one something to chew on.

Lawton went easily on a fly ball. But then second base-man Brent Gates battled to a full count before grounding out to Tino Martinez at first. The next hitter was the Twins' best hitter, future Hall of Famer Paul Molitor, the DH that day.

"I think the best thing about David Wells, even now, he doesn't give up a lot of walks," says Posada, getting more and more animated about remembering the game. "We went right after [Molitor]. We made a great pitch at 3–1, we wanted to throw him a little sinker away, try to get him to hit a ground ball or try to get him to pop out. Even then we were trying to make a pitch. But if it was meant to be, it was meant to be, no matter what, so that's why we went with the pitch. David went right after him."

"David was so basic, it was great to see," said Torre. "The first time he went 3-and-0 [to Lawton in the fourth], it didn't bother me that much because it was too early to even think about [perfection]. But when he went 3-and-1 on Molitor, that's the one memory I'll take from the game. Because once he got Molly out, he was going to pitch a perfect game. That's being tested by a big-time hitter, when you go 3-and-1 [and then get him]."

"When I fell behind in the count [to Molitor], I just tried to throw it right down the middle," Wells said after the game. "Then I threw a sinker and it sunk. It was probably one of my best pitches of the game."

An enormous cheer carried Wells to the dugout and once more into the company of a team that was avoiding him at every step.

Wells had by this time established a routine of going into the clubhouse until the Yankees had made one out, then returning to the dugout. Of course, no one was talking to him, but this was not exactly what the gregarious, oddly nervous Wells needed. Fortunately, David Cone, who would, of course, find himself in a similar situation only a year later, was there with just the right remark and created his own opposite version of a Cone of Silence in which talking about the (shhh!) perfect game was allowed.

"After the seventh, I told him it was time to break out the knuckleball," Cone said. "He let out a big laugh at that."

After the game, Wells added, "I just told Girardi that I was looking for Jorge to come by and talk to me between innings. Joe said, 'Are you kidding? He was as nervous as you were.'"

Posada wasn't alone, as Chuck Knoblauch remembered.

"I think we were all getting a little tighter out there," Knoblauch said. "You have to want the ball to be hit to you in that situation, but you want a nice, easy one-hopper, not a screamer you have to backhand."

With one out in the eighth, Knoblauch didn't get his wish. Ron Coomer smashed a screaming one-hopper, and all Knoblauch could do was knock it down. It was hit just to his right, and that saved it; any more distance to either side and it would have taken a tremendous play to get the out. As it was, the ball dropped to Knoblauch's feet, and he had plenty of time to throw out Coomer.

"Wells was so overpowering," says Sterling. "In the seventh, Coomer came up, a good line-drive hitter. Wells fell behind 2–0. Late in a no-hitter, if you've walked guys, then you can work to preserve it by just pitching around a good hitter. But in a perfect game, you don't have that luxury. You've got to go at them. So Wells got to 3–1 and Coomer hit a hot shot toward Knoblauch."

"It was a hard-hit ball, and when you're catching, you're playing like a second baseman, you're trying to catch the ball or something," Posada remembers. "When he knocks it down, you say, 'Throw the ball!' and all that stuff. I think a lot of emotions were involved. And he threw it. And I'm saying, 'All right!' But you're back in there to regroup and try and get the next guy out."

That they did, getting right fielder Alex Ochoa to pop out to Martinez. Wells was three outs away from history and finally having a very, very good reason to close every bar in Manhattan.

Meanwhile, Cone kept things light by confronting Wells after the eighth.

"Come on, man, you're not showing me anything," he said, laughing. But he knew different.

In the bottom of the inning, Twins manager Tom Kelly changed pitchers after one out, bringing in Greg Swindell to replace Dan Naulty, who had taken over for Hawkins to open the eighth.

"He's trying to ice me," Wells told anyone who would listen. "But it's not going to work."

As the ninth inning began, everyone on the field and elsewhere battled emotion.

"The fans were going crazy, which was great, but I kind of wanted them to calm down because they were making me nervous," Wells said. "By the end I could barely grip the ball, my hand was shaking so much."

"I was nervous," Torre said. "I am not normally someone who is superstitious, but I didn't want to mess anything up. We were all really quiet. That last inning was pretty intense."

The fans joined in the intensity.

"When Knoblauch made that play, coupled with the great work Wells did against Molitor, then I started to believe it was possible," notes fan David Fischer. "I was sorry I had waited so long to begin enjoying the historical possibilities.

"The ninth inning was spent on our feet, and the people in our section seemed to be on top of us. We seemed to close ranks subconsciously in a group hug of hope."

Out in right field, Paul O'Neill was drifting back to being on the field for Tom Browning's perfect game 10 years earlier.

"You want the ball hit to you," he says. "But you don't want a line drive in the lights or in [the backdrop of] the fans, or something like that. A fly ball is great. It's an easy play to make. The last out of a big game . . . is always fun to catch."

"I remember by the ninth inning, I felt like I was almost diving for foul balls," Brosius says, "because you want so hard to keep it alive if the ball's hit to you. That's what I remember more than anything else, just the tenseness as an infielder, because you want to make sure you're not the one who screws it up."

Earlier Brosius had made sure that he wasn't the one to screw it up psychically. From his third-base position, he would toss the ball back to Wells 18 times during the game, after the first two outs of each inning.

"I made sure to say the same thing, 'Way to go,' each time I threw the ball back to him," Brosius said.

On the bench, Yankees coach Don Zimmer had his own unique take on things.

"Sitting on the bench at 67 years old, I'm not going to be too nervous," Zim says. "If I'd had to catch it, I might have been nervous. I was rooting inside for him to do it."

Zimmer had the unique distinction of also being in uniform for the previous Yankees perfect game, by Don Larsen. He was an infielder with Brooklyn in 1956, though he wasn't activated for the World Series.

However, he says, "I don't think I thought of Larsen much during that [Wells] game. It wasn't much fun for us during that [earlier] game, but when it happens to your team, it's 10 times more fun to root for your guy. It's a big difference."

Another big difference was the coverage of the event. While a few fans might have called friends and neighbors to tune into the broadcast of Larsen's game, now technology brought the whole of Baseball America (and we don't mean the newspaper) into the fold. The last inning was broadcast live on video screens in San Diego and San Francisco. In the clubhouse in Detroit, Wells' former teammates didn't miss a pitch on TV. ESPN broke in to show the end of the game, too. The universe of people who can say that they "saw" a perfect game expanded instantly and dramatically.

Finally, on the mound, Wells was in total focus.

"The only thing I saw was Jorge's glove," he said on the MSG Network show *A Perfect Night*. "Thank goodness for tunnel vision."

Into the tunnel he went to face the Twinkies in the ninth.

Third baseman Jon Shave flew meekly to O'Neill.

Valentin struck out for the third time.

Every bear in the Stadium was roaring at this point, and the people were making a pretty big noise, too. The rumpled, frumpy, lumpy Wells took a deep breath at the bottom of this bowl of sound and faced Pat Meares, the kind of scrappy slapper who seems to make a living busting up dreams like this.

But this was one dream that came true. Meares swung and lofted the easy fly ball that O'Neill had prayed for. He camped under it easily and made the catch, though if he'd then followed through on his first thought, he'd have also made an enemy. "I joked with Boomer later that I was going to throw the ball into the stands," O'Neill said. "But I gave it to him, of course."

And that was that. David Wells, welcome to the club that you can join by accomplishment only, no matter how big or small you are, how many beers you drink after the game, or how many tattoos you have. Wells gets a spot on the list by dint of success, and he should receive no asterisk based on personal style.

Frank Sinatra's recording of "New York, New York" blared amid the Beanie- and Wells-induced cacophony, a perfect ending to a perfect day.

The Yankees poured out of the dugout, Wells pumped his left fist and pointed at the sky, to Mom's special seat. He also immediately looked for Posada, his Yankee nostalgia dictating that he and the catcher hug à la Larsen and Berra. But Jorge was halfway up the first-base line.

"When that ball headed to right field," Posada said on MSG, "I started running that way. I could have run out there and caught it myself, I was so nervous."

Instead, Wells looked up to see infielder Luis Sojo.

"Luis got there first, and he wouldn't leave me alone," Wells laughed. "I wanted to embrace Jorge, and I couldn't get him in there."

Clutching onto his hat and with his glove firmly on his hand, Wells soon was floating above the grass on the shoulders of Strawberry and Williams, supporting him then as they had earlier supported him with runs.

The "imperfect" perfect pitcher had thrown 120 pitches, 79 strikes, and 41 balls. He had lowered his ERA by nearly a run to 4.45 and kicked into gear a slow-starting season that would see him finish at 18–4 (a league-best .818 winning percentage), make the All-Star team, lead the league with five shutouts, and help the Yankees win the World Series (he went a combined 4–0 in the postseason).

It wasn't just the Yankees who appreciated Wells' effort.

"As much as we were fighting to win the game, deep down I was hoping to see something special," Twins manager Kelly admitted. "I like the guy, I really do. He has the charisma for something like this and I guess his stars were in alignment that day."

Kelly appreciated Wells' pitching as much as his "charisma."

"We let some fastballs go, we chased some curveballs. To pitch a perfect game, you have to have all of your pitches working. It doesn't happen by accident. We got to see a real workhorse sort of pitcher do something really special."

"I had never seen a perfect game in my life," says Kay, a former New York sportswriter before moving behind the mike. "All those years of writing and I didn't see even a no-hitter, and since becoming a broadcaster, I've seen four no-hitters, including two perfect games."

Kay also made sure to keep his scorecard, which he later had players on both teams and all four umpires sign, and which now hangs proudly in his office alongside a similar keepsake from the Cone game he would call a year later.

In the crowded and giddy clubhouse, Wells was called to the phone several times to take some special calls. One came from his fellow Point Loma Pointer, Don Larsen.

"I'm honored to share this with you, Don," Wells said as reporters listened in. "I mean two guys from the same high school doing this? What were the odds? Who would ever believe it?"

Larsen later revealed his end of the conversation.

"Oh yeah," Larsen said. "I told David we have to have a few drinks this summer and raise a little hell."

Larsen wasn't the only one to recall that first Yankees perfecto.

Yogi Berra heard about the game after arriving on a flight from Pittsburgh. At home, his wife, Carmen, told him what had happened and then she asked why he hadn't heard.

"They didn't have a radio on the plane," he said Yogically.

But he immediately took another trip, this into his memory, according to Mike Lupica in the *Daily News*.

"As soon as my wife told me, I went right back to that day in 1956," he said. "How could you not?"

After Wells made his curtain call and returned to the clubhouse, the fans could finally take their memories home.

"Walking down to the exits everyone was in no hurry," remembers Fischer. "They were smiling at one another, making contact with strangers and nodding as if to silently acknowledge that you, too, like me, were witness to something special. Something you'll never see again in your life."

(Memo to David: stick around.)

This being New York, the celebrity quotient was pretty high in the postgame celebration. Comedian Billy Crystal, a huge Yankees honk, stopped by to get his ticket stub signed.

"I got here late," he joked. "What happened?"

New York mayor Rudy Giuliani called to tell Wells to come to City Hall and enjoy "David Wells Day" and be presented with the key to the city.

"Do you think that's a good idea?" Wells joked with Hizzoner.

Trailed later by prying reporters, Wells hit the Upper East Side to toast his special day. He headed with fellow Yankees Graham Lloyd and Dale Sveum to Dorrian's Red Hand, where they stayed until the doors closed.

"It was a very good night," Lloyd said. "When we went into Dorrian's, everyone in the place applauded. It was a long night, but fairly tame. We went to a few places. It was exciting to be out in New York under those circumstances. I still don't think David realizes what he has accomplished."

Not that anything got out of hand. "You've got to go celebrate," Wells said, although he also allowed that he didn't appreciate the entourage of scribes.

"I wouldn't have wanted to be downtown with him after the game," Zimmer laughs. "I wouldn't have been able to keep up with him!"

The next morning, the party continued. Wells kept a commitment to Stottlemyre to play in a charity golf tournament in honor of the pitching coach's late son. Wells was a bit late, but he got in about 10 holes, chipping in for an eagle on the last, before he returned to the city to keep the show going—in this case, the *Late Show with David Letterman*, a by-now de rigueur appearance for any major sports success.

"I was nervous during the game," Wells admitted. "But I was more nervous going onto [Letterman's] show. Even though I've seen that show in person a couple of times, once in the audience and once in a room backstage. But to be out there in front of everyone, well, that was something else."

The next day was David Wells Day in the city, and Wells faced another crowd of Yankee lovers from the steps of City Hall, another addition to the modern celebration of the perfect game . . . Charley Robertson, for instance, didn't get the key to the clubhouse, let alone the city.

Under sunny skies that his perfect game seemed to have cleared up, Wells received his key outside City Hall. A band played, flags flapped, and Robert Merrill sang "Take Me Out to the Ball Game."

"It's all changed my personal life for the last 48 hours," Wells told the crowd. "I'm enjoying it while I can, but now it's time to go back to work, back to basics."

Later he said about the stadium, "This is like a sanctuary for me. I feel very comfortable coming to the park, and honestly, it's where I'd prefer to be 24-7 right now. It's crazy out there. Believe me, I'm flattered by everything that's going on . . . but I want to go back to playing baseball and cheer my teammates on. Today's a new day and we have to think about playing baseball instead of what happened Sunday."

Wells wouldn't do an interview for this book, saying that he wanted to save all his stories for his own book, according to the White Sox publicist who passed the message along.

But on the MSG show, Wells said, "I'm very proud to hear people talking about my perfect game. I go to my son's Little League game and I walk past people and hear them say, 'Hey, there's that guy who pitched a perfect game.'"

Wells' pride and memories are all that he retains of the game, for now, apparently. In 2001, Wells told *Penthouse* magazine that in the three years since that glorious Beanie Sunday, he had not once watched a tape of his perfect game.

"No, I've never watched it, never gone back and looked at it," he said. "That's all in the past. I'll worry about that when I retire. I'm looking forward, not back."

Well, pardon us for taking a short look back, Boomer, at the only perfect game witnessed by twenty thousand white, fuzzy bears.

As disbelieving as the fans behind him are ecstatic, David Cone awaits the embrace of Joe Girardi as the conclusion to the final perfect game of the twentieth century in 1999. *Photo courtesy of AP/Wide World Photos.*

CHAPTER 16

David Cone

July 18, 1999

Oh, come on. This is ridiculous.

David Cone, beloved by all in baseball, pitches a perfect game in Yankee Stadium on Yogi Berra Day while Don Larsen sits in the stands and watches?!

Larsen throws out the first pitch to Berra, just as they teamed up in 1956?

Cone uses exactly 88 pitches, and Yogi's number, of course, was 8?

And Cone was the comic relief for David Wells only 14 months earlier?

And oh, yes, did we mention that it was also Yankee manager Joe Torre's 59th birthday? And that Torre had not only been at Wells' game but had been in the stands for Larsen's as a 16-year-old Dodgers fan?

No way, that's all just too much to believe.

Believe it. That's why baseball is so great . . . you can't make this stuff up. You just have to love that it sometimes just happens this wonderful way.

Yep, July 18, 1999, was Yogi Berra Day. The Hall of Famer who had said he would never return to Yankee Stadium as long as George Steinbrenner owned the team had reached a rapprochement with The Boss. Finally, Lawrence Peter Berra could return to the place from which he had helped the Yankees win 10 World Series, along the way setting all-time records for most Series games played and most malapropisms uttered.

The old-timers came to honor him, among them Bobby Richardson, Gil McDougald, and a not-so-old-timer, Don Mattingly. Berra got gifts, trips, adulation, and a $100,000 donation to his new Yogi Berra Museum in New Jersey. Painted on the field in front of each dugout was a large number 8.

Another former Yankee made a special appearance: Larsen, who threw out the first pitch to Berra, who stood in his familiar spot behind home plate. Berra wore a mitt loaned to him by Yankees starter Joe Girardi. Yogi caught Larsen's pitch on the fly and instead of leaping into his arms, met him halfway for a handshake. Berra gave the mitt back to Girardi, a piece of leather now filled with Yankee mystique and laced with the stuff that dreams are made of.

The author of the only World Series perfect game and the soon-to-be author of the latest Yankees perfecto met and shook hands. Did some magic slip between them? No, more like a slip of the tongue.

"I shook Don Larsen's hand after he threw out the first ball to Yogi," Cone said on the MSG perfect-game show. "I jokingly asked him if he was going to jump into Yogi's arms like he did in 1956. He just looked at me and said, 'Kid, you got it wrong. It was Yogi jumped into my arms.' I felt about this tall."

As several reporters noted, it was the last mistake Cone made all day.

Meanwhile, the soon-to-be-chastened Expos stood on the top steps, watching in awe, like the Little Leaguers they were in comparison with the defending World Series–champion Yankees.

The dignitaries retired for a cool drink in the shade of the stands, while Cone made his way to the mound.

He entered the game at 9–4 in a season in which he had earned another All-Star selection, his fifth. Oddly, he was mostly ineffective for much of the rest of the season, and was knocked out of the rotation briefly later that summer; he won only 12 games. However, he returned to win Game 2 of both the ALCS and the World Series, giving him three rings in four seasons with the Yankees. He added a fourth in 2000, though he pitched but one inning in that Series, a memorable punch-out of Mike Piazza.

Coney always did have a flair for drama.

For instance, in 1992, he joined the Blue Jays as a hired gun and won four games to help them make the World Series. In that Series, he had no decisions, but he started the epic Game 6 that ended with Joe Carter's famous homer. In 1996, in his first start since returning from a nearly career-ending aneurysm, he had a no-hitter through seven innings before he was pulled for the safety of his arm.

"A couple of years before the perfect game, it looked like he wouldn't pitch again," says Don Zimmer, who at the time was about to watch his third perfecto at the Stadium. "I remember meeting a doctor at a restaurant once and he said he had read about what Cone had [the aneurysm]. I'll never forget, he said, 'Your pitcher will never throw another ball.' I said, 'You might be right, but if there's anybody that will beat that, it'll be David Cone.'

"That is what I remember about that game. Here's a guy who probably shouldn't have even thrown again, and he threw a perfect game. He is among the top competitors I've ever met. He's a real battler."

By 1999, Cone was 36 and had battled through 14 seasons. He had changed from the fresh-faced youngster who won 20 games with the Mets in 1988 and a Cy Young Award with Kansas City in 1994 into a clubhouse leader and a gritty oldster who many thought was relying as much on guile and smarts as on a still-biting slider and occasionally wicked fastball. However, he had won 20 games the year before, his first time reaching that total since 1988, his third big-league season.

As he stood on the mound on that historic July day, the air was steamy and humid; temperatures neared 100 degrees as the afternoon wore on. Pregame announcer Michael Kay says he had sweated through his suit while making introductions ("At least the old-timers got chairs," he joked. "It was really sweltering out there.") But the heat helped Cone loosen up. He was ready to go.

As the ceremonies wound down, Cone remembers being happy that no one was paying attention to him.

"It was great to warm up and relax before a game and have all the attention on them, not on me," he said on MSG.

Montreal manager Felipe Alou claimed to have had a pre-monition of something happening (though even he didn't predict exactly what did happen), when he filled out his lineup card.

"As I finished writing in the last batter, I realized that not one of the hitters had ever faced Cone," Alou said. "Not one."

Their bad luck . . . and Cone's good fortune. It almost wasn't fair that the hitters had no point of reference, no insights, no preview look at one of baseball's most intelligent, versatile, and crafty pitchers. Trotting out nine first-timers against Cone was like bringing out the ballboys to receive serve against Pete Sampras or letting the JV field the kickoff against the varsity on Friday night. (Also, this being an inter-league game, it was the first perfect game pitched by one league against the other since . . . all together now . . . 1956!)

The second batter of the game almost ended this fairy tale right then and there, but of course no one knew it at the time. Montreal center fielder Terry Jones blooped a ball into short right-center field. Paul O'Neill raced to his right and dove to make the catch, extending his glove hand, his right, to catch the ball just before it hit the grass. If O'Neill was a right-handed thrower, it would have been an even tougher back-hand catch; of such small things are perfection made. He tum-bled ass over teakettle until he came to a stop, still holding the ball.

"You can't see the ball right off the bat," O'Neill remem-bers. "It's sometimes hazy out there. I was glad that play was in the first inning and not the ninth."

As Cone began mowing down Expos, one group of fans was experiencing some serious déjà vu. David Fischer was in his regular Sunday seat, surrounded by dozens of people with whom he had watched Wells pitch perfectly only 14 months earlier.

"It was obvious immediately that Cone was dominating," Fischer remembers. "We sit in the front of the upper deck directly behind home plate, and you could see Cone's slider was moving incredibly, and his splitter was really diving and acting as a great change of pace, too. With Cone, even though he retired the Expos in order, the thing that stood out was how few pitches he was throwing."

In the bottom of the second, Cone received something few perfect-game pitchers have ever gotten: a comfortable lead.

With one out, Ricky Ledee, who would later make a memorable, if scary, play in left field, slugged a monstrous two-run homer in the third tier in right field, scoring Chili Davis ahead of him.

One out and four batters later, Derek Jeter hit a three-run home run deep into the bullpen in left-center, scoring Knoblauch and Brosius ahead of him.

All of a sudden, it was 5–0 Yankees.

Unlike most perfect games, Cone would move through this game with a big pad; in fact, it was the most runs scored that early in any perfect game. But whereas other perfect-game pitchers feel as if they benefited from tight games that kept them sharp, Cone enjoyed the pad.

"Once we got that big lead, I really relaxed," he said. At least until later, that is.

"I remember we got a lead in that game," says O'Neill, who was like a lucky charm for perfect-game pitchers. "So it wasn't like a one-run game where if you have to dive for a ball and miss it, it costs you the game. That's the big thing, to get a big lead so you can go all out and not worry about the out-come of the game."

"This was my first game after coming back up from the minors," remembers Montreal starter Javier Vazquez. "I went out early to see the ceremonies and I felt good out there. But I figured out that I didn't have my good stuff early in the game, and I later tried to be more perfect and throw more strikes."

He had a good teacher to watch while his team batted, or at least attempted to bat. (Observers also note that Vazquez became a much better pitcher following the game, improving steadily into one of the N.L.'s best young pitchers, evidenced by his August 2001 Pitcher of the Month Award.)

Then, as happened to Richmond in 1880 and Browning in 1988, Cone patiently waited through a rain delay. With one out in the top of the third, the heavens opened up. The humidity had coalesced into a thunderstorm that rolled over the Stadium a few minutes before 3:00. The umpires cleared the field, the tarps came out, and Cone and the Yankees began a 33-minute wait for the rain to stop (conspiracy theorists will note that David Wells wore number 33). Though catcher Joe Girardi worried ("David's not 22, anymore," he said), Cone had no problem going back out on the mound after the delay, mostly thanks to the weather.

"It was so humid, I had no problem staying loose," Cone said.

Michael Kay adds a wonderful footnote to the afternoon that occurred during the delay.

"During the rain delay, Cone warmed up with a batboy named Luigi, who the players all called Squeegee. After the season, Cone made up gold watches for all the players, and he gave one to Luigi, too, plus a signed ball."

"David looked so comfortable out there right after the rain delay," Torre said. "When he went three up and three down in the fourth inning [using only seven pitches], I was thinking no-hitter."

Cone was so comfortable after the delay that he actually threw harder. He was clocked around 85–87 through the first three innings and was hitting 88–91 by the ninth.

Also comfortable with what they were doing were Kay and John Sterling.

"Anyone who tells me that I can change something about the game by talking on the air, then I want to get paid a whole lot more money," Sterling says with a laugh. "So we don't pay any attention to those superstitions. We talked about Cone's game very early. We started building the drama probably in the fourth inning."

That was for fans who weren't there. Fans in the stands were right on top of it, too.

"Our section was definitely in tune to the perfect game from the 4th inning on," says fan David Fischer. "On Yogi Berra Day, with Don Larsen there, and the perfect-game aura was in the air. All the people around me had shared in Wells' perfecto, so we knew it was possible, if not probable. We were counting outs down from 10 outs to go."

Another 1-2-3 in the fifth got the crowd on their feet, thrilled and quickly cognizant of the march of zeros. "You can't help but get caught up in the emotion of the crowd," Cone said. "But I had to fight it after the fifth inning. That's too early."

It wasn't too early for a certain honored guest to think about taking a powder.

"After the fifth inning, I was going to my hotel," Larsen told *Sports Illustrated*. "Someone told me 'You can't leave now, he has a perfect game.' I'm glad I stayed."

"Cone had unbelievable stuff," remembers Kay. "But his breaking ball was breaking so much, they would have walked if they'd just taken pitches. But being a young team, the Expos were swinging at everything. The right-handed batters were swinging at balls that ended up in the left-handed batter's box."

That was the view from next to the plate as well.

"From the beginning, his slider was breaking so hard and away from the plate," remembers Montreal shortstop Orlando Cabrera, still shaking his head with amazement two years after the fact. "He throws a strike with that, then a fastball. And it wasn't that hard a fastball, but it just seemed to come on you so fast.

"He was throwing pitches you couldn't believe. His fastball seemed like it was 100 miles per hour, and his slider was like a Frisbee. He seemed like he had special stuff that day."

Zimmer says now, "For him to pitch a perfect game was really surprising. He wouldn't give his mother a ball down the middle. So he's even more apt to walk a hitter in a tough situation than a guy like Wells. Cone is what we call a nibbler. Somewhere along the line, he'd get to 3–2 and walk a guy."

That didn't happen in the sixth, even with none of Cone's relatives batting. He needed only five pitches to clear away the Expos, one of four innings in which he needed fewer than 10 pitches.

"By the time we got to the fifth or sixth inning, we all knew," said Expos catcher Chris Widger. "Because we hadn't even had any good swings against him."

Cabrera made the last out of the sixth . . . and started counting.

"We didn't realize he was throwing a perfect game until the sixth. Then I did the math and realized that if he kept doing what he's doing, I'd be the last hitter."

Cone made his way into the dugout and headed right toward the clubhouse through the connecting tunnel.

Every inning after the third, Cone changed his T-shirt. After the sixth, Torre says he passed Cone near his office, which he told Cone he could use. Thereafter, Torre made sure to pass Cone after every inning.

"The only time I talked to David was before the game, to go over the hitters," said Girardi. "We talked about pitch selection, and I didn't say another word to him the rest of the day until I ran out to the mound. Nobody was brave enough to joke."

You can bet, however, that had David Wells still been with the club, he'd have had something to say to Cone, just as Cone had helped him out in 1998.

However, while Cone's teammates weren't saying anything, the pitcher knew what was going on.

"Cone told me after the game that between innings, he would leave the bench and go to the clubhouse for a change of shirt," says John Sterling. "And the radio was on loud back there, blaring away. 'Forget the superstitions,' he said, 'I heard John and Michael mention it a hundred times. I heard it every time I was back there.'"

Sterling and Kay had company.

"[Columnist] Joel Sherman of the *Post* was actually jogging and listening to the game," says Sterling. "And as he heard the game go on, he ran home, called the *Post*, 'I'm going up there!' And he ended up in our booth before the seventh inning, and he claimed that Montreal had no chance against Cone, having seen them a week before."

Another writer of more significant note also tuned in at this point. The great baseball man for *The New Yorker*, Roger Angell, had been working at the magazine's offices. He returned home, as he writes in *A Pitcher's Story*, his book with Cone, after the sixth inning to the cries of his wife Carol: "You're not going to believe this."

Angell, like so many others around the country who watched as ESPN switched later to the game, was transfixed by the scene. Perfect games are like that: you can't help but pull for the guy, no matter who you root for. The chances of it disappearing with each pitch, with each batter are so great, that the relief one feels as each batter trudges back, fruitless, is that much more magnified.

As Cone took to the mound to warm up for the top of the seventh, he noticed something missing: a catcher.

Girardi had been on base the previous inning and was busy getting himself dressed. In one of those little things that wouldn't matter a lick in any other game but become oddly magnified in a game like this one, designated hitter Chili Davis played a minor but important role. He got a mask and glove and jogged out to warm up Cone.

"I didn't want to go out there," Davis said afterward. "But there was no one else and he was just standing there. I didn't want to break up the karma between him and Girardi. I'm looking over, thinking, 'C'mon Joe, I don't want to be out here.' David threw three pitches and Joe finally came out."

"[Chili] put on the mask and sat back there," Cone says. "He said, 'You can go ahead and let it go. I used to catch in the minor leagues.' It might not sound that funny, but some little comment like that helps break the ice and gets you talking a little bit. It can help. It was nice that Chili was there and wasn't afraid to do something. I'd rather Chili come out there than me just sort of hang around out there waiting."

Wilton Guerrero grounded out to third to open the seventh, and James Mouton came to the plate, batting for Jones. He went to 1–2 and the fans were on their feet, urging him on to strike three. Cone broke out his sharpest slider and had young Mouton diving after a ball that was a foot outside to record the second out.

One member of the Expos with some experience in these things compared Cone's stuff to the other perfecto he had witnessed. Coach Tommy Harper had been a coach with Montreal in 1991 when Dennis Martinez went 27-for-27.

"The Dodgers [in 1991] had two strikes against them before they got to the plate against Dennis," Harper said. "This one was like Dennis'. Cone had everything working. He was hitting all his spots and never with the same arm angle."

Up in his suite watching the proceedings, Berra decided this was the point to start the countdown.

"You're always thinking about it after the seventh," he said. "You only need six more outs."

The first of the final six was Vladimir Guerrero, perhaps the only significant threat in the lineup and one of the best young hitters in the National League. But he popped out. Cone next faced .315-hitting second baseman Jose Vidro. The pitcher, sweating heavily in the heat, was quickly behind 2–0 (the last time that a Montreal hitter would be ahead in the count).

"I thought to myself, 'I got to go for it here, I'm just going to challenge him,'" Cone remembers about the sequence. "We had enough of a lead that I could go after a guy. I was certainly going for the perfect game. I wasn't going to end it with a walk.

"I got the better part of the middle of the plate and he hit it up the middle. As soon as he hit that, I said, 'There it goes.'"

Vidro hit Cone's third pitch sharply, a hard ground ball through the box that had a chance to sneak through for the Expos' first hit. But Chuck Knoblauch sprinted to his right, caught the ball on the backhand, planted his feet, and fired to first to nail Vidro.

"When Chuck made that great play, I decided there was some kind of Yankee aura," Cone said on MSG. "Maybe this was my day."

"With that count, I moved a little to my left expecting him to maybe pull it, but he hit it up the middle," Knoblauch said afterward. "In that situation, I'm thinking of diving for it, but I was able to get to it on my feet. I think I was on the grass as I caught it. [I took an extra step to get set, because] in that situation, you don't want to have your feet slip from under you and I just planted and threw."

"After Knoblauch made that great play to throw out Vidro, we just said, he's going to do it," Cabrera remembers. "When he made that play, and he was having those throwing troubles, we knew we were in trouble ourselves. We just tried to keep swinging the bat, but we never did get that hit."

Knoblauch's throw was the key, of course, because the second baseman was in the midst of a horrible throwing slump that would cause him to be switched to left field only a season later. His sudden, Steve Sax–like inability to find first base from his relatively close-by position baffled him and everyone else. But he avoided becoming the goat in this game.

His later throwing problems rarely surfaced on tough plays or plays where he was moving, usually only on easy tosses off balls hit right at him. So maybe it was better for Cone that the second baseman had to cover a lot of ground to make the play. An at-em ball might have ended up six rows back.

"Whenever Chuck would move to his right, that was when you held your breath," says Kay. "But on that one, it was like everything was erased. All the problems he'd ever had throwing went away on that play. It was, well, it was perfect. It was almost weird."

Finally, on a day filled with more déjà vu than a convention of French spirit channelers, it was noted that Knoblauch had made his play on a tough ground ball with one out in the eighth, exactly the same situation in which he had aided David Wells 14 months earlier.

Spooky.

In the bottom of the eighth the Yankees had men on first and third with no outs when Chili Davis grounded into a run-scoring double play, extending the lead to 6–0, but, happily for Cone, shortening the game.

"I've never been happier to see a double play hit by one of our guys," he said, not wanting to sit on the bench any longer than he had to.

Yankee Stadium was a madhouse as Cone walked to the mound, his T-shirt fresh and history awaiting him.

One Yankee veteran actually felt a little sorry for the young opponents.

"The pressure is more on the Expos than him," mused Chili Davis afterward. "They're the ones having the game thrown against them. They've got to go up there and be a little selective and aggressive at the same time. It's a tough situation to be in."

But Cone felt the pressure, too, he admitted. "My heart was just about pounding through my uniform.

"I've wondered if I'd ever get a chance again [at a game like this]. Going into the later innings, that was running through my mind, about how many times I've been close and how this might be the last chance I get."

Widger led off the ninth and could just as well have stayed in the dugout. He looked at fastballs for strikes one and two and then waved feebly at strike three, an outside slider.

Pinch hitting for Shane Andrews was Ryan McGuire, a left-handed batter. He worked the count to 2–2, the fourth and final time an Expos hitter got two balls against Cone. On the fifth pitch, he dropped down and sliced a line drive toward left field.

As the drive headed toward Ledee, 41,000-plus sucked in their collective breath. Ledee was pretty worried, too.

"As we were talking during the game, by the sixth or seventh, I told them if they hit a ball at me it might be trouble because the sun was very bad," he says. "The sun's always bad in left during day games. It was an easy play that I made hard because I couldn't see it. Any other day, it's an easy line drive, but I didn't see it."

"Ledee bobbled it and he never saw the ball," remembers Michael Kay. "The ball was talked into his glove by Brosius, who told me later that he was yelling the whole time, 'Go to your right, go to your right, put the glove down.' And Ledee didn't know where it was until it hit the glove."

"He took a zigzag path to the ball," Cone says. "We were all worried. Somehow, miraculously, the ball found its way into the glove. I could see it snap back the way it looks when you catch the ball but don't see it."

"I was hoping that no one would hit the ball on a line," Ledee goes on to say. "And that's what happened. I knew when it was hit and I just ran in that direction. The third baseman was yelling. I knew the angle, but I never saw the ball. But all of a sudden, I saw it, it hit my glove, and I caught it."

What if he had missed it? It almost wouldn't matter. At that point, only perfection would have sufficed. Even if the official scorer had ruled a misplay an error, the perfect game would have been over the moment McGuire stood safely at first. The razor's edge that divides the perfect from the nearly perfect is always sharp and doesn't allow for "almost." But Cone and the Yankees stayed on the edge for one more batter, at least.

As soon as the ball was hit, "Zimmer said, 'It's caught,'" Torre said afterward. "I said, 'No, it isn't.' I'm glad he was right."

Two outs now, and the lattice of coincidence is nearly complete.

"I consider Cone a friend, I really like him, we have a lot of the same tastes," Sterling says. "So this bullshit about you're not supposed to root . . . well, if you think I wasn't rooting for David Cone to get a perfect game, you're crazy."

"When I came up, I thought, this is the biggest at-bat of my career," says Cabrera, whose math skills had proved better that day than his hitting talents. "If I break up this perfect game or the no-hitter, it would be awesome to do it in New York. Of course, I may not get out alive if I did. I went to hit, and I said to Girardi, 'This is it. Throw whatever you want. I'm up here to swing.'

"I could hear the crowd . . . they were going nuts. In the Bronx, there are a lot of Latino people screaming at me. I could hear stuff like, 'If you get a hit, you're not getting out of here alive,' and stuff like that. [Cabrera was too polite to list the Spanish curses hurled in his direction as well.] New York is one of the biggest intimidations in baseball with that crowd up there. I was trying not to pay attention, but I could hear them.

"If I'd gotten a hit, I would have needed bodyguards to get out of there."

Call off the bodyguards.

Cabrera took ball one, then strike one. Cone was in a complete zone, staring intently in toward Girardi, never looking around at the waving maelstrom surrounding him. He raised his arms above his head, turned, kicked, and threw.

It was a slider, swinging away from the right-handed-hitting Cabrera. The shortstop swung, and the ball flipped off the end of his bat. It was just what Cone needed, an easy pop-up. The ball drifted foul, and third baseman Brosius drifted down to meet it.

Brosius claims he felt no significant butterflies.

"No, not really. At that point, I was just telling myself there, if it's hit to me, make it an easy two-hopper. I don't want that nasty, short-hop, tough play. So it went up in the air, and I had a pretty good idea I was going to catch the pop-up. The funny part was, I was watching it again on the replay, because it was kind of hit between Girardi and me, and I'm thinking I want to make sure that we don't run into each other. So I'm just screaming for it, and then I looked later, and they're already hugging each other. They're nowhere near the play, and I'm on my own to catch it, so that kind of struck me as funny."

Yankee fans around the area heard Sterling's call.

"It's 1–1. Pitch. He popped him up. He's gonna get it. Brosius down from third. Brosius . . . makes the catch! Ballgame over! A perfect game! A perfect game for David Cone!"

Cone's reaction was the most dramatic, I think, of any perfect-game final outs that I've seen. It was almost balletic in its motions.

"I remember thinking," says Cone, "'He's going to catch it, now what do I do?'"

He pointed straight up, even though every eye in the place was on the ball (including Cabrera's, who jogged a few steps up the line toward first, then stopped to watch the drama). Then as the ball plopped into Brosius' glove, Cone put both hands on his head, and instead of leaping, as many victors do, he seemed to collapse under the weight of history and the amazing thing he had just accomplished. He fell to his knees, his glove and pitching hand covering his head as every eye in the place followed his fall to the ground.

Girardi sprinted out to the mound and stood next to Cone, waiting for a couple of beats for the pitcher to pull his head up, to come back from his private place of joy into the public arena of celebration. Cone looked up, finally, it seemed, beaming, and Girardi fell to his knees, too, and they joined in a massive hug. Then Girardi pulled Cone down on top of him.

"I have been under a lot of piles," said Girardi. "I didn't want him to be at the bottom."

"He was like my guardian angel under there," Cone laughs.

The pile roiled and rumbled and pounded, the music blared as it had for Wells just 14 months earlier, the fans cheered and screamed and wept, and the Yankee gods looked down and smiled.

Finally, Cone was raised up, he was carried, lifted, on the shoulders of Girardi, Knoblauch, Chili Davis, and Bernie Williams. His cap gone, the ball clutched in his right hand, his gloved left hand upraised, Cone shouted his joy, thrusting his arm up over and over again.

Even Red Sox fans were smiling.

The totals were simply awesome: 88 pitches, only 20 balls, first-pitch strikes to 20 batters, a two-ball count only three times. Stunning.

Cone, not surprisingly, knew he had pretty darned good stuff.

"That was my best slider of the year," he said amid the craziness of the clubhouse. "It was quick and hard, like I used to throw it. I had a good fastball, especially to left-handed hitters, but my out pitch was the sharp slider, which I haven't had in a while."

His backstop agreed.

"That's as good as Coney has ever been," said Girardi. "His slider was great and his fastball was great. We didn't use the curve or the forkball much. He didn't waste any pitches. He was ahead of everybody."

In the stands, one man knew better than anyone in the place what Cone was feeling.

"I was just thinking about my day," Larsen says he thought as he joined more than 41,000 delirious fans cheering their hero. "I'm sure David will think about this every day of his life."

He also knew how this would affect Cone.

"By doing this," he said, "people don't care about the mistakes you made. All they think about are the good things."

Also up in the stands, the 41,000-plus stood as they had for the entire ninth inning and filled the air with sound. Among them were many who probably acted as David Fischer did.

"When Cone got the final out, my father and I hugged for a long time," says Fischer. "This time around, I didn't feel if anybody was slapping me on the back as I did with Wells. I felt so emotional. Here I was with the guy who taught me the game, had a million catches with me, left work early to watch Little League games, took me to so many Yankee games, and now I had taken him to a game, and it was payback plus. I shared history with him on my dime.

"I had a tear in my eyes and made a joke to deflect the emotion. 'Dad, we've hugged and cried three times: my bar mitzvah, my wedding, and a perfect game. And each time it happened in a place of worship.'"

Another former Yankee who had stood in Cone's perfect shoes in that church of baseball had watched the last two innings in the clubhouse of his new team, the Toronto Blue Jays.

"I've got goose bumps larger than his right now," David Wells said. "He has been trying to get one of those. He had a lot of opportunities pass him by."

"I talked to Boomer and he welcomed me to the club," said a giddy Cone. "He said he wanted to fly down here and party with me all night."

Many in the stands, in the clubhouse, and elsewhere, reflected on the site of the game and its special place in baseball history.

"It was just one of those strange deals where you're just like, 'What else can happen here?'" says Scott Brosius. "There have been so many magical moments anyway here at Yankee Stadium, for it to happen on a day like that, it just makes you wonder, you know. It was a pretty cool deal. This is the one ballpark, and only ballpark, really, that I've ever been to, where you show up and you just kind of half expect something special to happen every day.

"And that day it did."

Another one of Cone's teammates also reached a special milestone, though typical of how he approaches the game, he made little of it in a later interview.

Paul O'Neill became the first player ever to play on the winning team in three perfect games. But he doesn't think much of the feat.

"The pitcher's the one doing it. It's not like as a player you're doing anything special other than taking your position. You feel lucky to be a part of it, but it's not like you're doing anything to contribute to it other than catching a fly ball once in a while. So it's a very personal achievement that a pitcher makes, a pitcher and a catcher, not really anybody out on the field."

Among the many things that stick out for Michael Kay was the evening of the game.

"I had tickets for Bruce Springsteen that night at the Meadowlands," he says. "First, there was the rain delay, so I knew I'd be later getting out there. Then as the game went on, I knew that if it was a perfect game, there would be more work, more interviews afterward. But I did all the interviews, then got to the Meadowlands on time. And as I walked through the parking lot, people were coming up to me like I'd pitched the perfect game. They'd been listening on the radio while they tailgated before the concert."

The effect on Cone was immediate and continuing.

"I asked him the next year," says Kay, "if he had to sell his soul to pitch that game and never be a good pitcher again, would he do it? He asked if it would have affected his team. I said no. And he said yes, I'd give it all up, except for my team's success, to pitch that game."

Cone's feat was the capper to his career. He suffered through a disastrous 2000 season and moved to the Red Sox in 2001, where, phoenixlike, he arose again from arm trouble to become a solid starter for the Red Sox before they imploded in August. But no matter what he had done before, or what he did afterward, Cone became the guy who pitched a perfect game. Cy Youngs were forgotten, World Series heroics downplayed, comebacks just a footnote to the story of July 18, 1999.

Cone's perfect game was the last of the 20th century. In it, the entire history of perfect games coalesced in one glorious, nostalgic, dramatic display of baseball's highest one-game individual and team feat.

Cone's game was interrupted by rain, as was Richmond's. Like Ward, Cone was for most of his career very active in the players' union. In 1994, Cone had won the Cy Young Award, named for the man who was perfect in 1904. As the leader of a team battling for another pennant, Addie Joss prefigured Cone, though, thankfully, Cone has already outpaced Joss in years. While there's not a good connection to Robertson, who is so much an anomaly, the parallels to Larsen are huge, of course.

Bunning was almost Cone's clone, a top-flight pitcher for many years, while Koufax had New York roots. Hunter, like Cone, starred elsewhere before joining the Yankees. Barker's game also featured rain, as did Browning's. Witt also was a Yankee later in his career, as was Kenny Rogers. And Cone, of course, shared in Wells' game. Randy Johnson's fireballing intimidation echoed Koufax's legendary speed, while completing a circle as a lefty reflecting Richmond 124 years earlier.

That connectivity through the years is what makes baseball so special. It's frankly just perfect that perfect games are like a series of stepping stones through history. Here's hoping you've enjoyed this trip, and here's hoping you're in the stands (or on the mound) for the next perfect game.

Johnson joined the ranks of perfection on May 18, 2004, and—at the age of 40—became the oldest member of the exclusive 17-member club. *Photo courtesy of AP/Wide World Photos.*

CHAPTER 17

Randy Johnson

May 18, 2004

The history of perfect games is dotted with numbers: 27 up, 27 down, 1904, 1956, and David Cone's numerologically correct 88 pitches. To this list, we can now add the number 40. That's how old Randy Johnson was on May 18, 2004, when he wrapped up the 17th perfect game in baseball history—and the first pitched by someone with four decades of life under his belt. Striking out 13, the second most ever in a perfect game, Johnson shut down the Atlanta Braves 2–0 and cemented his already solid place as one of the top left-handed pitchers the game has ever seen.

Want more numbers? Johnson has them in spades. Also in 2004, he became only the third pitcher with more than 4,000 strikeouts, finishing the season with 4,161 for his career, the most ever by a lefty. No pitcher ever, perfect game or not, has stood taller than the Big Unit's 6'10". His five Cy Young Awards, including four straight from 1999–2002, are the most behind

Roger Clemens. He has more 300-strikeout seasons (six) than any other pitcher in history (and just missed a seventh in 2004 with 290 Ks). He had three wins in the 2001 World Series, which helped him earn co-MVP honors with Curt Schilling.

And then came a sultry night in Georgia after which, said Arizona manager Bob Brenly, "Everything he's done up to this point pales in comparison." Added Arizona general manager Joe Garagiola Jr.: "Now there's nothing missing on Randy Johnson's résumé. Every box is now checked."

Some baseball experts thought Johnson had instead checked out after the 2003 season, when he pitched in only a handful of games because of two stints on the disabled list. The criticism continued as he started 2004 by taking an un-RJ-like 4–4 record into a May start against the Braves.

Of course, a "bad" beginning to a season for Johnson would be a career year for most pitchers. Though he had lost those four games heading into his perfecto, he led the league in Ks per inning with more than 11, and opponents were hitting a paltry .156 against him, the lowest mark in either league.

The Diamondbacks' first contract with Johnson, four years at $52.4 million, had paid off enormously for them as he led them to their first championship in 2001. His second contract, a two-year, $33-million job signed before 2003, was looking like a less-than-solid investment. But Johnson proved on that May night, and throughout the rest of 2004, that anyone who counted him out had counted too quickly.

It was hot and steamy in Atlanta the night that Johnson took the mound against the Braves. "With the humidity, you get loose pretty quick," Johnson said.

Not so the Braves, apparently. Only two nights earlier, the once-mighty Braves had watched Milwaukee's Ben Sheets whiff them 18 times, which made their futility against Johnson doubly frustrating. ESPN.com's Jayson Stark passed along this tidbit from Ken Hirdt of the Elias Sports Bureau: "This was the first time that a team had been struck out that many times and been no-hit in consecutive games . . . ever."

Atlanta's first batter, Jesse Garcia, tried to push a bunt toward first for a hit, but Arizona first baseman Shea Hillenbrand charged the ball and lunged to tag a headfirst-sliding Garcia for the first out. Sitting behind home plate, Gariagiola recalled that play later in the game, noting that, "Maybe the toughest play of the night was the first one of the game. Who knew then what would happen?"

Johnson then struck out six of the next nine batters. "I felt my velocity got better as the game progressed," Johnson said. "My slider was the best it's ever been, velocity wise. I threw a few split fingers; not many."

Perhaps the most crucial at-bat of the game came in the second inning, when Braves catcher Johnny Estrada, the only Atlanta player to see ball three all night (only seven others even got to ball two!), fouled off three straight 3–2 pitches before fanning. Estrada actually saw 22 pitches in three at-bats, nearly 20 percent of Johnson's total of 117 pitches.

Behind the plate, young catcher Robby Hammock was almost in awe. "Last year [2003] he had a one-hitter against the Rockies, gave up his one hit in the fifth. I remember his stuff that day was unbelievable. He was on. It was the same thing against the Braves. The first time through the order, no one put a good swing on the ball. They looked horrible. His speed and movement are always there, but his location was impeccable. After that long at-bat by Estrada, I just worried about his pitch count getting too high."

In the second inning, Johnson got all the offensive help he would need when Alex Cintron (who was all of 10 years old when Johnson made his MLB debut in 1988) doubled home Danny Bautista.

The third went quickly: a pop-out, a fly-out, and a K of opposing pitcher Mike Hampton. Johnson was through three innings unscathed. "I remember looking at my scorecard and noticing that lovely progression of three, three, three," Garagiola said.

Things just got nasty after that. Johnson simply had his way with the Braves, who could neither figure out the slider nor catch up with the fastball, which was timed in excess of 97 mph more than half a dozen times that night.

When Johnson is on his game, he is untouchable. His focus is dynamic, a living thing. Perhaps more so than his stunning left arm, his mental attitude has let him achieve his nearly unprecedented success. He was Nuke LaLoosh–wild as a young pitcher. Then, by the age of 40, he had evolved into more than a dominant fireballer; he had become a dominant pitcher, an even rarer breed.

As he wrote in his book for young pitchers, *Randy Johnson's Power Pitching*, "I've been able to dig deep within myself to produce an almost callous, stone-faced approach to my craft. This stern mentality has worked for me, but it isn't something that works for every pitcher. The point is that you must find something within yourself to motivate you and push you past your physical limits."

The Braves knew they had reached *their* limits, continuing to flail at Johnson's pitches like blind men threshing.

Garcia and Chipper Jones struck out in the fourth, sandwiching a Julio Franco fly-out to center.

Thom Brenneman was watching from above and calling the action for the fans back in Arizona: "Looking back now [several months later], the only word I can think of is *unbelievable*. As the game went on, it became obvious that something special was happening. In situations like these, you look at an inning with a couple of their guys hitting the ball hard, but right at someone. In the fifth, they all hit rockets. Then you say to yourself, that might have been their inning. Those were the only batters in the game who had shown any ability to put the bat on his ball that night."

One of those rockets was a line drive to right by Atlanta's J. D. Drew. Bautista roved toward the corner to snag the liner underhanded to end the inning. Not a "Web Gem" highlight, but a nice catch. "We hit the ball right at them," Drew said. "Things were falling into place for them."

As the mowing down continued, Brenly and the other Diamondbacks players and staff dove headlong into the superstition pool. "It wasn't foremost on my mind until after the sixth," Brenly said. "From that point on, everybody on the field, everybody in the dugout, was on pins and needles trying to make sure we sat in the same place, did the same things, and didn't do anything to disrupt the rhythm." For his part, Brenly stayed rooted to his seat on the bat rack in the dugout. Beginning in midgame, he tapped second baseman Matt Kata's bat with each Johnson windup.

"We all stuck with the superstitions, for sure," said outfielder Luis Gonzalez. "Went to the same place, talked to the same guys. Baseball players are so superstitious. We just pretend there's nothing going on, even when everyone does know what's going on."

Catcher Hammock had the sticky job of having to speak with Johnson between every inning. "We did our normal chatting between innings about the next hitters, like we always do. No mention of perfect game, of course."

The fever spread up to the press box, where team public relations director Mike Swanson was facing his own sort of struggle. "I remember the superstition aspect of it a lot. At some point, everyone started staying right where they were, not daring to move. From the third inning on, I had to go to the bathroom, but there was no way that was going to happen. Their PR guy came up to me in the eighth and asked if I needed any help. But there was no way I was going down there early, no way I was going to leave my seat. If I went down there and he gave up a hit, they'd blame me."

For his part, Brenneman was throwing caution to the airwaves, so to speak, much as other broadcasters we've spoken to for this book have done. "No, I don't follow the jinx," he said. "I talked to my father [longtime Reds' announcer Marty Brenneman] about that and to Vin Scully years ago. They both made the point: you broadcast for the fans, not for the players or the team or the manager. If a person turns on a game, on radio or TV, for five minutes or three hours, you owe it to them to tell them what's going on."

Marty and Thom Brenneman became, of course, the first father-son duo to each broadcast a perfect game. Thanks to Johnson in 2004 and the Diamondbacks in 2001, they also matched up on calling 4,000-strikeout games and World Series championships at home.

Superstitions or no, Johnson and Hammock were playing the same tune all night. "The job Robby did back there was amazing," Johnson said. "I shook him off two or three times.

That was in the eighth and ninth. It's nice when you're on the same page as your catcher." It's also nice when you wrote the book; Hammock called the shakeoffs "more like stareoffs."

With two outs in the Braves' sixth, Cintron turned in what was perhaps the only great defensive play of the game. Hampton, batting left-handed, topped a ball that bounced past the mound. Cintron raced in and made a bare-handed throw and catch that just nipped Hampton, who had gotten out of the box very quickly.

Johnson smacked Cintron on the back as he ran by in thanks for the nice glove work. But Cintron did not realize exactly what he had done. "After I made that play in the sixth, I looked at the scoreboard and saw that I had helped preserve the no-hitter. But I didn't know it was a perfect game until afterward."

The young shortstop then doubled in the seventh and scored the game's second run on a single by Chad Tracy, who was feeling a little extra pressure himself as he came up to bat, thanks to a loud Atlanta fan. "I didn't realize he had the perfect game going until the top of the seventh," Tracy said. "I heard someone in the stands say something about perfect game. I usually don't hear people, but I did hear that. I looked up there and saw what was going on."

Veteran baseball man Garagiola was worried as much about the win as about the perfect game. "We were up by two runs, and then in the eighth, we had runners on and didn't drive them in. I remember thinking that that's got a chance to be a big run. The way we were doing that year, *seven* runs wasn't a good number, let alone two. I mean, how often have you seen, in a no-hitter situation, that first hit gets in and then in the blink of an eye, it's 3–2." The way Johnson was pitching, though, he needn't have worried.

Garagiola was not the only one among the 23,281 people at Turner Field that night who realized what was happening. "When the Braves went out in the seventh," he remembered, "it was like the whole stadium collectively had the same thought. 'You know, we've seen the Braves win a lot, but we haven't seen a perfect game.' So when he went out in the eighth, the crowd had switched around totally. That was probably uncomfortable for the Braves, but it was just really the neatest thing to see the crowd recognize a historic moment."

For their part, the Diamondbacks were well clued in, too, and knew that they had a big part to play behind their Big Unit. "In the eighth and ninth, I started thinking, I gotta make a play," said Cintron. "You knew that you had to risk everything to make a play," said Tracy.

"Whatever you have in the tank, you've got to give him. No mental lapses, no mental mistakes. I wasn't taking any chance on playing back [at third]."

And it wasn't just infielders. On the wide green grass of Turner Field's outfield, three Arizona players were trying to think like one. "We kept in communication a lot in the outfield, more intensely than we might normally do it," remembered Gonzalez. "We made sure we were all on the same page. He wasn't going to pull anybody to me [in left], the way he was throwing. And a fastball was going to center or right. A slicing liner might go to me, though, from one of their lefties. I was also thinking, 'If you hit it to me, make it one I can make a play on.' If you're going to be a part of it, you want to be a good part!"

In the eighth, Johnson got Andruw Jones to send one of those fastballs to center. Estrada struck out again, and Drew grounded weakly to second.

Three outs to go.

"You could see it in Randy's eyes that he was going to get it," said Tracy. "We had no doubt he was going to get it. When he gets like that, he's untouchable."

The Braves had realized this some time ago. "A lot of guys came back to the dugout shaking their heads," Chipper Jones said in the quiet losers' clubhouse. "It was a situation where a dominant pitcher caught a struggling team."

The ninth was played amid as much noise as twenty-three-thousand-plus could muster. Mark DeRosa led off and grounded easily to second. Young second baseman Nick Green made it an even dozen strikeouts. Eddie Perez, pinch hitting for Mike Hampton, who had allowed only two runs on eight hits for his best performance of a disappointing season, thought he might have a chance to break things up. After all, Atlanta's backup catcher had six hits against Johnson in 13 career at-bats, including a homer and a pair of doubles.

That night, however, he didn't have a prayer. Johnson started him off with a strike, the 17th time in the game he had started out that way on a hitter. Then it was quickly 0–2.

And here's another dazzling number: the final pitch Johnson threw that night zoomed by a swinging Perez at 98 mph. Literally moving faster than any other pitcher in history, he rocketed onto the short list of perfect-game pitchers.

Hammock sprang from his crouch, the ball locked in his glove. He bounced up and down about five times between home and the mound. Says Hammock: "Every once in a while, I'll see highlights of me jumping around after the game, and I think, 'I look like an idiot.'" Reaching the star of the night, the youngster quickly whipped off his mask and helmet so he wouldn't bruise Johnson's chest, because that's about how high he reached on his towering pitcher. "I remember he was laughing at all my jumping around," Hammock said. "I took off my helmet and was just saying, 'You were perfect, tonight, perfect!' But it quickly turned into, 'Don't dog pile, don't hurt him, be careful!'"

The rest of the infield joined them. Said Gonzalez, "We had the longest run . . . the celebration was almost over by the time we got in from the outfield!")

Johnson, for his part, pointed his glove at the sky, as he does after all wins, a gesture that speaks to his continuing relationship with the beloved memory of his father, Bud. He then was surrounded by the Diamondbacks, a tower of power looking down on a party.

The fans were into it at the end, too. The cheering that had started in the seventh and eighth innings reached its loudest at the conclusion of the game. As the Diamondbacks bounced around the infield looking like Little Leaguers surrounding a grown-up coach, the Turner Field crowd chanted, "Randy! Randy! Randy!"

The celebration quickly moved from the field to the D-backs' clubhouse. Champagne magically appeared. "I walked into the clubhouse and saw Randy getting hugs, with a big ol' grin on his face," said Mike Swanson. "Randy was pouring champagne into Gatorade cups for everyone. And then they all had the champagne and they did a toast to him."

After enjoying many more congratulations and getting his shoulder wrapped in ice, Johnson moved to a crowded room down the tunnel, where the media had assembled to meet the hero of the night. In keeping with his generally low-key personality, Johnson was almost laid back at the news conference, deflecting his feat slightly, and calling the win for the team the big news.

"Obviously I knew what was going on," he said. "I've been in that situation before and I knew. That's a lesson for young pitchers. Don't lose your focus. . . . On days when I pitch, I'm very focused. It's me and the catcher and I know what I want to do. This was special."

He also noted that he was especially happy for Hammock: "He was probably the most excited one out there." Hammock was excited again later in the season when the future Hall of Fame pitcher presented his young catcher with a one-of-a-kind keepsake of the historic night: a beautiful silver Rolex watch. On the back is inscribed: Perfect Game 5-18-04 From RJ. "That's easily the greatest thing anyone has ever given me," said the still-awed catcher.

Johnson was not the only one, of course, to realize how special the game was. "After the game I realized I had helped with both runs. I realized I'd have a place in history," said Cintron months later. "Plus the play I made, that was really exciting. That was something we might never see again. That was something I'll remember the rest of my life. No matter what happens in my career, I'll always have that memory."

The best line of the night came from the Braves' usher working the section where Garagiola was sitting. "We finally started to make our way to the clubhouse. And this guy says, in all seriousness, with no trace of irony, says, 'Well, we'll do better tomorrow night.' I said, 'Well, I like your chances.'"

Veteran baseball man Bob Brenly was nearly giddy after the game. He said, "This is one of those nights when a superior athlete was at the top of his game. There was a tremendous rhythm out there. His focus, his concentration, his stuff— everything was as good as it could possibly be."

Believe it or not, a few nights later, Johnson actually disagreed with Brenly's assessment. Before his next start at Florida, Johnson told reporters, "I don't feel my stuff against the Braves was better than certain games I've pitched over the past five years with the Diamondbacks. I've felt I've had better stuff before."

Chipper Jones, a three-time strikeout victim that perfect night, would probably argue that point. "He's gotten better with age," said Jones after the game. "He's starting to use the outside part of the plate and has added a pitch over the last year or two."

That ability to continue to improve can be traced to Johnson's phenomenal workout routine and his God's gift of a left arm. "A lot of people said, 'He's not going to be the pitcher he was,'" Johnson told the *New York Daily News*. "Anybody that knows me knows I'll give everything I can to be the pitcher I've always been." As Johnson wrote in his book, "Regardless of what I have achieved, all the records and the awards, until my final hour as a baseball player I will continue to work to get better at what I do."

Still, the age at which Johnson pitched his perfect game will remain as the most remarkable part of his feat until someone tops it (as if!). Heck, he knocked Cy Young out of the top spot in that category. Even David Letterman brought it up. The night after his perfecto, Johnson was asked by the late-night show to read the Top 10 Best Things about Pitching a Perfect Game. Number 8 was, "Shows everyone that even though I'm 40, I can still . . . I'm sorry, I lost my train of thought."

Unfortunately, by the time the season had ended, the entire Diamondbacks train had come off the tracks completely. Brenly was gone by early July, and the team's major league–worst final winning percentage of .315 was the lowest in history by a team that included a perfect game among its meager win total. It had been .310 back on May 17, 2004, also an all-time low by a team at the time it won a perfect game.

Though Johnson led the National League in strikeouts (290), and opponents' batting average (.197), and was second in ERA and innings pitched (2.60, 245.2), he finished only 16–14 (though that was more than 30 percent of Arizona's 51 victories!). During one especially painful stretch in August, the Unit went three straight starts allowing four or fewer hits and striking out 14, 11, and 15, respectively. And yes, you guessed it: the punchless Diamondbacks lost all three.

In the game prior to his perfect game, Johnson allowed only a leadoff homer to Kaz Matsui, but lost the game 1–0 to Tom Glavine and the Mets. Combine the rest of that game with Johnson's perfect one and he allowed only two base runners in a stretch of 47 batters. No wonder Garagiola was worried back in the seventh.

May 18, 2004, was simply unforgettable. At an age when most of us are happy not to creak when we bend over, Randy Johnson reached the pinnacle of success in his chosen field. A career that, at one point, was headed for trivia-answer status had wound up on the sure and certain road to the Hall of Fame. He was 40 years old. The Braves and the National League all hope he can't do it again when he's 50. Frankly, I wouldn't put it past him.

After the historic game, Johnson joined many of his teammates in the Ritz-Carlton bar in Atlanta late that night. The big man was buying and laughing it up with kids who were in T-ball when he was first firing BBs. "You guys keep saying I'm old," he had told reporters earlier that evening. "And someday I will be." But not tonight, baby. Not tonight.

Randy Johnson's Perfect Night

- The 14 years (and 219 wins) between Johnson's two no-hitters (his first was with Seattle in 1990) were the most ever.

- The feat made him the fifth pitcher to throw a no-hitter in each league, joining Cy Young, Jim Bunning, Hideo Nomo, and Nolan Ryan.

- Jayson Stark of ESPN.com noted that only Johnson and Cy Young have thrown a perfect game "more than 200 wins deep into" a career. It was win number 234 for Johnson; it was Young's 381st.

- Getting better with age? From the day he turned 40 through the game against Atlanta, Johnson started 12 games. Among them were a one-hitter, a two-hitter, and the perfect game.

- Johnson threw the first no-hitter in the history of two different franchises: Seattle in 1990 and Arizona in 2004.

- His was the first perfect game thrown on a Tuesday and was the first of the 21st century, exactly 100 years and 13 days after Cy Young's was the first of the 20th.

In the gloom of a Milwaukee evening, Pittsburgh's Harvey Haddix fires in another pitch on his way to retiring 36 consecutive batters— and later losing the game. *Photo courtesy of AP/Wide World Photos.*

APPENDIX
Nearly Perfect
by David Fischer

For of all sad words of tongue or pen,
The saddest are these: "It might have been."

—JOHN GREENLEAF WHITTIER, AMERICAN POET 1807–1892

This chapter is about exactly the situation we started off
with: a seemingly perfect day "broken up" by one tiny detail.
You've just read about the 17 instances of pitchers stepping
carefully along the razor's edge with nary a nick or cut, but
there are dozens more instances of pitchers who slipped off,
either early in their walk along that edge or just as they
reached the far end. The agony of that one final misstep is
simply magnified by the difference between those who have
completed it and those who have not. You don't get your picture on the front page, the key to the city, a place in the
record books, or a chapter in this book for just coming close.
Nearly perfect isn't good enough. And that's a hard thing to
have to say, but that's how it is.

The razor-thin margin between perfection and just another great outing also seems to shrink smaller and smaller as you look at these instances of pitchers who came within one batter of perfection. Some of them are more heartbreaking than others; some are bizarre (see Hooks Wiltse!). Their names come up only when yet another unlucky soul joins the fraternity of Almost Gotta Zero. And then they disappear once again into the mists while those perfect boys remain above, secure in their antiseptic ring of zeros.

Thanks to that most harsh dividing line between perfect heaven and nearly perfect purgatory, there is now an almost giddy, desperate search for perfection that pervades any broadcast of a game in which a pitcher gets through the lineup a bunch of times with seeming ease. Fans watching at home and in the park, broadcasters looking to anchor their careers, even pitchers wanting to cement their reputations, all start to wonder, "Will this be the day?" as a hurler cruises untouched through five.

It happened again in 2001, and if not for Carl Everett, the Yankees would have added their fourth perfecto to the list, thanks to the pinpoint control of Mike Mussina.

"Moose" mowed down Red Sox with little fanfare, and in fact, with little help. He struck out 8 of the first 13 Boston batters. After five innings, ESPN wasted no time in calling attention to Mussina's perfection, noting that he led the American League at the time by having retired the side in order 78 times that season. (Who keeps track of this stuff?!)

On TV entering the seventh, commentator Joe Morgan noted that the spin on Mussina's breaking pitch was "so tight that hitters couldn't pick up the rotation."

Mussina was through seven with no trouble, but the Yankees still hadn't bothered Cone. In the eighth, Mussina went to 3–2 on Manny Ramirez, only the second 3-ball count of the night, but Manny popped to Derek Jeter. As that happened, the graphic came up noting that Mussina had twice finished the eighth inning with no-hitters, including eight and one-third perfect innings in 1997. Dante Bichette flew to Williams, and Brian Daubach looked at strike three.

Jon Miller and Joe Morgan on TV knew what was up and had no problem talking about perfection. Obviously, they weren't alone.

"I thought about it every inning," Mussina told ESPN.

He thought about something else, too.

"It actually flashed through my mind that I'm going to go nine innings and we're not going to score and I'm going to get one of those asterisk jobs somewhere, because we'd play 11 innings or something."

Of course, at this point, Babe Ruth made an appearance, thus dooming the Sox to another disappointment. Tino Martinez singled to center, and Jorge Posada popped out. Then Paul O'Neill hit a routine 4-6-3 to Lou Merloni, who turned it ineptly into an E-4. That noise he heard was not the fans yelling "Looooo." In a bit of foreshadowing, Clay Bellinger ran for Martinez at third. He then scored the first run of the game when Enrique Wilson drove a double that kissed the right-field line. Cone (who, *The New York Times* noted, once had the Yankee Stadium locker that was now Mussina's) was taken out to a tremendous cheer, and Derek Lowe got Chuck Knoblauch to ground out (though Hillenbrand's throw pulled Daubach off the bag, but he made the tag).

Now Mussina had his chance. He had a run, but did he have the stuff? The camera followed him as he gathered his gear and mounted the steps. Not one Yankee even glanced in his direction as they milled about, gathering gloves and caps. During a commercial break, Dan Patrick previewed *SportsCenter*, saying that they'd have highlights of the (and here he mouthed, rather than spoke the words) *perfect game*. Superstition lives . . .

With Fenway's fans oddly quiet (what did you expect, a standing O for a Yankee?), Troy O'Leary went to 2–1 and then drove a hard grounder that seemed ticketed for right field. But pinch-runner-turned-first-baseman Clay Bellinger dove full-out to his right, snared the ball, and got it to Mussina for the out.

"After Clay made that play," Mussina said afterward, "I thought that this might be the time that it happens." (See Brian Holman, later, for similar thoughts.)

Second baseman/goat Lou Merloni came up and became Mussina's 13th strikeout victim with little trouble. Now Mussina was just one batter away, but that batter was Carl Everett, pinch hitting. Bing, bing, it was 0–2. Now Mussina was in very rare territory, one strike away. Along with the guys who made it through the wall of perfection, only five other players have gotten this far.

Everett took a ball high.

"You never think it's going to happen," manager Joe Torre said later, "until there are two out and two strikes. Then you feel like he's going to get it."

On the next pitch, Mussina left the ball a bit high and Everett swung. The ball flew on a looping line into left-center field and landed safely. Base hit. Clean, no chance for a play. Perfect game over. Trot Nixon grounded out to follow and the game was over, too.

"I guess I'll be second-guessing that pitch until I retire," Mussina told ESPN afterward. "And yeah, I was disappointed. That's the second time I've been to the ninth, and I didn't get it either time. So it's probably not meant to be.

"Hey, Mike Mussina," said Harvey Haddix, "come on down!"

Although Mussina's is the most recent in this string of near-perfection, Harvey Haddix will remain the captain of the Almost team. On May 26, 1959, Haddix, of the Pittsburgh Pirates, retired the first 36 Milwaukee Braves batters in a row. That's right . . . 36. Twelve innings. A game plus three.

But even that wasn't enough for him to pitch a perfect game, for the simple reason that his team couldn't score a run.

Haddix's unprecedented string of consecutive outs is a feat that ranks with the most unassailable in baseball. Yet nowhere in the official record book does Haddix receive credit for 12 innings of perfect pitching. In 1991, an eight-man committee on statistical accuracy voted unanimously to define an official perfect game as a game of nine innings or more that ends with no batter reaching first base. Because Haddix and the Pirates eventually lost the game, 1–0, in 13 innings, Haddix's otherworldly performance was deleted from the list of perfect games.

"In the long run," a philosophical Haddix said before his death in 1994, "I got more notoriety for losing the game in thirteen innings than if I'd have won it in nine."

So the greatest game ever pitched is no longer a perfect game. But it was still a hell of a game.

During a pregame meeting, Haddix and his catcher, Smoky Burgess, were reviewing the scouting reports and planning their pitching patterns against the powerful Milwaukee batters. The Braves, who were coming off back-to-back World Series appearances, boasted a potent lineup featuring the future Hall of Fame sluggers Henry Aaron and Eddie Mathews. Pittsburgh third baseman Don Hoak, who was eavesdropping on the strategy session, said to Haddix, "Harv, if you pitch like that, you'll throw a no-hitter."

As Haddix warmed up for the game in Milwaukee against Lew Burdette and the Braves, he was not throwing particularly hard, his breaking ball was not especially sharp, his control was not exactly pinpoint. But once the game started, Haddix just got outs. Lots of them. The Braves were swinging early in the count and returned to the bench quickly; Haddix went to three balls on just one batter. When he set the Braves down in order in the seventh, it was apparent that this was more than a no-hitter. But while Haddix was flawless, Burdette pitched just well enough, holding the Pirates scoreless, too.

Though rain was falling throughout the evening at Milwaukee's Country Stadium (hello J. Lee Richmond, Len Barker, Tom Browning, David Cone . . .), foul weather could not dampen Haddix's masterful form. By the end of the eighth inning he had retired 24 in a row. Three outs to go for a perfect game, but the Pirates still weren't helping out much, either.

Haddix, bearing down for the ninth inning, struck out two of the three men to face him. The crowd of 19,194 was screaming with every pitch. When Haddix fanned Burdette for the third out in the last of the ninth, he had done something no National League pitcher had accomplished in 79 years—retire the first 27 batters of a game. As Haddix accepted congratulations from teammates, he knew his night's work was far from over.

The scoreless game entered extra innings, and Haddix retired the Braves in order in the tenth. He got them 1-2-3 in the eleventh. And he did it again in the twelfth. But the Pittsburgh batters repeatedly failed to deliver the key hit with runners in scoring position. Pirates standouts Roberto Clemente and Dick Groat were given the night off by manager Danny Murtaugh, and for reasons Haddix never did understand, neither player got into the game as a pinch-hitter.

"I don't know why Clemente and Groat were out of the lineup," Haddix said. "When you consider we had 12 hits and couldn't score a run, Groat and Clemente might have made the difference."

Superstitious people view the number 13 as unlucky, and in the bottom of the thirteenth inning, the Haddix fortunes changed. He got two strikes on leadoff batter Felix Mantilla, then threw what he thought was strike three. The umpire disagreed. On the next pitch, Mantilla slapped a routine grounder to the third baseman. Hoak fielded the ball cleanly but threw a short-hopper in the dirt that first baseman Rocky Nelson was unable to handle. Hoak's throwing error ended the perfect game.

"I'll never forget that play," said Haddix. "Hoak had all night. He picked up the ball, looked at the seams—then threw it away."

Haddix's hypnotic pitching spell had ended, but the feat remains legendary today, in an era when pitching a complete game, much less 12 perfect innings, is almost unheard of.

Ironically, Hoak's pregame prediction held true, for Haddix still had a no-hitter intact. "I wasn't concerned about perfect games and no-hitters. I just wanted to win," said Haddix. With runs tough to come by, the next batter, Mathews, sacrificed

Mantilla to second base, and then Aaron was intentionally walked to set up the double play. On deck was Joe Adcock, who was 0-for-4 with two strikeouts. Haddix had handled him easily with inside sliders. This time, however, Haddix made the mistake that would haunt him forever. He left a slider too high in the zone, and Adcock smashed the ball over the wall in right-center field for a home run. The no-hitter was gone, the shutout was gone, the victory was gone, all with one swing of the bat.

But a bizarre coda simply added to this game's place in history.

As Adcock went into his home-run trot, Mantilla touched the plate with the winning run. Aaron, assuming the game was over, then headed across the diamond to celebrate the improbable victory with his teammates. The umpires ruled that Adcock was out for passing Aaron between second base and third. Mantilla's run was the only one that counted and Adcock's home run was changed to a run-scoring double. The official score of the game is 1–0, but to Haddix, the score is unimportant. "It didn't matter to me whether it was 1–0 or 100–0," he said. "We lost the game, and that's what hurt me most."

Following the game, Burdette joked that he would seek a raise because the greatest-pitched game in baseball history wasn't good enough to beat him.

"Obviously, I had no right to win that game," said Burdette. "But that's baseball for you." Indeed, had the Pirates been able to push one runner across home plate in regulation, Haddix would have hurled and won a perfect game. And he would have retired just 27 consecutive batters instead of 36 in a row. What poor Harvey Haddix needed was a run.

One lousy run is also all that stood between Pedro Martinez and a perfect game on June 3, 1995, when the 23-year-old right-hander, then with the Montreal Expos, became the second pitcher to take a perfecto into extra innings. Like Haddix, Martinez is not included among the list of perfect-game pitchers. Yet anyone who was there at San Diego's Jack Murphy Stadium saw a performance that was one for the books. Martinez stifled the Padres with a performance that foreshadowed his later domination of the American League with Boston.

Of the first twenty-seven outs, nine came on strikeouts, eight on fly balls to the outfield, two on line drives caught in the infield, four on ground balls, and four on infield pop-ups. After nine scoreless innings, the Expos broke through for a 1–0 lead in the top of the tenth, giving Martinez a chance for the first extra-inning perfect game in baseball history.

Unfortunately, the 28th batter spoiled the fairy-tale ending. Bip Roberts broke up perfection leading off the bottom of the tenth with a line-drive double that landed just inside the right-field foul line. The hit came on a 1–1 changeup that was Martinez's 96th pitch of the game. Three outs later, Martinez had a 1–0 victory, but under the amended rule, he receives no credit for a perfect game or a no-hitter. Joe Kerrigan, who was then the Montreal pitching coach and was later Martinez's coach and manager in Boston, was opposed to the amended rule on perfect games.

"For Pedro not to get credit for a perfect game is a shame," he told *Sports Illustrated*. "This belongs in the annals of baseball. You can't pass this off as just another game, but that's how it will go down—as just another game."

For all that he didn't get right in Boston in his early, unpleasant days as manager, Kerrigan got that right: even the great Pedro is only nearly perfect.

To be sure, baseball fans appreciate great pitching performances for the remarkable achievements they are. It doesn't matter where they rank in the record book. On June 23, 1917, the Red Sox hosted the Senators at Fenway Park. Boston's starting pitcher Babe Ruth walked Washington leadoff batter Ray Morgan on four pitches, complaining bitterly to plate umpire Brick Owens after each pitch. When Ruth approached the umpire after ball four and then punched Owens in the jaw, Ruth was booted from the game. Ernie Shore rushed in from the bullpen and took eight warm-up tosses. On his first pitch, Morgan attempted to steal second and was thrown out. Shore retired the next 26 batters in a row with machinelike consistency and was credited with a perfect game. Seventy-four years later, the amended rule robbed the hard-luck Shore of his perfecto.

The amended rule is appropriate and necessary, for official guidelines protect the sanctity of a perfect game. In 1919, Boston's Waite Hoyt pitched 11⅓ perfect innings against the New York Yankees. The 19-year-old right-hander gave up three hits in the second inning but didn't allow another base runner until surrendering a hit in the thirteenth inning. Hoyt's single-game mark of 34 consecutive outs ranks second to Haddix's record of 36, yet it pales in comparison to Haddix's achievement because Hoyt never had to pitch under the mounting pressure of a perfect game in progress.

"Baseball can be a strange game," said Dave Stieb, who seemed particularly jinxed during his 16-year major league career, losing three no-hit bids with two outs in the ninth inning, including one near-perfect game (see page 292–93). "Sometimes, it's easier to pitch when you give up an early hit. It takes the pressure off the whole team and lets you concentrate on what's really important—winning the game."

Winning, however, is anticlimactic when the result is heartbreak and disappointment. No pitcher had immortality snatched away as tragically as Hooks Wiltse, a left-hander who won 139 games for the New York Giants between 1904 and 1914. Wiltse's most successful season was in 1908, when he won 23 games with seven shutouts. The southpaw's best performance that year was a no-hitter he pitched against the Philadelphia Phillies on July 4 in the first game of a double-header. Wiltse won the game, 1–0, in 10 innings, but it could have been a perfect game. In fact, it should have been.

With two outs in the bottom of the ninth, Wiltse was facing the opposing pitcher, George McQuillan, and with a two-strike count . . . Wiltse hit him! He hit the opposing pitcher with a pitch, reportedly a curveball. That just boggles the mind. Sure, pitchers hit back then, and some of them weren't too bad. But my gosh, hit a guy with a perfect game on the line? Sure, it wasn't called that then, but everyone knew the rarity of the "no-hit, no-run, no-man-reaches-base" game.

It was the only time a pitcher lost a perfect game by hitting the final batter. In 1960, Lew Burdette pitched a no-hitter and missed perfection because he also hit a batter, but his only base runner came in the fifth inning, not the ninth. The difference is palpable. In the later innings of a perfect game, spectators grow progressively more fidgety with each pitch, edging forward in their seats, as the seemingly unperturbed pitcher tries to hold the burden of accumulated tension upon his shoulders. Wiltse and Burdette each faced 28 batters en route to a no-hitter. In the box score, each pitched a similar game. But by taking a perfect game into the ninth inning, the pressure on Wiltse's psyche weighed more heavily as he attempted to achieve the impossible.

———————

Nothing is more bittersweet than a pitcher having to settle for a no-hitter. Imagine having a game that pitchers dream about, only to be pinched by the 27th batter.

"The controversy surrounding my no-hitter still lives today," says Milt Pappas, who won 209 games during his 17-year career. On September 2, 1972, Pappas was working on a perfect game with one out to go against the last-place San Diego Padres. It was a dreary day at Chicago's Wrigley Field, and the last man up to face the Cubs right-hander was a left-handed pinch-hitter, Larry Stahl. With a 1–2 count, umpire Bruce Froemming called the next two pitches balls.

"Those pitches were on the outside corner," says Pappas, an outstanding control pitcher who that season led the major leagues in fewest walks per nine innings. "Froemming could call either pitch a strike and nobody argues. Those pitches were a heck of a lot closer than the last pitch of Don Larsen's perfect game."

Pappas once asked Stahl how he could possibly take such close pitches with two strikes. According to Pappas, Stahl said he had decided to keep the bat on his shoulder and let fate decide. "He stops swinging after the 1–2 pitch and never tips me off," says an incredulous Pappas. "I could've grooved a strike, right down the middle, but he never gave me a sign."

It all came down to a nerve-racking 3–2 pitch. This was the first time Pappas had gone to a 3-ball count since the first inning. He had to get this delivery over the plate. Catcher Randy Hundley called for a fastball, and the pitch apparently cut the corner of the plate, depending on who is telling the story. Hundley framed it, but the umpire never lifted his arm. Ball four. The perfect game vanished into history. Pappas retired the next batter to preserve the no-hitter and an 8–0 victory, but sorry, Milt, you don't get a dinner.

The next day, Pappas confronted Froemming. According to Pappas, Froemming insisted that the perfect game never entered his mind.

"He's an arrogant umpire," says Pappas of Froemming. "I asked why he couldn't sympathize with a perfect game and call a strike. I said, 'You could have been famous as one of a handful of umps who ever called a perfect game.' He said, 'Oh yeah? Who are the others?'"

Pappas won't soon forgive Froemming. "He's not on my Christmas card list," says Pappas, 62, who now works for a Chicago-area building supply company.

While Pappas may hold a particular grudge against the home-plate umpire, Dick Bosman of the Cleveland Indians has nobody but himself to blame. Bosman kept the world champion Oakland Athletics in check with a no-hitter on July 19, 1974, but was denied perfection by his own throwing error in the fourth inning. Sal Bando hit a chopper back to the box and Bosman threw wildly to first. "It's a play I make a hundred times," said Bosman. "But that time I didn't."

Next to a perfect game, a near-perfect game—coming within one pitch of perfection only to be burned by the last batter—is a rare pitching feat, even tougher to pitch than a no-hitter.

"I'd rather not be so rare," says Billy Pierce with a laugh.

Pierce won 211 games, mostly for the White Sox, during a solid 18-year career. On June 27, 1958, the 5'10", 160-pound left-hander beat the Washington Senators, 3–0, at Comiskey Park in Chicago. Pierce retired 26 batters in a row, and just missed a perfect game when Senators pinch-hitter Ed Fitz Gerald doubled with two outs in the ninth inning. Although a close friend was in the ballpark that night, Pierce has no keepsake from his memorable game.

"A buddy was keeping score," says Pierce, 74, retired and living in a suburb outside Chicago, "but after I gave up the hit he threw away the scoresheet. Souvenirs weren't a big deal back then."

Fitz Gerald, who was pinch hitting for the pitcher Russ Kemmerer, was a first-ball, fastball hitter, according to Pierce, so catcher Sherm Lollar called for a curveball, low and away.

"Fitz Gerald flicked his bat out, and that was that," says Pierce. The soft line drive into right field landed inches inside the foul line. "It wasn't hit well," says Pierce, "just well enough."

Pierce fanned Albie Pearson to end the game, and then he refused to second-guess himself. "I threw the pitch I wanted to, where I wanted it," says Pierce.

Another near-perfect pitcher, Milt Wilcox of the Detroit Tigers, is still second-guessing a pitch he threw on April 15,

1983. Wilcox was pitching superbly and leading 4–0 over the Chicago White Sox at Comiskey Park. He was one out away from a perfect game when Chicago's Jerry Hairston hit a clean single through the box with two down in the ninth inning.

"It was the worst pitch I made all night," said Wilcox, who doubled over in disappointment on the mound after Hairston broke the no-hit spell. "Pitch a perfect game and you go in the Hall of Fame. That's the only way I'd go there," said Wilcox, who compiled a 119–113 record from 1970 to 1986. "You've got to be lucky or good to get as close to a perfect game as I did, and I was both," Wilcox told *Sport Illustrated*'s Jerry Green. "I was able to put the ball where I wanted. You wonder why you can't do it all the time. I was throwing the ball and it seemed like something was taking control of me. It was as if I was sitting there and watching the game."

The near-freezing game-time temperature certainly contributed to Wilcox's numbing display of consistency. He ducked into the clubhouse between innings to keep warm and heard the radio announcer repeatedly refer to the perfect game. Hairston, according to *The Baseball Research Journal*, was also keeping warm in the dugout in the ninth inning when the phone rang. It was the radio announcer, who was calling to invite as a guest on the postgame show the player who might spoil the perfect game.

"Tell him I'll be there," said Hairston, grabbing a bat to pinch hit for shortstop Jerry Dybzinski. "I'm going to jump on the first pitch."

It was a fastball, and Hairston drilled it past Wilcox for a single.

"It would have been embarrassing to have a perfect game pitched against us," Hairston told *The Sporting News*. "It would be like someone taking off your clothes in front of a thousand people."

Pitchers who come close to perfect games are destined to share the stage of history with their antagonists. Tommy Bridges, a 5'10", 155-pound right-hander who won 194 games for the Detroit Tigers from 1930 to 1946, had everything going his way on August 5, 1932, against the Washington Senators. He had set down 26 batters in a row, striking out 7, inducing 14 ground-ball outs, and allowing only five balls to be hit out of the infield. Bridges also had an advantage of being able to concentrate solely on the perfect game because the Tigers had a commanding 13–0 lead. Despite the lopsided score, Washington manager Walter Johnson, who knew a thing or two about pitching himself, refused to be a spectator to history. To bat for the pitcher Bobby Burke, who had thrown a no-hitter of his own the previous August, the Senators' skipper sent up Dave Harris, a part-time outfielder who was one of the best pinch-hitters in the league. When Harris appeared in the on-deck circle at Detroit's Navin Field, the Tiger fans began to hoot and holler, incensed that Johnson was still maneuvering at the end of a hopelessly lost game. Bridges would've been better served by the partisan crowd had they been cheering for him—their hometown man—rather than booing the opposing team's strategy. Harris entered the bat-ter's box, dug in, and took a swing at Bridges' first pitch, hit-ting a clean single to left field. The jeers continued as Bridges retired the next batter, Sam Rice, on a ground-out to end the game. There was some postgame grumbling against Johnson's overzealous managing. However, one of Johnson's defenders was Bridges himself.

"I would have done the same thing if I were in Johnson's place," Bridges told *The Sporting News*. "It was the thing to do. Besides, any pitcher would prefer a bona fide one-hitter to a gift no-hitter."

Pinch-hitters often swing at the first good pitch they see, especially if it's a fastball, because they fear falling behind in the count. On April 20, 1990, Brian Holman lost his bid for a perfect game with two outs in the ninth inning on Ken Phelps' pinch-hit home run in the Seattle Mariners' 6–1 victory over the Oakland Athletics. Holman remembered that the Mariners' scouting report on Phelps said that he was a low fastball hitter who never swung at the first pitch. So Holman started him off with a high fastball, and Phelps clubbed it over the right-field wall at the Oakland Coliseum. Despite the stunning loss of his perfecto, no-hitter, and shutout all in one blow, Holman retired the next batter to end the game.

"I didn't think he was going to swing at the first pitch," says Holman. "You can second-guess that forever. Maybe I should have thrown a breaking ball. But I'm glad it happened that way and not with a bloop single."

Holman, a 25-year-old right-hander who had been acquired from Montreal the previous season in the trade that brought Randy Johnson to Seattle, used a sinking fastball to baffle the first 26 Oakland batters.

"[Catcher] Dave Valle and I were totally in synch," says Holman. "Wherever he put the glove, I hit it."

Holman had pitched brilliantly, so dominating the defending World Series champions that his teammates were not forced to make so much as one difficult defensive play. He struck out seven, and went to 3-ball counts just three times on a lineup that included Rickey Henderson, Mark McGwire, and Jose Canseco. Holman admits that he realized he was working on a perfect game after the seventh inning.

"Everybody in the dugout acted as if I had the plague," he says. "There was silence, nobody looked at me. Then I saw all those zeros on the scoreboard and it kicked in."

Holman's rhythm may have been broken in the top of the ninth when a defensive shift that eliminated Seattle's designated hitter forced him to take a turn at bat, a rarity for a pitcher in the American League. He reached first on an error and advanced to second on a two-run single.

"I would rather we went down 1-2-3 and go back out there," Holman says. "But we scored some runs, and against that Oakland team you never could have enough runs."

With two outs in the ninth, there was a brief delay as the pinch-hitter was announced and Phelps appeared in the on-deck circle. Holman's mind began to wander.

"I'm thinking to myself, 'You're one out away from the Hall of Fame.' I actually began to think, 'Will my glove or my jersey be on display in Cooperstown?' It was an out-of-body experience. The Oakland fans were cheering for me, and though I was a part of what was happening, I was watching it all take place from somewhere else."

He should have stayed where he was instead of taking that trip to nowhere. Holman threw 103 perfect pitches and one that missed by an inch. Phelps turned that inch into a

370-foot homer. It was Phelps' only home run of the year and the last of his major league career.

"That was the only time I ever faced him," says Holman, "so I guess he's batting 1.000 against me." Holman, a financial planner in the Seattle area, admits that he didn't sleep at all the night after his near-perfecto.

"In the hotel room at 4:00 in the morning I realized I'd never get that close again. I put a pillow over my face and screamed."

Ron Robinson of the Cincinnati Reds was supposed to be on a pitch count the night he came within one out of tossing a perfect game, May 2, 1988, just eight weeks before teammate Tom Browning would complete his own perfect game. Robinson, a 26-year-old right-hander, was coming back from his second elbow surgery and wasn't expected to pitch deep into the game against the Montreal Expos at Riverfront Stadium.

"It was Glove Night in Cincinnati so the stadium was packed with kids," says Robinson. "I had no stuff in the bullpen and thought, 'I won't last long tonight anyway.' But everything started falling into place between [catcher] Bo Diaz and me. I never shook him off. The manager that day was Tommy Helms; Pete Rose had just had knee surgery. With a perfect game going, there was no way Tommy could take the ball away from me. The crowd would've gotten mad and booed like crazy."

Robinson had his perfect game in hand with two outs in the ninth and a 2-strike count on pinch-hitter Wallace Johnson.

"Johnson fouled off a good 2–2 pitch," says Robinson, "and then I curved him." Johnson punched the ball into left field for a single. Move over Billy and Tommy, and welcome Ron.

"The ball bounced right at the feet of Kal Daniels," says Robinson with a tinge of regret in his voice. When the ball landed safely, "I was drained of all power. Drenched. My strength was zapped." Stunned and dejected, Robinson served up a home-run ball to the next batter, Tim Raines, although the Reds hung on to win, 3–2.

"You never live that down," says Robinson, who had taped the game on his VCR and replays it about once a year. "I still get chills down my spine whenever I watch it. The feeling always gives me goosebumps."

That's not necessarily the case for every member of his fraternity. Dave Stieb, who accumulated 175 career victories, is the winningest pitcher in Toronto Blue Jays franchise history. If ever there was a hard-luck pitcher, it's the ace of an expansion team. The 6'1", 195-pound right-hander was in top form and as tough to hit as ever over six days in September 1988, when twice a no-hitter eluded him with two outs in the ninth inning. Stieb was the first pitcher ever to lose a no-hitter to the last batter in back-to-back starts.

Amazingly, it happened for a third time on August 4, 1989, and this time he went himself one better (or one worse, depending on your point of view), because this time, he was working on a perfect game.

Stieb was cruising. He pitched a perfect game for 8⅔ innings against the New York Yankees at Toronto's Skydome. Of the first 26 batters he faced, just four made outs to the outfield. He struck out 11 and reached 3 balls on just one batter. With two down in the ninth, Stieb fell behind in the count, 2–0, to Roberto Kelly.

"I didn't do myself any favors by falling behind," said Stieb. His 84th pitch of the game was a slider down and away. Kelly lined the ball sharply to left field for a double, ending Stieb's bid for a perfect game and a no-hitter. When Steve Sax followed with a single, that ended the shutout, too, but the Jays and Stieb held on for a 2–1, two-hit victory. In 1990, Stieb won a career-high 18 games and finally earned his no-hitter, becoming the only member on our list of near-perfect-game pitchers to regroup, come back, and throw a no-hitter.

"It's funny," said Stieb, who ironically titled his autobiography, *Tomorrow I'll Be Perfect*, "When I finally did get the no-hitter, I didn't have as good stuff as I did the other games. I guess that time it was just meant to be."

Ending our tale with this nod to fate might be the very best way of all to explain just how perfect games happen.

Sometimes, they just do . . .

Selected
Bibliography

Angell, Roger. *A Pitcher's Story: Innings with David Cone.* New York: Warner Books, 2001.

Appel, Marty, and Tom Seaver. *Great Moments in Baseball.* New York: Birch Lane Press, 1992.

Browning, Reed. *Cy Young: A Baseball Life.* Amherst, MA: University of Massachusetts Press, 2000.

Carmichael, John P., ed. *My Greatest Day in Baseball.* New York: A. S. Barnes Co., 1945.

Coberly, Rich. *The No-Hit Hall of Fame.* Newport Beach, CA: Triple Play Publications, 1985.

Dickey, Glenn. *The Great No-Hitters.* Radnor, PA: Chilton Book Company, 1976.

Dickson, Paul. *The New Dickson Baseball Dictionary.* San Diego: Harcourt Brace, 1999.

Di Salvatore, Bryan. *A Clever Base-Ballist.* New York: Pantheon Books, 1999.

Holway, John, and John Thorn. *The Pitcher*. New York: Prentice Hall Press, 1988.

Hoppel, Joe. *The Series*. St. Louis: Sporting News Books, 1991.

Hunter, Jim, and Armen Keteyian. *Catfish: My Life in Baseball*. New York: McGraw-Hill, 1976.

Kahn, Roger. *The Era*. New York: Ticknor and Fields, 1993.

Larsen, Don, and Mark Shaw. *The Perfect Yankee*. Schaumburg, IL: Sports Publishing, Inc., 2001.

Libby, Bill. Catfish: *The Three Million Dollar Pitcher*. New York: Coward, McGann & Geohegan, 1976.

Longert, Scott. *Addie Joss: King of the Pitchers*. Cleveland: Society for American Baseball Research, 1998.

Mayer, Ronald A. *Perfect*. Jefferson, NC: McFarland, 1991.

Pappas, Milt, et al. *Out at Home*. Oshkosh, WI: Angel Press, 1999.

Reichler, Joseph. *Baseball's Great Moments*. New York: Crown, 1974

Santa Maria, Michael, and James Costello. *In the Shadows of the Diamond*. St. Paul, MN: Elysian Fields Press, 1992.

Shaw, Mark, with Don Larsen. *The Perfect Yankee*. Champaign, IL: Sagamore Publishing, 1996.

Solomon, Burt. *The Baseball Timeline*. New York: DK Publishing, 2001.

Stieb, Dave. *Tomorrow I'll Be Perfect*. Toronto: Doubleday Canada, 1986.

Stout, Glenn, and Richard A. Johnson. *Red Sox Century.* Boston: Houghton Mifflin Company, 2000.

Thorn, John, Pete Palmer, and Michael Gershman, eds. *Total Baseball* (6th and 7th editions). Kingston, NY: Total Sports/Sports Illustrated, 1999–2001.

Ward, Geoffrey, and Ken Burns. *Baseball: The American Epic.* New York: Knopf, 1998.

Westcott, Rich, and Allen Lewis. *No-Hitters: The 225 Games.* Jefferson, NC: McFarland, 2000.

INDEX